Tru Blu!!
Love for
Man!!
keep sweet!

Jason
Williams
6-4-09

# ZERO CHANCE

*Power of Love...Love of Power*

Jason Williams with JM and Anthus Williams

authorHOUSE®

AuthorHouse™
1663 Liberty Drive
Bloomington, IN 47403
www.authorhouse.com
Phone: 1-800-839-8640

First published by AuthorHouse     5/5/2009

ISBN: 978-1-4389-8397-4 (e)
ISBN: 978-1-4389-8396-7 (sc)
ISBN: 978-1-4389-8395-0 (hc)


Library of Congress Control Number: 2009904407

Printed in the United States of America
Bloomington, Indiana

This book is printed on acid-free paper.

Dedicated to my sons Jay and Kyle,
the stars in my world
Acknowledgments to Lane Blackmore for the FORE-
WORD,
and to
Suzanne Johnson for the AFTERWORD

# FOREWORD

In 1963, my parents began the naturalization process to become citizens of the United States. Centered around a small rural farm in southwestern British Columbia, Canada, our social and religious circle consisted primarily of half a dozen families who also believed in fundamental Mormonism. My parents were hardworking people of principle who had carved out a relatively stable existence in spite of the harsh economic conditions they faced in Canada. Our family ended up moving to Hildale.

In a short time, my family went from full community acceptance and involvement to almost zero association. To make matters even more challenging, my parents chose to relocate to LaVerkin, Utah, some thirty miles away from Hildale. Because of our past affiliation with this fundamentalist group, we were not welcomed into this predominantly Mormon town with any degree of enthusiasm.

Trapped between two philosophically adverse communities, it was extremely difficult to make a living. Our family had lost everything to the United Effort Plan trust (UEP). I tell this story here for one reason only. This experience did give me the perspective, empathy, and awareness to appreciate the difficult experiences which many of my family and friends have since been subjected to. One by one, I saw some of the best people on earth get stripped of their social and economic stability by the same religious hierarchy which over time has become even more insidious.

On a positive note, as my relatives became branded as "apostates," we were able to once again begin a working relationship with each other. A warm, constructive, and respectful association exists between us now, in spite of the pain each of us has endured. I have been blessed to have become acquainted with Jason Williams when he was just twelve years old. I watched him grow up, get married, and I saw the joy and enthusiasm he had when his children were born. I felt his passion as he discussed his plan for the future with his wife Suzanne. He also talked with me about the conflict which he felt because of the community pressure directed at his wife. He, at one time, told me that he intended to do his best to stay affiliated with the group for the sake of his marriage and family peace. From everything I knew of Jason, I knew him to be hardworking, loving, cheerful, and dedicated to his wife and family.

I was saddened when Jason came to me with the story you will read in the following pages. He needed help. He was threatened with losing his wife and children. For several years, I witnessed Jason put everything he had on the line to defend his legal rights to be a father to his sons. I witnessed his heart break, his tenacity, and his quest to preserve all that he could of his family. Jason has since found comfort in knowing, that in the end, love conquers all.

Lane Blackmore

# TABLE OF CONTENTS

# I
# DEAR JASON

The cold January rain ran in rivulets down my windshield. Sitting in my car outside the Post Office, I stared down at the letter my wife had mailed to me after she kidnapped my two little boys. The darkness made it hard to read, but I needed answers. I knew I could trust no one in the community to give them to me. I was not just dealing with my wife Suzanne. My wife would never steal my children from me; she would know the things that might make me do. Tears of rage and frustration filled my eyes. I sobbed in the car, relieved it was raining. Now passersby could not see my grief. I knew if I made an angry demonstration, it would not help me see them any sooner. Suzanne had my boys; she held the power, for now.

I had to play this cool. Gather in my emotions. Act smart. A come-apart would ruin my relationship with my children. I would play this out. I would be patient, knowing this would not be a sprint. It was shaping up to be a drawn-out and grueling marathon. Glancing at the letter, I could hardly focus on the fragments of sentences. Choking back tears, I read again the note that changed my life forever.

Dear Jason,

I need to be alone for a period of time and would really appreciate you respecting my wishes to do so. I don't want to make you angry by doing this. Please understand that it will be good for both of us. I know the boys are a big part of your life right now but know they are being taken care of by me. I am sure it won't be too long before I get in touch with you again. I have put myself in the prophets hands I cannot say what will happen one way or the other.

I do know that alot depends on
you proving yourself faithful, your
prayers and your connection with him
who holds the Keys. I am going to
go through with the divorce wether
or not some time down the road
we are remarried. I feel that it
is better you don't know where
I am, only remember it wont be
very long and that the boys are
getting the things they need.
I wish you the best, You
are in my prayers.
                            - Suzie &
                              the boys

I sat, helpless, stunned, wondering whether I would ever see those boys again. This was not like my wife. Suzanne wouldn't use phrases like "him who holds the keys." Or "I have put myself in the Prophet's hands." She wouldn't even write "I wish you the best." Instead, two weeks ago, she had written "I ♥ you, baby." And now here she was using lines out of the sixteenth century? Whoever was behind this, it was not my wife.

My wife did not steal those boys. It was the religious leaders of the community I was once part of who were screwing with my family. I had to act fast, or Kyle and Jay would disappear. This sect had refuges in Salt Lake City and Canada. I had heard of children disappearing into some other family and of fathers despairing of ever finding them again. I had to stop this.

That church had grown arrogant and greedy. They were used to people giving up and giving in, because they made life just damn hard for them. But I was just as stubborn as they were. This time they had broken the glasses of a kid who wasn't afraid of bullies.

But I was caught in a dilemma. How could I challenge what I believed? What *did* I believe? I believed in the FLDS church, and I had since I was a kid, which was what made my belief possible. I don't think an adult can *convert* to the FLDS.

That's why they wanted *my* kids, while they were young, so they could start the process, just like they started it on me when I was young. I grew up believing entirely in what the "Prophet" said. Then I was forced to watch the maliciousness of my benevolent church, and I realized the incompatibility.

Most of my family expected me to obey. My father had been through the same thing with *his* wife, and twelve of *his* children, but his protests were like a whimper in a hurricane. They failed. He lost his kids, and he was finally, sadly, reduced to accepting it. I knew that I was going to try to talk Suzanne into coming back. I was going to try to find my children, peaceably. But, failing that, I was determined to start a cyclone of my own.

My dad shared empathy for my situation, but he wasn't likely to come to my aid. There were a couple brothers who were long on support but short on means. I had a lot of poor relatives who would lend a sympathetic ear, but that was it.

Many members of my family were linked to the church in various ways, and the FLDS is very good at convincing people that salvation sometimes depends on betraying the ones you love most. Even now, there were some members of my family trying to convince me that my own salvation would involve sacrificing my will and abandoning my sons.

I knew my own mother, for example, would resent anything I did in the way of protest or retaliation. Her attitude was that I should meekly submit. The "Prophet" was never wrong. It was this kind of attitude that gave the church its formidable power.

My parents' position made my predicament difficult, because the concept of the infallible "Prophet" went back a hundred and seventy years. Any objections to the words of the "Prophet," or even the title "Prophet" had its consequences. I knew any protest at this point would bring the full brunt of Rulon Jeffs power, money, and influence right at me, and any friend or associate who stood by me. I had seen it before, and I had no illusions about what this man could do. Still, no one was going to push me around.

This man wielded a frightening power in the minds of the people. The peculiar belief held by this church is that all women and children belong to the "Prophet." He could assign them to men he favors, and he could *reassign* them to men he favors *more*. He could take the wife away from the husband and "give" her to someone else. He could take the man's children, and shuffle them around, like playing cards. Pimps dream of this kind of power.

# II
# THE 'CRICKERS'

The "Prophet" was a powerful figure in the Short Creek community. The people living there have been suspicious of the outside world. You cannot change a century and a half of isolation and fear very easily, but that was what I faced. It may not seem like much of a foe to those who are unfamiliar with the workings of the FLDS, but it is no easy thing to challenge generations of cultural indoctrination.

This cultural indoctrination started in the early 1800s, when the Mormon Church was founded. They endured a good deal of prejudice from their neighbors, and ultimately, under Brigham Young, they gathered their belongings and trekked across the plains into Utah, which at the time was still being contested militarily as part of Mexico.

The old-school Mormons were a lot like the FLDS today. They practiced polygamy and communal living, and believed in a "one man doctrine" which held that Brigham Young was a prophet, seer, and revelator, the same way that Warren Jeffs is viewed as the "Prophet" by the FLDS today. In both cases, it is a bit of a faulty appellation, since modern prophets seldom, if ever, prophesy.

The Mormons adhered to their biblical social practices for some time, despite federal attempts to quell that type of cohabitation. In the 1880s, many followers of the LDS faith were jailed because the Edmunds Tucker Act made polygamy illegal. Church members and property were severely impacted by the aggressive enforcement. Then finally, in 1890, the LDS church formally renounced polygamy in a bid to achieve statehood. Polygamy became a felony in both Utah and Arizona. Even though the Edmunds Tucker Act was eventually repealed, it didn't affect these two states because of specific anti-polygamy language in their Constitutions.

There were a lot of sects who splintered away from the Mormon Church so they could still practice polygamy and communism. In the 1930s, one such group established Short Creek and billed it as a safe refuge for covenant people. There the "true" Mormons flourished in the desert, away from any competing ideology and the watchful eyes of the government. For a while it remained a ward of the LDS church, but eventually they were excommunicated en masse for refusing to sign an oath declaring the LDS Church President a prophet. Now the LDS church excommunicates polygamists as a matter of course.

Polygamists have always been something of an embarrassment to mainstream Mormons, because people, unaware of the intricacies of history, tend to equate the two, even though it is a matter of public record that Mormons have been strictly monogamous for over a century.

Because of the embarrassment though, there were anti-polygamy crusades that took place on several occasions, including a small state raid in 1935 and an FBI raid in 1944. The raids made the Short Creek inhabitants even more close-mouthed and isolationist than before.

The largest raid occurred in 1953, when Arizona's Governor Howard Pyle launched a sting into Short Creek, arrested nearly every adult male inhabitant, transported the women to hospice in the southern half of the state, and actively sought adoption for the minor children. My dad was there, very young at the time, and had to experience being put up to auction with his mother and siblings in a Phoenix Greyhound lobby and sold—literally, sold for the substantial welfare check, with people checking his teeth and testing his musculature like a miniature slave child.

After the men were released on plea bargain, they returned to deserted homes and streets, a community entirely emptied of its inhabitants. It took two years of legal battles at an immense cost, but at last, every person was returned to the community. Governor Pyle suffered intense scorn for the crusade and eventually lost his bid for re-election because of it. The resultant paranoia and general distrust of outsiders in the Short Creek area pushed the group further into the shadows of the Tumurru Mountain Range. They changed the name of the town from Short Creek to the twin cities of Hildale, Utah, and Colorado City, Arizona.

Because of these raids, a rumor had circulated that the place was due for an anti-polygamy raid every time the last two digits of the year could be added to make the number eight. There had already been one in '35, '44, and '53, and we were due for another one in another nine years. However, 1962 came and went, as did 1971 and 1980, so at last the rumor died down. Interestingly enough, the state of Texas raided the Yearning for Zion compound in El Dorado in the year 2008.

At the time the FLDS church was not really a church—it was just considered to be a group of informal leaders who met in one another's basements to argue theology. It was never organized into a legal entity until 1987, when certain civil disputes forced the"Prophet" Rulon Jeffs to formally found the Fundamentalist Church of Jesus Christ of Latter-Day Saints.

During the same period, a business trust, the United Effort Plan (UEP), was founded. It was an instrument of Mormon communism, a corporation that held the property of all the residents of the Short Creek area. The trust was controlled by the FLDS church, which meant that the "Prophet" had the right to dictate who was allowed to dwell upon it. The UEP caused me a wide variety of problems over the course of my life. Sometimes I would assert that *UEP* was really just an acronym for the *Ultimate Evil Powers*.

I was born into this area and grew up thinking most of the peculiarities had come directly from God. That sort of thing was taught to me since the day I was born. Many people I meet wonder how I could accept some of the ludicrous conditions and styles. Many who read this book will probably consider me to be among the dumbest of fools. Our problem was that we were only aware of how we fit into our narrow existence. The reason why it works is because the believer adapts to an idealistic quality of being childlike.

The secret to a cult is to capitalize on this –the follower's ability to believe whatever you tell them, and then you add a patriotic or religious fervor that declares an unquestioning belief is an ideal to strive for. It is hard to break away from a cult like the FLDS because it actively works to keep you in the mental state of a child. There are people in that area who go their entire lives without ever evolving beyond the vulnerable psyche of an eight-year-old.

Really, for the first twelve or so years in that church a child has no reason to doubt what is taught. We couldn't judge or weigh the evidence because we had no standards of meter against which to compare them. As I got older, and more integrated with the rest of the world, I started to wonder about the nature of the religion I was part of. Stephen Colbert said in his book that the secret to figuring out whether or not you're a member of a cult is simple: if you're wondering if you're in a cult, the answer is yes. For me, the answer was most certainly a yes, loud and resounding.

The other phenomenon was the evolving nature of the men who led—when I was a child the FLDS was nowhere near as crazed as it is today. The path to insanity is noted more clearly from a distance than in the midst of it.

The FLDS congregation is a group of very frightened people. Warren Jeffs, and those who came before him, have done their best to capitalize on that fear. There were all manner of terrors to navigate when these leaders spoke—the fear of hell, of the apocalypse, of anti-polygamy law enforcement, of losing one's family and home, of corruption and apostasy, of the influence of Gentiles. The Jeffs regime fed off this fear until they successfully transitioned the group away from a council of leaders and toward a one-man demigod. As fate would have it, I was among the first people to publicly gouge a hole in the Jeffs narrative, and for that, they tried their best to run me down, like an asphalt roller in pursuit of a field mouse. I was expected to forever be a fossil.

Thankfully that battle didn't come until I was more prepared to fight it. For the first part of my life I was fairly well-integrated into the FLDS society, and I didn't realize how odd it was. First, the look: if we were to be God's people, apparently, we were supposed to look very, very strange. We had a look that was a hundred and fifty years old, so that it could match a lifestyle the same age.

The women in the community wore nineteenth century prairie dresses, heavy hiker boots, and opaque hose. When I was younger the dresses were allowed some variety—calicos with flowers and embroidery for example, or pastel colors, or a ribbon or some other piece of flair. In the early days of Mormonism, a pioneer named Eliza Snow had developed a flowing pantsuit for modest women to wear—however; it never really caught on with the 1870s fashion divas. Here in Short Creek, the thing was not formally banned, but was considered far too modern wear for a church that was trying its hardest to resist the passage of time.

After the church fell into Warren Jeffs's hands, he became the personal style icon as well as the "Prophet." Pants for women were banned. He demanded the mid-calf-length dresses, outlawed embroidery and required the dresses to be of sturdy fabric in one solid color, such as blue or brown or a dull pink. In many cases the girls were expected to wear blue jeans underneath their weighty dresses. To top it off, he outlawed variations on hairstyles, so that the French roll Victorian pompadour became an obligation for the faithful.

The men were a little luckier in their required garb, in that they could sometimes blend in with people in other areas, especially in the winter, when longer clothing was more common. They were obligated to wear nondescript blue jeans in a straight cut with a long-sleeved flannel shirt. This was intended to cover the full body underwear that was handed out as pseudo sacred temple raiment and became mandatory undergarments for every member of the FLDS church, including small infants.

Twenty years ago or more, the Short Creek polygamists affectionately referred to Salt Lake City polygamists as *Lakers*; they were, in turn, labeled *Crickers*. Ever since then, the people of the Short Creek area have been known by the colloquial term, Crickers, or, if not a current follower, ex-Crickers. The name *Cricker* has since been adopted as a derogatory epithet among locals, along with the term *plig*, short for polygamist. In short, as of the writing of this book, I am an ex-Cricker plig kid.

In the FLDS, marrying more than one woman is considered a commandment, one which the highest degree of glory in heaven hangs upon. Therefore, whoever controls the assignment of women decides which follower is a candidate for salvation. That's a lot of power in a mortal hand, and so it became essential to kiss up to the "Prophet" in order to get as many wives as possible.

Warren Jeffs always taught that a man had to have at least three wives to get to heaven, and the more wives a man has, the closer he is to heaven. Warren Jeffs himself, by the time he was arrested, had over 70 wives. This meant that for every wife he had beyond the required three, he was preventing someone else from being saved. As far as I was concerned this meant that he wasn't being charitable, even by his own ridiculous standards, let alone the standards of the poor women who were forced to be shackled up to him.

And they were certainly forced into their marriages. The idea of placement marriage meant that the "Prophet" could arrange a union between a husband and wife, who didn't meet one another until a few days before the wedding, or in many cases, moments before the ceremony. It is a shotgun wedding in that the bride-to-be is brought up to fear that objecting to the marriage meant inviting a curse from God, because God was guiding every action the "Prophet" took.

Worse than objecting was choosing for yourself whom you wanted to marry— this was a cardinal sin; one I eventually ended up guilty of. We weren't allowed to date, or even really talk to girls at all, for that matter. It was a tough rule.

Members of this church are required to live "at the feet of the priesthood" which means that they have to live in an area owned by the UEP. The right to have a building lot or a home on land owned by the UEP is decided solely by the "Prophet." who can take away the wife he had formerly assigned and remove or evict you from your home, which is a real incentive for a member to continue faithful to the "one man" worship.

For men, priesthood is essential. In other religions a priest is an elite class, but in the FLDS the priesthood is an office granted to all its (male) lay members. It is defined as ordained authority to act for God, and it is essential. It means nothing, because only the "Prophet" can act for God, but it is still essential. This third arm of control is capricious in nature; priesthood can be taken for any variety of reasons, known only to the "Prophet," or restored just as suddenly.

All members are believed to belong to the "Prophet," including the women and all the minor children. These too, can be confiscated by him for a perceived indiscretion. If he felt you needed to be handled, he would instruct your wife to divorce you and to marry someone else. This meant that you had lost your shot at collecting three wives and were now doomed to hell. The "Prophet" could stop up your eternal progression like the Hoover Dam halts the Colorado River.

Argument or debate about anything was not looked at with much tolerance. When God's word had been revealed, discussion was pointless. "Reason and debate are some of the devil's sharpest tools," Sam Barlow once told us when he was teaching our priesthood class.

There are quite a few odd ideas and doctrines the church claims. I could list them interminably; however, a few will convey the concept of odd. For instance, the color red is evil, and the people are instructed to avoid it; not to drive it, wear it, or develop a regard for it. One doctrine argues that nonmembers, or Gentiles, are all wicked and will be destroyed once the apocalypse hits. Rock music and nearly every other outside influence are tools of the devil. The children are taught that dinosaurs never actually existed, man never landed on the moon, evolution was an utter lie, and that God would place Southern Utah as the ruling seat of the entire world. They even prophesied that the Chinese would swoop up from Panama, conquer the nations of Central America, and invade the United States, at which point Short Creek would stop them using nothing more than their faith in the Lord. Also, most recreation is considered evil, but work, of course, is always good, especially on common projects, because common projects are not really communally owned; they are part of the corporate estate, owned, naturally, by the "Prophet."

People of authority within the FLDS church are often referred to by the title of "Uncle" or "Aunt." This was a cut above the "Brother" and "Sister" that applied to lay members of the congregation. The result was names like "Uncle" Rulon, "Uncle" Fred, "Aunt" Lydia, or even "Uncle" Warren, even if Warren Jeffs happened to be twenty years younger than half the community. It is true that inbreeding is a problem in the town, but that didn't mean that every "Aunt" really was one. Sometimes the "aunt" was the term used to address your dad's other wives, and she might have really been one.

Because of the level of inbreeding, Hildale and Colorado City log the world's highest incidence of fumarase deficiency, according to a local Dr. Ted Tarby, who treats the disease. Before 1990, only thirteen cases of this disease had *ever* been reported worldwide, out of six billion people. Since then, an additional twenty have occurred in this single community, out of six thousand people. Fumarase deficiency is a genetic disorder that causes severe mental retardation (the estimated average IQ of these patients is about 25) and facial malformations that make the afflicted look very strange. It is sometimes referred to as "Polygamist's Down's."

The major differences between mainstream Mormons and fundamentalist Mormons extended beyond the plural marriage, clothing choices, and attitudes about the outside world. Crickers love coffee, for example, while Mormons ban it. Wine and beer are used with discretion by Crickers, but Mormons ban that as well. They both agree on the evils of tobacco use.

Mormons have temples; fundamentalists postpone the activity,--fundamentalists have celestial wives, traditional Mormons postpone the activity. 'Crickers' don't believe in facial hair for men, but have no policy for women; Mormons don't believe in facial hair for women, but have no formal policy for men. Mormon women have short sleeves, pants, cut hair, make-up and sometimes get to make out. 'Cricker' women have long hair, longer dresses, no make-up, and always get to make do.

Fundamentalists are concerned about pure and faithful blood, and they are sure their relatives have some, which is why there are so many marriages that take place between first cousins. Mormons will proselyte to anybody, no matter their bloodline. Mormons tend to downplay their polygamous history; they are very concerned about shaking the family tree, in case some polygamists are discovered there.

As a culture, the FLDS is helpful to its own, but distrustful of all others. People have always been expected to work for the good of the church, even if they were very young. It was routine to see an eleven- or twelve-year-old boy operating heavy equipment. Unlicensed little drivers often roared around town in heavy-duty trucks, cement mixers, and backhoes. Children manned manufacturing stations, worked professionally out on contracts, or in plants, farms, or other services. By the time I was in fourth grade, I was proficient at setting radial arm saws, working geometry and calculating angles for a local truss shop. This area thrived on child labor; without it, many families would starve. So many financial issues or mandatory donations to church projects drained the coffers of local families that children had to be sent off to work.

This led to dropouts from the educational system and a void of college-educated youth. The community generally mistrusted higher education, anyway, because the few lucky kids that got to go would usually learn too much to ever want to come back. The entire community had pitched in once to send a promising young man through law school. After a year or two of study, he disappeared and was never heard from again.

Most college diplomas that were obtained were in general education. For a lot of years, accredited teachers were needed to manage the local school system. Then the Jeffs regime boycotted the local community college and the public schools; requiring teachers to find different work.

In the summer of 2000, Warren finally prevailed on the faithful to withdraw their children from public schools and start up several different private and parochial schools throughout the area. I think one of the reasons Warren liked this idea was because he had developed a priesthood-approved curriculum while he was the principal of a private school in Salt Lake, Alta Academy. Perhaps he considered his curriculum grand enough to foist on the entire FLDS community, rather than just the few who volunteered for Alta Academy. Besides which, the curriculum charge was about $300 per student, which was a nice little ancillary income. He had both spelling and connotation surrounded; profit and prophet are natural bookends in the library of life.

For many years the law enforcement stayed out of the hands of the FLDS. An old cowboy named Dolee Nyborg owned just about the only piece of property in the area that was not controlled by the UEP. He was a deputy sheriff of Mohave County, and stayed active in the community until just after the 1953 raid. At that point, a local churchgoer named Sam Barlow went through the police training and became deputized.

Sam considered himself the law north of the Grand Canyon. The city could have been named "Sam's Town," except a Las Vegas casino beat him to it. He was a "good ol' boy" to his friends and a man you didn't want for an enemy. Very often, he seemed to get a little confused between the tenets of the church and the statutes of the state. He was a two-holstered lawman, with a Bible in one holster and a six-gun in the other. Our family always thought he drew from the wrong holster in almost every situation. On one occasion he arrested a kid for urinating by the side of a public road, and on another he preached repentance to a burglar, whom he then released.

He spent many years as the sheriff in Colorado City, but eventually he was discredited and disarmed, because the county found out he was a polygamist and took his badge away. Then another Sam took over. Sam Roundy and his deputies had gotten their start as enforcers and bodyguards for Warren Jeffs. Once they moved into the realm of official law enforcement, they basically kept their old job and just did everything with badges this time. Eventually they ended up in trouble with the real law. My family and I would have a lot of trouble with the two "Yes mighty" Sams and their deputies over the years.

Another method of enforcing the peace started out as a neighborhood watch group and eventually ended up as a vigilante patrol on steroids. Ervil Lebaron, a leader of a rival polygamous group, arranged the murder of a third leader, Rulon C. Allred. Short Creek was worried about similar attacks on LeRoy Johnson, so Sam Barlow organized a special night watch crew to record everyone who entered the town. This group eventually became an FLDS goon platoon under Sam's brother, Nephi Barlow. They would run people off the road, interrogating visitors and congregants alike of suspected wrong-doing; their greatest contribution was a public nuisance. This group had no official name, but my family always referred to them as the God Squad, because they took it upon themselves to do God's work for him.

# III
# THE WILLIAMS CLAN

I was a natural enemy for Warren Jeffs, when it comes down to it, because I was a Williams. My family has always been a poor fit in the FLDS community. We were always free thinkers, every one of us, and we made enemies quickly because we slaughtered sacred cows on a regular basis.

I come from a long line of people with a propensity for protest. My ancestors were Scottish and Welsh and English, with a dose of bluster from the hills of Arkansas thrown in as well. My great, great grandfather came directly from England and settled in the Cache Valley area north east of Salt Lake. His son Thomas took advantage of the Homestead Act and staked out a farm in the Mud Lake part of Idaho.

He was one of the first settlers in that region, scraping a subsistence farm out of the flatland. He was known to challenge the powers that be, taking on the powerful farmers, ranchers, or even the local government in his effort to build a living for his family. Once he ended up in a massive quarrel with one of the local politicians in the area, and argued with him into the night until they were both sore and lost for words.

"Congratulations, Mr. Williams," huffed the politician when they were finished squabbling. "That was the first argument I ever lost."

"Oh, hell!" roared my ancestor. "That's the first argument you ever heard!"

My paternal grandfather, Jerold Ray Williams, was born in that region, in a little town called Treasureton, carved out of the frontier by men with grub hoes. He migrated southward to get his masters degree in education administration from the University of Utah. Then he ended up teaching school in Iona. He was a 35-year-old bachelor, when he met a Canadian girl his sister had invited to the ranch. He fell in love with her and followed her back to British Columbia to marry her.

My paternal grandmother, Fayila Blackmore, accepted his offer and they started eking out a life in Creston and Lister, and various other parts of British Columbia. She had been born Canadian, in Cardston, Alberta and was descended from one of the early Mormon pioneers to Utah, Edwin Woolley, who himself had a rebellious streak. He became notorious among the Mormon settlers for frequently daring to challenge Brigham Young, the leader at the time, over his penchant for land-grabbing.

"Well, Brother Woolley," Brigham Young challenged him. "I suppose you'll just go off somewhere and apostatize now."

"If this were your church, Brother Brigham," old Woolley rejoined, "I most certainly would. It belongs, however, to the Lord, so you can just go to hell."

Every one of us was due to spend our lives listening to the growling of the bears at night, stuck in the frozen tundra by day, but for a chance meeting my grandfather had with a few polygamists who had come to speak with some Mormons in the area. They had a message that an LDS elder named John Taylor had set apart a few followers to keep the system of plural marriage from dying out. They needed an accredited school manager and teacher for the little town of Short Creek, Arizona. My grandfather thought that certainly sounded better than cutting Christmas trees in the cold.

My dad and his four older brothers had already been born in Canada by this time, and they were brought down into the United States without any kind of customs officials to halt their progress. The result is that the entire lot of them is now considered by the United States to be illegal immigrants. They have all been in the country for just about their entire lives, but they struggle to get United States citizenship. Canada refuses to readmit them and grant them citizenship either, since they have been out of the country for so long, so they are mostly men without countries, classified as 'permanent alien residents.'

My dad was very young when he and his family moved into Short Creek. It was February of 1953, and no one knew of the danger lurking in the state law offices. In July, after my dad had been in the area all of six months, Arizona launched the raid. Arizona police troopers and the Army National Guard stormed into town and jailed my grandfather and all the other men, including some bachelors, and two soldier's home on leave from the Korean War.

My dad and his siblings spent a week after that, trying to avoid the spite of the soldiers, who were camped in a nearby grove of ancient cottonwoods. Every morning, my dad, with his older brother John, had to go on a milk run to the local dairy. To get there, they would go down through the creek and clamber up through the grove, giving their best attempt to play it calm in front of armed strangers who didn't think much at all of either of them.

A week after the initial arrests, a convoy of buses arrived and pirated the women and kids to Phoenix, Mesa, Snowflake, and Tucson in an effort to spread them all over the state so they could no longer be found.

Meanwhile, in the Kingman county jail, my grandfather was becoming unpopular with the police very quickly. He spent almost every waking moment in a state of cathartic fury, haranguing his jailers with a fervor that rivaled Thomas Caine. He railed them all about the Constitution, illegal seizure and holding, kidnapping, habeas corpus, and some other fine points of law in a free land. The authorities soon grew very tired of him; they had not expected to see an outback polygamous farmer carry knowledge of constitutional law. Finally his fellow inmates urged him to calm down and accept whatever plea bargain they offered in order to get out of prison.

When they returned to the community, it was completely deserted, and so a lengthy court battle ensued. It took two years of legal posturing before the Williams family case, the first one on the docket, hit the Arizona District Court. By this time, my grandfather's involvement with the community went beyond his job as a schoolteacher. He was woven into the social, religious, and economic fabric of the congregation.

When the Williams family finally had their day in court, my three-year-old father escaped my grandmother's clutches and scampered up behind the judge's bench. A moment later he clambered up the back of Judge Lorna Lockwood's chair and grabbed a fistful of her hair. She screamed in fear and rage as the bailiff scrambled to pull the child away from her. Judge Lockwood certainly didn't want to see much of my dad after that. He was probably a major factor in getting my grandfather acquitted.

Toward the latter end of his life, my grandfather started to cement his status as a firebrand rebel. He had written several essays and papers on the raid of '53, and these went far to recommend him as a suitable candidate for the local Justice of the Peace. After that, he made a reputation for himself as a judge who would not kowtow to anybody. His nickname had been *Jud* the whole while, and so by this time they all changed it and started to refer to him as *Judge*, even when he was not fulfilling his official capacity.

During this time, he and his son John were actively involved in negotiations with the two county commissions to construct a television booster tower on the outskirts of town, so they could watch football. They were both sports enthusiasts who sometimes went so far as to drive into St George or Salt Lake and rent a motel so they could watch the Dallas Cowboys play.

They had gotten permission from the FLDS leaders of the time, but they did not have permission from Sam Barlow, who dubbed them "public enemy number one." Sam was certain that television was "a slippery slope that will lead an entire generation of young people into hell."

They tried unsuccessfully to appease him, but he was adamant about the evils of television. He considered that a VCR was a good investment, since we could select the movies we would allow our children to watch. In reality, network television was censored far more heavily than any film on videocassette, but Sam knew he could control the movies that came into the town, whereas with network TV, anyone with a remote could watch whatever was playing. It was the control that was important to him, not the content.

"No one's forcing Sam to buy a TV," Uncle John declared. "He could just do without one, if he wanted, or if he felt compelled to own one, maybe he could familiarize himself with the on/off switch."

Needless to say, Sam did not find this suggestion particularly appealing, so he enlisted the help of "Uncle" Fred Jessop, a sort of bishop in the town. He was one of those "uncles" that was not really related to me at all. Fred spent every ounce of energy he had trying to combat the inevitable.

His heaviest ammunition came one summer morning when, after a heavy rainstorm, a flood ripped down the creek and sloshed through the town. Fortunately, nothing in the town was destroyed, except Fred's garden. Fred went up in church the following Sunday and declared that the flood was the Lord's punishment on us for trying to get TV. This was always a favorite tactic of his. Like certain other evangelical preachers, he always claimed the dubious ability to communicate directly with God, and would always assert that every natural disaster or bit of tragedy was a punishment from God for a totally unrelated crime.

The people fighting to get television generally saw through this particular ploy. "I notice," Uncle John wrote to the local paper, "that the only thing God chose to destroy was the garden of the person fighting *against* getting a booster tower set up. It could be that Fred Jessop is misinterpreting God's message."

In large part they laughed off the attempts to block the tower. Our family was particularly concerned about the lack of TV in the lives of the children of the community; because they were so culturally unaware it baffled every schoolteacher in the area. One local education administrator brought several of the children in the area to Kingman for a standardized pre-kindergarten test.

He was shocked at the results. He would show the children several images, such as the one below, and ask them if they knew what it was.

Some of the children guessed it was a "cowboy." The body of the test results displayed many recurrences of that sort of phenomenon. My uncle and grandfather, like the county commissioners, were very concerned about what this might portend when these children grew up. For this reason, plus sports and news, they worked tirelessly to get the permits approved and eventually procured a decent signal for the area.

"You're a *revolutionary*, that's what you are," Fred once spat to Uncle John during an argument they were having. "Every time there's something you don't like, you scramble like hell to get it changed! This church can't trust that kind of man!"

Perhaps Fred didn't appreciate the compliment inherent in his words, but we certainly did. We were all revolutionaries who challenged some of the actions that were taken, which you cannot do in that group. Sooner or later, we were all doomed to fall into disfavor.

As time progressed, the church broke down into a power struggle between the ordained apostles and the Barlows in the area. Both sides were allied in their unique dislike of anyone with the name Williams, because we fought hard against their tactics of revisionism. History was frequently edited and retold in this area. Events that were common knowledge were disavowed, and religious doctrine was twisted and reinterpreted to the point of ridiculousness.

We fought against it, as long as we could. My grandfather stood up in city council one morning and raised a mighty din about the lies that were being spun. "You damn Barlow bastards!" he swore. "You think you can change what happened, but some of us were around from the beginning! Some of us are smart enough to know what really went on and your prevarications will not stand scrutiny or the test of time!"

The Williams voices were often raised in defense of logic and compelling evidence. My grandfather sowed a legacy of people that did not respond well at all to force or intimidation. He had an entertaining sort of wisdom and a grand generosity that did its utmost to defend people, ideas and truth, which did not make him a favored person in the eyes of those who thrived on lies.

Whenever I visit the grave of my grandfather, I'm always a little in awe of what appears on the headstone. It says *"Freedom to think—Freedom to speak"* in block letters, carved indelibly into the granite. He left behind an echelon of people who were ready to defend the downtrodden, no matter what type of demons were thrown at them.

One such case took place early on, when the Williams bunch took on the community at large in defense of a tourist from Greece who was so awfully mistreated during his visit to Colorado City, I always thought it was a wonder he never came back and shot everybody, like Sylvester Stallone did in *Rambo*.

The Greek appeared at the local grocery store one morning looking for a motel or campsite where he could stay. Claiming to be an anthropologist, he said he had heard of the place and wanted to study it. The God Squad followed him everywhere he went, demanding he leave town because it was all private property. While he was parked in front of the local grocery store, they attacked his car, kicking in his grille and smashing his headlights.

He had a name that no one in the community could pronounce or spell. My dad once took a stab at trying to write the name down. He came up with Essasyphololus, which the Greek said was getting close. My uncle John always joked with him that his name sounded like some sort of awful STD, a concept he found to be hilarious. Neither my dad nor my uncle could read the name aloud though, so he just told us all to call him Ess. Ess was a short, curly-headed fellow with a full-length beard. He was very soft-spoken and mild, but harbored a few unorthodox views that did not sit well with the FLDS. You could write an entire book on him alone, and the way he was treated.

In reality, Ess did no harm except loiter about the town, but something about him infuriated the God Squad. He was harassed, beaten, arrested several times, detained by the law, jailed at Kingman twice, and generally treated like so much shit. He expressed a desire to go to church with us, and attend our local baseball games (limited athletic competition was allowed at the time). Sam Barlow organized security to keep him out of church and beseeched my uncle John, the athletic director, to cancel all the scheduled games until "Esshole" went away.

"Well, Sam," my uncle said, "tell you what. He wants to go to church too, so if you get that cancelled, I'll postpone the games. Otherwise, hell no!"

So Ess did show up at the softball game after all, and the God Squad was ready for him. They grabbed him by the beard and yanked him down to the road, where a mob of more than fifty people dragged him off to the police station. Some of my relatives were there, and they always attest the thing they regret most about their lives was not rescuing poor old Ess, but it had happened too quickly for them to really do anything anyway.

By the time Sam Barlow got to the scene, the mob around him had grown to a hundred. He took Ess into custody, detained him, and charged him with inciting a riot. Ess spent some time in a Kingman prison, but upon his release he came hotfooting right back up to Colorado City once again.

By this time Sam had checked every police database he had, and found Ess had been arrested once, for skinny dipping in Canada. So Sam broadcast to the town that he was a rapist and a sex offender, and the whole town would have nothing to do with him. The local store even refused to sell him food.

My uncle Roger invited him to Sunday dinner once, to show him that there were residents here who were considerate, decent people. He always maintained he found Ess to be intelligent, funny, and entertaining, playing his flute for the children and philosophizing as grandly as any Greek has ever done. My uncle caught a lot of flak for that kindness to a stranger, but that is how my kin were. We got along with people and rarely took the stated view about anything. This hardly contributed to our popularity within the community.

Eventually Ess got tired of the trouble and disappeared for a year. The next time I saw him, I was riding on a truck on the way to our work project. The project manager gave me a shove and told me to ignore him because he was "one of the most wicked men on the face of the earth."

I watched him covertly anyway. He looked tired and worn, like he had been run over a few times. He was dressed in a gunny sack robe, pushing an Albertsons' grocery cart with all his belongings in it. A hand lettered sign on each side of the cart said, in big letters: *REPENT, COLORADO CITY.* I've always thought he had the look of a prophet nailed. Warren Jeffs, for his part, never tried the robe and cart; instead, he opted for a metallic red Escalade.

After that Ess disappeared, never seen again. Sam Barlow still maintains that he was the screenwriter of a film that came out a few months later, called *The Child Bride of Short Creek.* It was a fairly interesting film, although instead of dealing with any real, complex themes, they went off on the "follow your heart" trope that Hollywood makes so much of. I don't think Ess could have written it though, because between his visit and the film's debut, there would not have been enough time to finish the writing and the photography. Also, there was no name that looked like an STD that appeared anywhere in the final credits.

Personally, I sometimes wondered if Ess could have been an angel. He never looked afraid or miserable, even when he was being ruthlessly beaten. I thought it was possible he was sent to weigh us in the balance and test the community— if that was the case, we certainly didn't pass. Our community mistreated that poor human being so impassively I don't know how the FLDS considers it has any moral fiber left. Interestingly enough, he later showed up on the news in Salt Lake City as a proponent for starting a nudist colony in the adjacent wilderness area, which I think is icing on the cake. Hell, angels are *always* nude, if you believe the paintings of Raphael.

The events surrounding Ess and his visits made the Williams' more stigmatized than ever before. They had done the unmentionable, defending a man who was a "rapist" and threatened every mother's daughter in the community. This did not endear us to the local leadership.

The Jeffs group had finally gained the upper hand in their power struggle against the Barlows. Some of the losers, such as Truman and Dan Barlow, ended up stripped of their families and their lavish homes, living lives that were so austere and lonely I wonder if they wish that they had died instead.

As soon as they had the popular support of the congregation, the Jeffs started to cement their power over the UEP and the local priesthood brides. They harbored a vicious grudge against the Williams clan and snubbed them routinely. By the time I was old enough to understand what was going on, the deck was already stacked. No one with the name Williams was likely to be dealt any aces.

We didn't mind being enemies of the public, though, because we were uniquely cut out for it. We were always very clannish and we banded together, which meant that it was close to impossible to destroy us. All of us were very persuasive in our way—some through eloquence and reason, and others (like me) through volume.

I don't know why I was handpicked among the Williams boys to be an example to those who challenged the "Prophet." It was a difficult war I ended up fighting, because I was among the first to fight it, which meant that precedent was lined against me. Also, in the large part, I would end up fighting the battle alone. Later challenges against the FLDS had the backing of lawyers, governments, safe houses, and charities, but when I fought, I fought alone.

Because of that, I'm glad to be a Williams, because I had the emotional and moral support of all my family on my side. They did their best to aid me when they could, but unfortunately, there aren't many of my family who are financially secure. But even without material aid, I know I could not have challenged the FLDS if I didn't have a web of emotional allies on my side.

The web was particularly large when it came to manpower, at least. I have a large family tree—a giant redwood kind of tree. As of this writing, I still have three paternal grandmothers, twenty-two paternal aunts and uncles, twenty-three siblings, over two hundred cousins, and about five hundred nephews and nieces. When I use the word *clan*, I am not being facetious—our last reunion in July of 2008 was an affair to see.

My mother had a network of family as well, but every one of them was an ardent member of the FLDS, and they generally leveraged a lot of pressure on her to disavow the members of her family who did not follow the true path. We were thought to be on the path, but going in an unsuitable direction, because we did not follow them over the cliff and into fanaticism like good little lemmings. The best way I can phrase our situation is to say that we were one of the congregation, but not one *with* the congregation, which made all the difference. The Jeffs family corporation, and those that supported it, had no room for the rowdy bunch of Canucks and generally wished we would all just go back up north and leave them the hell alone.

# IV
# THE LITTLE KID WITH THICK GLASSES

I was born in Hildale, Utah in 1976 to Robert and Susan Williams. My mother had twelve children all told. I was the fourth. I had one brother and two sisters who were born before I was. My mother often used to tell me that it was a good thing I wasn't the first child, or she might not have wanted any more. When you grow up in a polygamous community, you often tend to differentiate between the children of your own mother and the half-siblings you had from various other mothers that happened to be married to your father at the time.

I always thought of myself as the special one. I wore thick glasses, was an extremely precocious kid, good at making friends, and I generally captivated (or annoyed) the adults I met.

As a child, I always had a unique ability to press all the right buttons and have most of my older relatives ready to murder me. Once, my father and I were watching a football game, and I had the audacity to celebrate when my beloved Bears intercepted a Cowboys pass and won the game. My father, a rabid Cowboys fan, heaved me bodily out the door and into the front yard. Then he promptly locked the door. If he had had his way I might never have gotten back into the house.

My mother had two more boys after I was born, and then my father married another woman, and we had the good fortune of having *two* mothers. This was called the correct order, and it apparently meant we were guaranteed a slot in God's primetime choir. After Mildred came into the family, our family started to increase much more rapidly. My mother had six more children, and Millie had twelve children of her own. I always thought it was interesting that my father had exactly twelve children with each wife—six boys and six girls apiece. My father was like that; he was all about balance. He even had one pair of twins who were perfectly balanced—a boy and a girl.

At the time we all lived together in a small house at the foot of a formidable mesa. With our own personal baby boom in the making, we were quickly running out of room, and so my father set to building a two-story box to serve as an addition to the home. We ended up finishing the bottom floor eventually, but financial burdens prevented us from fixing the upper portion of the addition. To this day the upper portion stands as little more than a wooden framework hulking over the house.

I got to have the first room in the addition because I was the first child to stop wetting the bed. I enjoyed having my own space for the first several hours, but after one night huddled frightened under the bed, I decided to ask my older brother to move in with me.

As I was growing up, we were subjected to a regimen of modesty requiring that our bodies must be covered at all times. One's arms and legs and neck were *never* to be revealed. This was because they were meant to cover long undergarments that were handed out to every one of us. These were full-length off-white underwear that made us look something like prisoners when we didn't wear clothes over them. We never had the agonizing dilemma of having to decide between boxers or briefs before a hot date. Shoot, we never got to go on a date.

By all accounts we were required to look peculiar, and we certainly managed to accomplish it. I would wear the heavy homemade long-sleeve shirts and pants with long sleeved underwear beneath my clothing every day, even in the worst of the summer when the high desert temperature was consistently in the hundreds. Our clothing requirements were worse than uncomfortable; they were downright oppressive.

When I was a child in Colorado City, we were only a little bit weird. The leaders had not yet completed the transition into total control, but they were starting the process along, and the fruits of their efforts were apparent in many aspects of my everyday life.

One of these efforts was the youth program. My brothers and I would always look forward to the summer. Any youngster old enough to hold a hoe or drag a rake was invited to join this youth program. The program was a massive assembly of children who provided clean-up projects around the town. It always helped if the kid had been potty-trained first.

A lot of very young kids would show up to the program, because it was touted as a great place to be if you wanted to demonstrate that you truly loved the "Prophet." The kids, and the unnamed program they all joined, eventually came to be called "Uncle Roy's Boys." "Uncle Roy" was LeRoy Johnson, the leader of the fundamentalist group. This was before it was founded as a legal entity under his successor, Rulon Jeffs. At the time, "Uncle" Roy was ninety-five years old.

This work crew basically functioned as an outdoor day care center, with the added benefit of child labor. It was led by several older boys, who served as platoon leaders and directed thirty to fifty young boys each. The elementary school principal, Alvin Barlow, donated his summer vacation to preside over this small army—and 'small' was indeed the operative word. I was only four years old when I first went.

We would meet as early as seven-thirty to be assigned to various crews which would work on different tasks throughout the town. The tasks generally included hoeing weeds along the community streets, collecting trash, or working in the communal garden. We would sit in the meeting hall until we were called to order, and then Alvin Barlow, or one of his lieutenants, would outline the projects for the day. Then we would line up and trudge halfway across town to the site of the project.

Sometimes if the destination was too far away to walk, we would pile into a truck someone volunteered and hang on as the thing bounced and clattered over the rocky streets. On many occasions there were ten of us or more, clinging to the racks on the back of a small truck. Once we arrived, we would bail out of the truck and start slaving away in the heat. I certainly didn't enjoy the work much; I went partly because my father asked me, but mostly for the free lunch.

We generally worked until just before noon. Then we would gather back at the meeting hall for a community prayer. Then we washed up and started on the short walk to the cafeteria. This was my favorite part of the day, as we gathered around the cafeteria waiting for lunch to be prepared. We usually had some moments of respite as we waited for the other work crews to wash and arrive at the cafeteria. When I first noticed this reprieve, I walked up to the front of the congregation and tapped our crew leader on the knee.

"Can I sing a song?" I asked him.

He looked down at me in surprise. "Wha-at?" he asked.

"Can I sing a song for everybody?" I asked him again.

He looked at his friends. I was clearly insane. "Sure," he shrugged.

I turned to face the crowd and broke into a masterful rendition of "Mary Had a Little Lamb." The applause was deafening, and I beamed with delight. This was my calling. Every day from that moment forward, I would always head up the front and lead them in various songs I had picked out. It was only later that I realized the applause was actually laughter. They thought the whole show was hilarious because I couldn't say my R's. After that, as Alvin Barlow led the crowd in a hymn (usually "Do What Is Right"), I would go down to the crowd and grin like a madman. Everyone wanted to give me a congratulatory slap on the back.

After I started those performances, I began to make a lot more friends in the work crew. They thought the little kid with thick glasses was a real hoot. I even got several of them to work with me on my speech problem. The progress would stall out frequently, because everyone would laugh hysterically every time I said the famous "Roger has a brown car with a round rubber tire" tongue-twister. After my first several concerts, there was not a day that passed without someone trying to get me to go sing a song. They loved it. Despite that, for some reason, my recording career never seemed to really take off.

The icing on the day was eating lunch in the cafeteria at the end of our half-day of work. After this we would be expected to go home and work on our own yards. Fred Jessop, a sort of unofficial bishop in the town, would arrange the meal. They would assemble a series of tables and create a de facto sort of café. We called the place "Permillia's Palace" in honor of the cook. "Uncle" Fred's no-nonsense wife, Permillia, had gathered a small army of ladies who would feed the massive crew each day. Lunch always consisted of turkey or chicken, a bit of mashed potatoes, some bread, and a cup of juice. Permillia was a true martinet; she was bound and determined not to let any of us have seconds.

The highlight of our summer came on the Fourth of July. The fire engines would start their circuit of the town at about four in the morning, with sirens screaming and wailing. Now that the community was awake, they were all expected to congregate at the School Center for breakfast. After this we saw a patriotic parade. The entire work crew marched along carrying our hoes or rakes. We held a massive banner aloft as we marched, declaring us to be "UNCLE ROY'S BOYS." The parade culminated in a series of speeches delivered by the church elders. The speeches were always too long.

---

It certainly was a strange childhood, when compared to the rest of America. That type of child labor would be unacceptable in many societies, but as a child, that was the only life I really knew. I had no inkling at all that there *were* any variations on the types of childhood people experienced. In retrospect, it certainly isn't something I would subject my boys to by any account, but for myself, I look back on it with a certain degree of fondness. Anyway, in the 1650s, I might have had a one in three chance of making it to age eighteen. Compared to that, the years I spent attached to a rake were nothing. My childhood was more enjoyable than that of 99.999% of all the people who have *ever* lived anywhere in the world.

My life took a turn for the worse once our other mother started to have children of her own. Before that she treated us fairly well, but after she had a bouncing baby boy herself, she transformed into a monster. She was one of those people that are always convinced she is not getting a fair shake. Even when all empirical evidence argues otherwise, she still feels she is being had. Aunt Millie (as she insisted on being called) was convinced that my mother's oldest son, Jeromy, was the favorite, at the expense of *her* oldest son, Joey. She would demand that he be taken to every event Jeromy was taken to, even though there was a substantial difference in age. This was symptomatic of the kind of domestic politics that put my dad in a very difficult situation. For a guy who likes balance, the power-sharing agreement was very dangerous and volatile.

My father generally retreated from the squabbles in an effort to find balance. He was always trying to balance his life, his family, his favors, his checkbook, and even his car. Every time they went anywhere, Millie and my mother would ride in front, and he would ride in back, reading, always reading. He was a voracious reader; that was the kind of thing that would get him in trouble later. He always recognized that ignorance is the greatest ally a dictatorship can have. That is why they always downplay the importance of knowledge, usually arguing for obedience or patriotism as a better value to uphold. Reading is to theocracy what light is to a vampire. My father always encouraged us to read, especially as the church slowly started to careen into a cult. The balance and free thinking my father instilled in us was a huge factor in breaking us out of the clutches of a greedy church.

At the time, my dad was having difficulty providing for his increasing family, so he started to take work farther out of town. When the commute was too far, he would take two children and one of his wives with him, for a week or two at a time. At first, I was frequently invited to travel with him, and I loved every second of it. He would set me up helping him work, teaching me what to do until I was fairly proficient at most of the building trades.

Like most kids, I loved being high up in the air. There is a sense of power children get from climbing on things. One day, I thought I could climb to the very top of a tall scaffold. My dad usually didn't like me to climb things, so I snuck over to a corner and scurried unobtrusively up to the top. Unfortunately, my dad and my Uncle John were just preparing to slide it over another six feet. As I threw my hands exultantly into the air, the scaffold suddenly jerked out from under me and I tumbled off and cracked my head open on the concrete floor some fifteen feet below. That blow to the head is perhaps a good explanation for some of my later behavior. Even today, it is a good excuse for some of the things I have been known to do.

After that accident, I was invited to go with my dad less frequently. Unfortunately, this meant I would often have to remain home with no one to protect me from Aunt Millie. She felt that I was some kind of favorite, and on these rare occasions she had us alone, she did everything she could to even the score.

# V
## AUNT DREAD

I don't recall who coined the name "Aunt Dread," but it was an appropriate description. She insisted on being called "Aunt Mildred", instead of Mother, or Mom, or Mama Millie. Mildred Barlow was the lady God sent into our lives to make our family a shoo-in for the celestial kingdom. For my part, I think it was well deserved too—if tribulations purify the human soul, we were on the road to snow white.

She was pretty enough—sort of a Molly Ringwald clone, with dark red hair and freckles. My dad was obviously in love, a phenomenon to us, but it enabled him to overlook a lot of her aberrant behavior. I'm sure my mom was a little jealous sometimes, but for several years the two of them acted like the best of friends. They went everywhere together; some of their friends thought that they were exemplary—the way sister-wives *should* live. Unfortunately, the demonstrated good will was short-lived from my perspective. She soon grew into the name the rest of the family seemed to prefer. She filled *me* with dread almost every day.

To us, this lady was Miss Hannigan. She would glare at us, filled with resentment of the idea that she was left home tending children that she didn't really view as hers. She wanted to show us just how foreign we were to her. I knew what was coming, so I would often beg my mom and dad to take me whenever they went somewhere. When I was told no, I would burst into tears.

After mom and dad had been gone for some time, Millie would make some special dessert and call all of the children in to enjoy. Invariably, when I reached for a helping, she would slap my hand with her serving spoon.

"Little *boobs* don't deserve a treat," she would sneer. Then she would send me to my room. I almost felt that she made the dessert specifically to *not* give some to me. She wanted to punish me for crying when my parents first left. She had an instinctive ability to torture. There is nothing worse for a little kid than to be deprived of a dessert everyone else is enjoying. Fortunately, my brother Bobby would usually save me a bit of his. That generally eased my suffering a little.

Every one of us suffered physical abuse at the hands of this evil stepmother. We all knew that if one of us fell into her clutches, we were expected to go to bat for each other. The one who had taken a beating always needed a little support after the kid had endured the wrath of Millie. Every one of us were aggressive kids, ready to fight each other over trivia. But we developed a lasting bond; we had to show solidarity in our war against Aunt Dread.

And she was determined to win her war against *us*. We were often known to sneak over next door to my Uncle Tom's house. I was really close with my cousins; we treated each other like brothers and sisters. In Millie's view, we were never to be over there because my cousins were part of the "2nd Ward." That was one of the reasons she hated us. We older children were too close to our "apostate" cousins.

Because she couldn't stop us from fraternizing with the wicked, she was determined to exact punishment in other areas of our life. I learned this lesson well one morning when Bobby and I broke out into a fight. I had finally pinned him. I was grinning victoriously, when I felt a stunning blow to the back of my head. I was not surprised to find the attacker was Aunt Dread, wielding a broom stick. I looked at her a moment, stars in my eyes. As my rattled brain tried to connect the dots, another blow rained down.

Before I knew what was happening, I had been hit five times in the same spot on the back of my head. Sitting in stunned silence, I looked at her for an explanation for such a violent attack. She just glared a moment, and without a word, stormed away. I felt a knot beginning to form on the top of my head. Running as quickly as I could to my room, not wanting anyone to see me cry, I shut the door and locked it behind me.

"Who is there?" I whimpered, when a light knock caught my attention. It was Aunt Dread—the Millie Monster coming back to beat me again.

Bobby answered. "Jase, it's me. Open the door." I hurried over and let him in.

"Sorry about that, dude," he offered. "I didn't even see her there 'til she was already swinging. I was just trying to stay out of the way so she couldn't get me too." I just sat there in silence, wondering when this kind of abuse was going to stop.

Later that day, a friend at school noticed the wound. He kept staring at it, long after it got on my nerves. "What's up?" I asked.

"There's a huge lump on your head," he said. "How in the hell did you get that?"

"Aunt Millie hit me with a broom," I answered. "Like five or six times in the same spot. I was really hoping she would just kind of take the broom and fly away, if you know what I mean."

It was a good joke, but it hurt to laugh. I was just hoping to look tough in front of my friends. After a moment, a black fear crossed my mind. What if it got back to Aunt Millie? She had vowed to make our lives a living hell if we ever told anyone about the beatings, especially our mom. I often wondered if we weren't there already.

This was not the first time that Aunt Millie had attacked us. She seemed to have it out for my mom's oldest children, which kept us walking on eggshells when we were around her. She would take to our heads with a stick or knife handle as punishment for little crimes, like chewing with our mouths open. We were forced to finish every scrap of food on our plates, even if the meal tasted like charcoal briquettes with cheese sauce. To top it off, under no circumstances were we permitted to scrape our plates. This sometimes affected our ability to eat everything. When it comes down to the last bit of food residue, you have to be given a little license, or there is no way you can get it on your fork. This fell on deaf ears with Millie, though. If we scraped our plate, we could count on a beating. She was a true dictator when it came to etiquette. Emily Post and Genghis Khan were now sharing the same body.

Every evening on the trampoline, we would sit in a circle and recount the stories of that day's beatings. The smaller the crime, the larger the punishment seemed to be. Sometimes we would reenact some of the things she had done to us that day. We always laughed long and loud at the stories. On certain occasions, I would grab my brother's hand and glare at him.

"Do you want to go the rounds with me?" I would challenge him, spinning him in circles and delivering an over-exaggerated spanking until finally I gave up in a fit of exhaustion. My siblings would laugh, telling me that I had delivered a spot-on impersonation of our Aunt Dread. Strangely enough, my acting career never took off either.

Everyone had "gone the rounds" with Aunt Dread, some of us more than others. Millie had discovered a secret when it involved spanking. When you hit kids in the behind, they always leap forward. It's too much work to follow them in order to strike again. She came up with the brilliant concept of grabbing our arm with one hand and guiding our leaping into a fitful circle around her. With the other hand she would whip at us ferociously, using a belt, stick, hanger, kitchen implement, or whatever happened to be nearby when she got angry.

We would move in a circle (hence "going the rounds") cringing under the blows. If we tried to block it, she would swing it hard into our heads or upper bodies. The beating would generally last until she was tired, or we were crying hysterically, or, more often, both. We learned early on that the best thing was to let her know she had hurt you. You always wanted to start crying as early as possible. Sometimes, though, I would start to cry before she had even hit me. That was never a wise decision on my part.

All in all, going the rounds with Aunt Dread was better than the alternative, which was grounding us. We could be grounded for crazy things sometimes. Once, when it was my turn to do dishes, I committed the crime of letting the dishes dry in the drainer, and waiting until the morning to put them away. Aunt Dread scooped up a glass and trudged over to the window. Holding the glass up into the sunlight, she found there were a few water spots on its rim. She rounded on the children with a furious screech.

"Who did these dishes?" she yelled in her most intimidating bellow.

The tone of her voice made me a little hesitant to confess. My brothers and sisters turned as one and shot me a look. They knew that if I didn't confess, we would all receive a beating. Jeromy elbowed me in the ribs.

Finally I could stand it no longer. "I th-think," I stammered, "I think I did the dishes last n-night." I cringed at the sound of my confession, knowing I had called down hellfire upon me.

She grabbed me by the roots of my hair and yanked me in a wide arc. "How many times do I have to tell you," she roared as she pulled my hair out by the roots, "that the dishes have to be dried with a *towel* before you put them away?"

After she was finished rattling me around the kitchen, I slumped, miserable, on the floor, knowing tufts of my hair were gone. My head hurt so badly I couldn't remember how many times she had told us that. Even my crying wouldn't stop her. It only served to energize her further. The Marquis de Sade would have smiled at the scene.

"Let this be a lesson to *each* of you," she threatened viciously, glaring at us all. "I will *not* permit you to leave these dishes with water on them." Her voice rose into a mad crescendo. *"Do you understand me?"* Then she turned her attention back to me, and me alone. "You have already been warned, Jason," she told me. "You are grounded, and you're required to do *all* the dishes for a month. Is that clear?"

I nodded in reply. I didn't think the punishment was particularly fair, but I knew that any word of protest would only serve to lengthen the punishment. It was a terrible grounding—true torture, especially because it was November. Thanksgiving landed in that month, and I was slave to the kitchen for two days afterward.

I felt like Cinderella, except she only had two ugly stepsisters. My situation was much worse—I had an ugly *brother*. After his initial fright, Jeromy took a little bit of delight in my punishment. It meant he was absolved of kitchen duty. On several occasions, he would stride into the kitchen, finishing his last swallow of milk. Then he would hold the empty glass up to the light.

"Jason," he would say, "I'd better not see any spots on this glass." Then, when with a smug grin on his face, he would hand me his dirty glass. He thought it was hilarious, but I saw no humor in the situation until many years later.

It was some time before I experienced the most embarrassing beating of all. I was taking a shower one early morning. I had just shampooed my hair, when I heard the bathroom door click open. Just then, I realized I had forgotten to lock it, which was a mistake I would never repeat. For a few moments I wondered who it was, and then the shower door was thrown open. There, in the wan light of the bathroom, stood Aunt Dread, mad as hell.

"You guys know you're not supposed to shower before *me*," she screeched. She grabbed hold of my hair and shook me ferociously. I don't know why it was always the hair with her. The loosening of follicles might explain the shiny knob I display today.

Startled and embarrassed, I tried my best to cover my exposed body. Her hands slipped away because of the soap in my hair. Not to be thwarted, she started slapping at my naked back with both hands. I couldn't fight her off because my hands and arms were busy protecting more important things. Fourteen year old boys are pretty shy about those things. I just let her slap away at my back until she finally tired of it.

Then she stormed out of the bathroom. "Tell the rest of them," she screamed back at me through the shower door, "they have to wait until *I* have showered."

I seized the respite to finish shampooing my hair, burning with rage and embarrassment. I wanted to fight back. I was finished with her thinking she had the right to strike us whenever she wanted.

I told my dad what had happened, and he promised he would talk to her. A few days later, though, she was at it again. I entered my bedroom to find her attacking Bobby with her trusty broomstick. After a few blows, I decided enough was enough. I rushed at her and the two of us succeeded in ripping the broom away.

Bobby glowered at her. "We're sick and tired of you hitting us for no reason," he said.

I nodded. This was a pact of solidarity between us. Looking her in the eye, I finally told her: "This is not going to happen anymore."

She looked at both of us in utter fury and stormed away. That was the last time she ever laid a hand on one of my mother's children. Aunt Dread was so livid that we had dared stand up to her that she demanded a separate house. She told my father she wanted to raise her children away from the influence of my mom's family. We knew that wasn't the problem though. The problem was that she had finally lost control. I think the moment we stood up to her, she began to fear us on some level.

My dad moved us back into the house proper and moved Aunt Dread and her children to the addition. Then he built a wall between the front room and the new house. We called it the Berlin Wall. She was determined to keep her children isolated from my mom and the rest of the family. Finally, we celebrated, the Wicked Witch was dead. Aunt Millie was no longer a part of our daily lives. We were no longer subject to her abuse.

My mom, however, was furious about the developments, because the separation meant that we were no longer living the correct order. Each family living in their own designated area was just not the same as sharing everything. The community was big on sharing. We had failed at 'celestial marriage.'

After the Iron Curtain, actually four and a half inches of frame and drywall, was erected, Aunt Dread still had a need to keep tabs on us. My dad had set up separate phone lines in each mother's apartment. This allowed him to make and receive calls without having to trot halfway around the house to do it.

Aunt Dread somehow arranged a bug on my mom's line, complete with a recording device. Like President Nixon, she used it to monitor her political enemies. Milliegate was uncovered when my dad accidentally pushed the wrong button and discovered a conversation between himself and my mother. After that, he did his best to repeal the surveillance. She claimed the spying was a matter of national security, to keep us from talking to girls. Still, I suspect it was just a method of spying on my mom, to make sure that she wasn't getting any special favors.

And she felt she was right to be suspicious. She accused my father of always spending his paycheck on my mom's family needs, and ignoring Millie. She did come up with one solution to the family finances. All us older kids, she argued, should get jobs and donate the entirety of our paychecks to my mom. Then Millie should receive my dad's entire paycheck to spend on her family. This, she felt, would be fair.

She pointed to *her* father's family as an example of this success. All his children would pay a modest amount each month into a fund for her father, almost like a familial tithing. Millie would spend money every month on her father's new Lincoln town car. She never did cut the umbilical cord—over coffee every morning, her mother and sisters would inject their opinions of right and wrong. Generally speaking, they interpreted righteous actions to be the opposite of whatever we did.

Aunt Dread's righteous paranoia soon found a more fertile field. Rulon Jeffs and his son told their followers that the Last Days were on their way. The Lord was going to destroy the wicked and lift the righteous up into the heavens. Destruction would pass over the entire earth. Preparations were underway to determine who the righteous were.

Millie was sure that living in our home would mean that she would be left behind. How could my dad and his first wife's wicked offspring possibly be ready to meet God? She made herself physically ill worrying about it. Her natural vindictiveness now was wrapped in the mantle of striving to become Godlike. She was determined to stamp out the idolatry of her husband and his miscreant progeny.

She would spend hours listening to recorded Jeffs sermons, and lie bedridden for weeks out of her fear. When it came time to be lifted up, the Rapture, of course, never happened. The near miss confused many of God's chosen few. Rulon Jeffs kindly explained that it was only because of the wicked among them that God didn't snatch them into the clouds. A lot of evictions from homes, reassigned marriages, and commands to get out of town were forthcoming. These false alarms occurred often—they predicted the rapture at least four times that I was aware of, the most famous one being in the middle of the Y2K furor.

Millie breathed a sigh of relief, now that she knew she had a few extra months to get out of the clutches of wickedness. This fear made her determined to take action. It was about this time a pamphlet was issued, compiled by Warren Jeffs. It was titled "Purity." This ultra-righteous reading material convinced most women who read it that reassignment was a good thing, that women were justified in marrying their way up the ladder of priesthood authority, a little like sleeping your way to the top of a corporation. The best part of this was that God was not only okay with it; he *insisted* on it. From then on, our other mother was in a hurry to become the other mother of another.

# VI
# CIVIL WAR

Between the years of age fourteen to eighteen, I formed most of my opinions about the world around me. The contradictions were extreme, and a lot of parties were in competition for my allegiance. On one hand, the church, with Warren Jeffs, demanded disassociation with the outside world, or Gentiles, and no contact with anyone—including my best friends and cousins—whom he had identified as apostates. On the other hand, I met people through work and sports who were very hard to go on hating. It takes a lot of energy to hate the world, especially when you're required to hate people so *likable*. Hating Gentiles always made me very tired. The dilemma taught me that the position of Warren Jeffs and his father was not justified in most instances.

Like most teenagers, I was subjected to a lot of peer pressure. But my peers were not trying to subject me to the temptations of drugs, alcohol, tobacco, vandalism, or any other teenage enticements (like *each other*, for example). Instead my peers were trying to get me high on good old-fashioned paranoia and isolation, which had been around a lot longer. My interest in sports put me in contact with people my dad had on his teams, with my uncles, and with other *bad* people. Bad, in this case, meant anything different than the teachings of the FLDS.

My very first taste of the outside world came with sports, when my dad started to take me to softball games. There, I met Clay Mills, who was one of the men playing on our team. Coming from California, he did not really know or understand the church and its background of polygamy. One of his first experiences was a simple phone call to my parents' home.

"Is Robert home?" he asked.

After a short silence on the other end, someone finally answered. "Which one?" they asked, "The dad or the boy?"

"The dad," Clay replied, chuckling.

"He's not home."

"Well, may I speak to your mother?" he asked.

"Which one?" asked the voice, nonchalantly.

This time the silence on the phone belonged to Clay. "I'll just call back later," he volunteered.

I had never imagined someone could be that shocked. There were a lot of juniors in this town, and many men had managed to grab themselves an extra wife to boot. I always thought nothing of it, but I nearly died whenever I heard Clay relate the story. Clay really took a liking to the Williams boys, and he thought it would be a good idea to immerse us in the outside world. I had never been on any kind of trip without the whole family in tow, but he invited me and my brother Jeromy to travel with him to California. We were going to watch an Angels game, go to Disneyland, and swim in the ocean. I was excited. I had heard all sorts of stories about how cool it was to hang at a beach in California. Our religious leaders always implied that kind of behavior merits a one-way ticket to hell, and I believed them, because I never thought I would actually have the opportunity to do it. Now that I had a chance to go to California, I didn't give a whole lot of thought about what this meant for my eternal soul. The idea never occurred to me. I was a kid, after all; I could only really think of one or two things at a time anyway.

We stayed with Clay's parents in their condo, and we loved it. Kay and Sandra treated us like kings. Every morning, Clay's mother served us heaps of pancakes slathered in syrup, grade-A bacon, and eggs cooked just the way we liked them. A few days of that and I wondered if I would ever be able to go back to cold cereal again. Jeromy and I agreed—Sandra was a godsend.

Kay and Sandra gave us full permission to use the tennis courts and other amenities the condo had to offer. Jeromy and I, along with our friend Bo Draper, who had tagged along, decided it would be fun to play tennis one summer morning. We had seen a lot of surfers and basketball players and beach bums and the like who went around shirtless, and we thought it would be fun to lose our shirts as well. It was a humid day anyway, we told ourselves; we would roast with them on.

It felt strange to go shirtless in public. Because of the dress codes the FLDS enforced, my skin had never before been exposed to the sun. My brother and I really got into the competition—another no-no in my community—and we lost track of time. We remained out on the courts for several hours.

That afternoon, we went off to the beach. Most people who spend their lives on the coast seem to grow a little desensitized to the power and the vastness of the ocean. But we had come from the northern Arizona desert, and now we were facing more water than we believed existed. Like most people, we had all seen photos of the ocean—we had seen maps showing a lot of blue space between California and Japan, but there is nothing that compares to actually seeing it. We could have sat for hours, just watching the waves and listening to them crashing in on the shore.

We had more important things to do with those hours though. We wanted to experience the water. We wanted to get in and splash around. Clay reminded us to be really careful, because the riptides would grab us and sink us like an anchor. I didn't have to worry about that because I wasn't going to go that far out. I couldn't swim.

I was ecstatic when we got back to the condo. I had gone shirtless in the California sun for an entire day. That was something I would never have been allowed to do in the strict community of Hildale and Colorado City. I felt joyful, I felt liberated, I felt—a throbbing pain that nearly crippled me. I quickly looked in the mirror. I was glowing red.

Kay and Sandra peeled some fresh aloe vera leaves and put them on our burns. That would give us enough relief that we might be able to sleep. The next morning, I found I looked a little bit like a beet and felt like I was on fire. They administered another dose of aloe vera and sent us off to a swap meet, with our shirts on this time. The three of us trudged around, stiff-limbed, taking in the sights and ignoring the pain. Then Jeromy noticed a particularly cool booth. Trying to call my attention to it, he gave me a sharp slap on the back.

Instantly a jolt of pain shot up my spine. Letting out a sharp cry, I bent over in agony, tears running down my face. Normally, I thought crying in public made me look like a sissy. I wanted to be tough, but this time, I didn't care *what* I looked like, because it hurt so badly. When you are in pain, all you care about is making it stop.

Clay's sister, Sue was with us at the time. She looked at me sympathetically. "Oh, you poor thing," she said. "Let's take you home and get this burn out."

Sue and Sandra laid the three of us out on a big sheet and mixed a sort of baking soda paste. With it smeared all over our whole bodies, we lay there all afternoon, watching westerns and looking like we belonged in King Tut's tomb. The paste cooked like a tortilla because of the heat in our bodies. I think I could have literally fried an egg on my torso that day. I might have tried, if it didn't hurt so badly.

In the next room I could hear Kay and Sandra talking about us. They were blaming themselves for letting us get too much sun. Any prairie dress-wearing FLDS mother would let us sit and burn to teach us a lesson rather than concoct a baking soda mix and turn us into human chimichangas in an effort to ease the pain. Hell, she might have even decided to "go the rounds with us," slapping at our sunburns with a willow stick or a wire hanger.

That line of thinking made me very ashamed at even listening to some of the silly things Rulon Jeffs had said over the years. In one sermon I remember, he told us how lucky we were to be living at this time. We were lucky to have a man who held the keys to our salvation. We were not to associate with Gentiles because they were all going to be destroyed.

Yet here, right in front of me, these people opened their hearts and reached out to strangers---really strange. To them, we had a really weird religion, and we did really weird things. We might as well have been from Mars. But they took us in and made us feel like part of their family. Rulon Jeffs himself, our "Prophet," wouldn't have done the same. If a Muslim, or a hippie, or a feminist, or someone else Rulon Jeffs found weird were to show up at his door, he would kick them back out into the street. No, I decided, these Gentiles were not *bad* people. They were the opposite. These people treated others so much better than the people with whom *I* associated every day.

There was another person I met in my early life that I was required to hate, and it was hard to hate him too. His name was Joel Timo, and the reason I was supposed to hate him was because he was black. His race was just fine with regular Mormons—in 1978, the mainstream Mormon Church finally relaxed its ban on blacks holding the priesthood and began ordaining black elders into various church positions.

But his race was *not* just fine with the FLDS. They already differed with the mainstream Mormons over polygamy and communal living, and now they added this to the pile. Warren Jeffs maintained the ban and preached that the exclusion was another proof that the FLDS had it right. In his sermons he often referred to blacks as "the race of mud" and told us to have nothing to do with them. He didn't think black people had any chance at salvation, because they were supposedly the seed of Cain. In one sermon he would tell his followers "you see some classes of the human family that are black, uncouth, or rude and filthy, uncomely, disagreeable and low in their habits; wild and seemingly deprived of nearly all the blessings of the intelligence that is usually bestowed upon mankind."

He wanted us to avoid blacks at all costs, so that we didn't become immoral too. He never allowed us to listen to rock music, because he told us "when you enjoy the beats, the rock music—maybe even toned down with an orchestra—you are enjoying the spirit of the black race."

I believed in that kind of intolerance when I was a kid, because I didn't have any experience to measure it against. My dad never really talked about the issue of racial prejudice, because he thought all races are equal, when it comes right down to it. It seemed like such an *obvious* thing, that it didn't have to be discussed. But because we never talked about it, the result was that, for a while, I believed that sort of racist trash. I wasn't ever really likely to go on believing it forever, though. Few people in the Williams clan ever really bought into the idea that some people or races were inherently better, or that a race was predetermined to be saved or condemned. We generally thought that was a silly notion.

Joel Timo was my eye-opener. I was a little apprehensive about meeting him at first, since he was basically the first black man I'd ever met. I was doing construction work for the Home Company in LaVerkin, Utah, about fifteen miles north of where I lived. Joel was employed there, and we did a lot of work together, talking about the world as we saw it.

Joel was a tall, muscular guy from the Bahamas. He'd been converted and baptized into the LDS faith, and had moved to Utah to be closer to his church. Over the years, he had had to endure a lot of racist comments and threats. We understood one another on that issue. In our community, I had run into a lot of harsh words because I was a Williams, and therefore reviled. Then, whenever I went *out* of the area, I encountered a lot of hostility just on virtue of being a resident *of* the area. Neither my name nor my birthplace was my fault, any more than Joel's race was *his* fault. We were sort of kindred spirits, Joel and I, because, since the day we were born, we had both been surrounded by people who told us, full of conviction, that we weren't worth shit.

Joel lived just down the street from a Skinhead compound in LaVerkin. They had set up shop next door to the church Joel attended every Sunday. The compound was run by Johnny Bangerter, a Skinhead who was made famous later for smashing a chair across Geraldo Rivera's nose on live TV. That group hated blacks and vowed to take over the nearby Zion national park and turn it into a Skinhead stronghold. They attacked Joel on several occasions. Once we were forming a concrete slab, and Bangerter's car drove up. Four of them barreled out of the car, taunting him and warning him to leave town before they murdered him.

"Take your crap and peddle it somewhere else!" my cousin yelled. "This is private property!"

One bald head was edging toward the car, where I presumed they were carrying a gun. The leader sneered at us. "What are you doin' tryin' to defend this monkey?" he asked us. "Aren't you proud of your heritage? You're blood traitors, that's what you are."

"Get out of here!" Joel roared back at them. He had a 22 oz. framing hammer and was ready to plunk the claws into the first shaved head that got close enough. In the Bible, Samson did a lot of damage with the jawbone of a donkey. Joel was just as strong, and his weaponry was upgraded. My money was on Joel.

My cousin held up his cell phone and told them he had the cops on the way. In the time it took him to make that statement, the Skinheads were gone, melted away into suburban Utah.

I had to admire Joel's outlook on life. He met racism in various forms almost every day. This meant that every time he woke up, there was at least one white guy somewhere who hated him and wanted to make sure he knew it. I would have gotten sick of that early on; I would have wanted to stuff the heads of the next ten white people I met. Joel never had that inclination, though. He took it in stride and behaved just as kindly to the next person he met, as though nothing had happened. Joel was a delightful human being, and I felt bad for ever thinking otherwise.

Another bone of contention within the FLDS was a lawsuit that was filed against them. Warren Jeffs, trying to purge the town of wickedness, decided to evict many of the people who had stopped going to church. A lawyer went through the literature surrounding the United Effort Plan, which was the trust that soaked up all the properties in the area. He crossed the dissidents' names off all the beneficiary lists and filed a disenfranchisement case against them, taking away their right to the homes they had built. Five of these people were related to me.

In retaliation, many of these opponents decided to sue the UEP to get their land back. They were branded as apostates who were fighting the "Prophet." Three of my uncles were involved in the lawsuit. The other two had withdrawn from the battle, saying that suing people wasn't the right thing to do in any situation. I guess that line of thought makes sense, if you file suing people in the same category as stabbing them.

About twenty five plaintiffs banded together to fight the actions of the UEP. One of my uncles, Roger Williams, had a side judgment, which caused the case to be lumped under his name. There was something a little fitting about *Roger Williams vs. UEP et. al.* The people of Rhode Island might still be watching.

The more I learned about the details of the trust and the fiduciaries that operated it, the more I realized the plaintiffs had a good gripe. They were not the wicked men we heard about every Sunday, but a group of men who were being cheated. The suit dragged on for several years, but in the end the UEP was doomed to lose. The District Court ruled that the plaintiffs had the right to stay in their own homes.

As I met more of the dissidents over the years, I found people that just wanted justice. Here again, the church I believed in was wrong in the way it dealt with its own people. It was yet another contradiction that I had to work out. It always seemed that the words were Warren's, but the deeds belonged to everyone else. For a while I kept score, but after it reached *Gentiles-10, Crickers-0*, I lost track of the point spread. It was obvious which direction the game was going though.

At this time there was a huge division within the church. The argument was about what was called the "one-man doctrine." This was the idea that at any given time, there was only one man with the authority to govern the priesthood. The belief basically meant that the spirit of Jesus Christ was sitting upon the "Prophet's" shoulder and instructing his every action. This meant that the "Prophet" could not make a mistake.

There was a lot of rhetoric and historical revision underway. Many people went off southward toward a nearby town called Centennial Park. They referred to the FLDS as the "1st Ward," and they formed their very own "2nd Ward." They styled themselves as the last remaining guardians of truth and firmly rejected the one-man doctrine. Interestingly enough, they later came to accept a one-man doctrine of their own. Their "Prophet" was a man named John Timpson.

Most of the Williams clan went off with the Centennial Park group (some later broke away from *that* too, but that's another story). Only my dad and my Uncle Jerold remained where they were. My dad had discussed the issue with LeRoy Johnson, who was the leader at the time, asking what he should do in the face of the split in the church. LeRoy instructed him "to stay in the middle of the road," which was a pretty good idea, but he forgot to tell him to look out for the trucks that are always speeding there. My dad did it to the best of his ability, though. The philosophy really worked well for him, because he liked balance so much. He never got terribly excited over doctrinal arguments.

Both my dad and my Uncle Jerold tried to stay loyal to the church, but only Jerold managed it. Jerold was the only member of my dad's family who went over to the dark side. He bought whole-heartedly into the Jeffs doctrine. Eventually he ended up spearheading an attempt to start a polygamous colony in South Dakota. From there, I don't know what became of him.

My dad, however, was never left alone. Nephi and Sam Barlow, as well as every member of the God Squad, harassed him continually. He was always accused of crimes against the church—his sideburns were too long, he didn't teach his family, he let his wives rule over him, he was an idolater, and on and on into a whole bunch of other shortcomings.

They always gave him a list of commands that he must meet, and he generally met them, or tried to, at any rate. One of the only things he was told to do that didn't sit right with him was to stop all contact with his parents and siblings. That was something neither he nor I could see as coming from God.

But it didn't have to come from God, apparently, because it came from the "Prophet," which was just as good. The FLDS decided it was time to take God out of the equation. The religious leaders began to argue that the faithful no longer *had* to pray to God; instead they should pray directly to the "Prophet." Not since the days of ancient Egypt had a mortal man been worshipped as God. This edict certainly caused some harsh words in our family.

The split in the church gave Aunt Dread the ammunition she needed to isolate herself even further. Her parents exerted tremendous pressure on her to leave my dad. There was a general reshuffling of wives going on amongst my relatives, and a plan was afoot for the "modernization of Millie."

Millie finally did get her wish. My dad had gone to Phoenix with his brother to watch the Cardinals play the Cowboys. My dad was a true Cowboys fan, and the "Prophet" didn't distinguish between fanhood and idolatry. Rulon Jeffs gave Millie a call and finally told her what she wanted to hear—that he was "going to teach Robert a lesson" by releasing her from the marriage.

So, while my dad was at work one day, Nephi Barlow and his army of young men arrived in a moving van. They packed up everything my dad had in the home and stuffed it in the van, driving off with a cloud of dust. Millie arranged for all the furniture to be trucked over to her new residence in an apartment at her mother's house.

When my dad and I came home, not a thing remained. The walls were bare, and the floor was empty, except for one framed photograph that lay face down on the carpet in the front room. I turned the picture over to see what it was, and my dad's jaw dropped. It was a color portrait of him, with fractures appearing in the glass. They had stomped his image down into the floor. This was the ultimate form of symbolism.

Rulon Jeffs ensured that his questions and pleas fell on deaf ears. The "Prophet" told him he must go to Joe Barlow's house, where Millie was living, if he wanted to see his kids. He was even told to attend the Barlow Sunday school. And he did. Every Sunday he went, sitting as politely as possible in the home of the people who had conspired to steal his wife and kids. He went through a lot of depression over this high-handed and sudden intrusion into his life. It hurt to watch. I fervently hoped nothing like that would ever happen to me.

I was experiencing some troubles of my own. My two closest friends were my cousins Thomas and Jared. They were the oldest sons of two of the plaintiffs in the UEP lawsuit. They had no belief in the Jeffs family's ability (or authority) to lead. They were not considered to be candidates for salvation. Consequently, they were branded by my friends at school as wicked, worse than the devil himself. Whenever my high school buddies' parents saw me in the company of my cousins, they made it a point to tell their children not to associate with me anymore.

Personally, I wanted to be friends with all of them. My cousins weren't a barrier to that; they didn't have a problem with my high school friends. They would show up at school for choose-up games of basketball. If I made a foul shot and was a team captain, I would pick my cousins for my team, not only because I was close to them, but also because they were just plain better at basketball than the gangly knots of limbs that made up the rest of the group.

Whenever I picked my cousins, though, my high school friends suddenly had things they needed to do. My cousins and I would end up playing basketball alone. Then, when school started the next day, my friends would give me hell about being an apostate-lover, claiming I was becoming an apostate myself. I tried to defend my cousins, and I asked my friends to get to know them. The most common response, however, was that all they needed to know about my cousins was that they didn't follow the word of the "Prophet."

On a few occasions, I felt like I had to appease my friends, so I selected *them* for my team. But then my cousins would be left out completely. They would feel betrayed, angry at me, and then *they* would leave the court. This was a real catch-22. I still remember Jared spinning out in his truck to make sure that I knew he was not pleased. I'm still hearing about that today.

When it came right down to it, I ended up wishing I'd chosen my cousins every chance I got. I liked both my cousins and my high school buddies, but it was only my cousins who actually cared about *me*. My cousins would lay down their lives for me in the blink of an eye. Regardless of peer pressure, there was a real difference between the two circles of friends, even if I was too dumb to realize it at the time. Sometimes, family is all we really have.

My pals from school didn't get tired of hating the world, the way I did. They seemed to get a kick out of it. It would seem that once people experience prejudice from the outside world, they would be forgiving of their fellow man, but that was not the case. My friends would meet a lot of intolerance for their religion, and then they would turn around and show more intense bigotry toward people from the same background over a slightly different set of beliefs.

Humans have a sordid history when you think of it in that context. The Pilgrims escaped persecution by fleeing across the Atlantic, and then they set up the Massachusetts Bay Colony and started dunking witches. As soon as a Protestant order was set up, which made allowance for many churches, Joseph Smith established the Mormon Church, which was persecuted until it's exodus to Utah. After the Mormon Church renounced polygamy in a bid to achieve statehood, they started to persecute those who still adhered to that order. The polygamists escaped to Short Creek, and some years later, started persecuting their own dissenters. It's always persecution and bigotry when it happens to you, but when *you* do it to someone else, then suddenly it amounts to defending truth and God and upholding the rule of law.

The truest words *I've* ever heard on this subject of intolerance came in the verdict of the UEP lawsuit. In his final ruling, Judge Bruce Jenkins had written very simply that "the only true litmus test of the progress of any society is in the way a persecuted group treats its *own* minority."

# VII
# SUZY Q

One minority that the FLDS treated very poorly was the young bachelors of the society. My oldest brother Jeromy had graduated from high school and got a job in Hurricane, a town twenty five miles north of Hildale. While he was there, he did the unthinkable and dared to hold a platonic conversation with a girl.

She was a really cute waitress who fell in love with his big, brown eyes. She was just younger than he, just happened to be from Short Creek, and just like that, they were in love. Young men are incapable of thinking while they're in love. They sweat nervously and react badly; their mouth disengages and they babble like a madman until the girl leaves. That's love, medically speaking. That was my sophomore opinion.

I was a sophomore in high school and had never had girl problems. I was a little fascinated watching my smart brother's brain turn to mush. Growing up in the FLDS, we all knew that dating was not tolerated. I guess sneaking out at night to talk to a girl qualifies as a date. Showing up at a girl's door with an armload of flowers meant only one thing in this town: you would at least have a bouquet on your grave. The main reason for this, of course, was that if a young lady were permitted to date young men, she might feel a little disapproval toward a placement marriage to an ancient relic, regardless of his pedigree.

Jeromy and Cherylynn fell hard for one another. Naturally, once the news got back to her parents, she was rushed into an appointment with the "Prophet." He convinced her to relocate to Salt Lake City. She could finish her senior year of school at the Alta Academy, a private religious school, presided over by the infamous Warren Jeffs. Being sent to Alta Academy was banishment, like being sentenced to Azkhaban.

Once she found she was sentenced to reform school, Cherylynn risked coming to see Jeromy with a plan to run away. He begged her to try the school; maybe they could negotiate through what the priesthood barons referred to as the "correct channels".

She was relocated to Salk Lake City and enrolled in the church's parochial school. Some times Jeromy would try to contact her. Once I went with him to the area to stay at my grandparents' home. I don't know if he wanted to send coded letters or flick pebbles at her window, but the weekend was fruitless.

When we got back, we found the FLDS leadership was up in arms. Jeromy was mandatorily invited to an interview with the "Prophet" Rulon Jeffs. "That girl is in training," Rulon lectured him sternly. "She is relearning the proper way to be a daughter of Zion."

"I am not trying to upset anyone," Jeromy replied. "I'm willing to wait until school is over. I just need you to know how we feel about each other."

"You might as well run off with her now," the old man spat. "I am washing my hands clean of the whole thing. As far as I am concerned you will be stealing from the Priesthood. Go on, take her!"

"I told her parents I would wait," my brother told him. "So I'll wait."

Once Jeromy was gone, Rulon spoke with Cherylynn and told her that he had offered her hand in marriage, but Jeromy had refused. The poor girl was heartbroken. Assuming my brother didn't care about her anymore, she agreed to a short exile in Canada. She later finally got married properly into the church.

After they finally managed to get Cherylynn back into lockstep, they expelled my brother from priesthood meeting. He was told he had zero chance at salvation and was instructed to leave the community.

I was determined never to have girl problems of my own, but my junior year in high school threw that vow out the window. I don't know why the guy always meets the girl at a dance; but Romeo's first glimpse of Juliet was nothing compared to the vision I saw across the floor. Suzanne was a shy, petite, blue-eyed, blond-haired bombshell, and I was smitten immediately.

Almost two times a month the community would gather for a dance at the Civic Center. They were a lot of old fashioned polkas, reels, and schottisches, with an occasional slow waltz mixed in. When it was my turn to choose my dance partner, I walked right up to this gorgeous girl and offered her my arm.

We didn't say much to each other, because what I was feeling had me a little embarrassed. I had not developed *any* skills for talking to the opposite sex, so I just danced clumsily around, tight-lipped and silent as a wraith. Worse, my hands were shaking, my palms were sweating, and I knew she could tell.

As the music died down, I trudged away, sure I had blown it. Later that evening, however, she picked me for a waltz. I was ecstatic. Dancing with the same partner twice was frowned upon, especially if it was a waltz. Since she had run that gauntlet, she must have some serious feelings for me. I blushed just thinking about it.

During the second dance we started to talk a little. It was the first time that I had been chosen by a girl who was actually beautiful.

"So where do you go to school?" I ventured, wondering why I hadn't seen this beautiful girl before.

"Same as you," she answered, smiling.

"Oh," I said, "I've never seen you around before."

It took another eight bars of music to finally work up the courage to ask who she was. Suzanne was just shy of ninth grade, and we were going into the same art class in the upcoming school year. The thought made me grin widely. I couldn't wait until the school year started.

I don't think I ever again had more fun drawing than I did that year. Suzanne was a wonderful girl, and I was so besotted, I could feel my brain turning to mush, just like Jeromy's had. But we had to tread carefully. If word got around that we had any kind of special feelings for one another, there would be hell to pay.

We made up some quick little nicknames, so that if our communiqués were intercepted, no one could tie them to us. She called me "Buddy," and my pet name for her was "Suzy Q." We thought we were geniuses. *No one* would crack this code.

After school, she would hang out at the court and pretend to be interested in basketball. That way we could slip one another meaningful glances in between jump shots. Sometimes, we would find a few moments in comparative solitude, and we could talk to one another a little more. In spite of our caution, we must have telegraphed our budding attraction, because the art teacher became suspicious of us and told her parents all about it.

Suzanne wrote me a letter and mailed it, trying to let me know how she felt about me. Like the famous missed communications in *West Side Story*, the note missed its target and became the centerpiece of ever-widening ripples of contention.

The letter ended up mailed to the wrong address, a different home just down the street. It's possible she had inadvertently jotted down the wrong address number on the same street. But more likely, Jim Allred, who ran the local post office, noticed the envelope was addressed to "Buddy," and reasoned that there was no one named Buddy at my dad's house, and he would have decided "Boyd," as in Boyd Roundy, was the closest name he could think of, and plopped it the Roundys' mailbox. I assumed this might be why I never got her love letter.

Naturally, old Boyd Roundy erroneously concluded it was *his* kids planning something, and after interrogating everyone in the house, decided to give them all a good old-fashioned beating, just in case they deserved to be punished.

One of the girls of the family, a classmate of Suzanne's, recognized my nickname on the back of the note, and for her own safety she told Boyd that the "Buddy" mentioned in the letter was Jason Williams, who lived up the street.

Boyd knew my dad very well, but he decided to land a few brownie points by taking it directly to the "Prophet." Our simple little friendship had just grown to the point it was too big for us. We were swept along on a current of over-reaction and pathetic assumption.

I knew the brown stuff was about to hit the fan when I met Suzanne in the Cooperative Mercantile Corporation, a grocery store whose name indicated it thought it was more important than it actually was. She cut over a couple aisles and asked if I had gotten the letter.

"No," I said, "where did you send it?" I was genuinely worried about the prospect of a lost love letter. The written word was evidence that was hard to explain away.

"My parents want me to move," she said. "I can't see you anymore."

"Why, what's wrong?" I asked.

"My parents are so worried of me turning out like my sisters that they are insisting that I go to Salt Lake City," she quietly replied. And that was the end of it. She had to leave without telling me much, not even what was in the letter.

I was utterly miserable as I clambered into the car with my brother Bobby. That really sucked. We drove around for a little while and discussed my problems. I could hardly believe that my actions meant Suzie was forced to move away from her family and friends.

"Don't worry, things will work out, dude," Bobby said reassuringly.

Just then we passed Suzanne walking along a side road. This was too good; too much serendipity for passing by. This was a moment of destiny, and I was not about to let it slip away.

"Stop the car and let me find out what's going on," I told my brother. He pulled the car over so I could to walk down the street with her.

"Why do you have to go?" I asked. "Can't we just be friends and not make any more problems?"

"My parent's minds are already made up," she replied. "They don't believe that nothing has happened between us. They are the most suspicious, stubborn and unreasonable couple God ever made."

Just then we could hear the rumble of a big diesel truck behind us. "Oh crap!" she exclaimed. "That's my dad's truck! You need to get the hell out of here!"

"I'm not going to run," I declared, knowing we had done nothing wrong. "Running will make us look guilty."'"

You don't understand," she said, more urgently. "He'll kick your ass!"

I was in for a true beat down. I hoped Bobby would come to my aid. I wanted to vanish, so badly. My mind was racing for all the possible ways to disappear, but I knew there was no escape. Relax, I told myself, you have nothing to hide.

Her dad's truck had just pulled even with us and the tinted window of a huge quad Dodge rolled down. "What the hell is going on here?" he demanded.

"We are just out for a little walk," I croaked. It was all I could think to say.

"Hasn't the Prophet asked you to stay away from the girls? You're supposed to treat them like snakes!"

Alarm bells were clanging in my head, but I charged on. The Jeffs regime often told us to "treat women like snakes" and "stay away from them," on the grounds that they were often poisonous. They interpreted Genesis to mean that women and snakes were together in working their wiles on poor unsuspecting men. Apparently women have seductive powers that *men* must guard against.

"Talking to a girl isn't a sin," I said warily.

That did it—I must have struck a nerve, because he immediately barreled out of his truck and rushed over to me. Grabbing me by the neck, he lifted his other hand ready to strike me. That big, strong, angry man could almost decapitate me with one hard blow.

I stood there and tried not to blink. "If I ever catch you anywhere near my daughter again, I will kill you!" he threatened in his icy voice.

"We weren't doing anything," Suzy screamed. "Just let him go!" She grabbed his hand and began to pull.

Frank finally loosened his grip. "I'm serious!" he warned. "Don't let me catch you around my daughter again!"

He shoved me into the dirt and disappeared with Suzanne. Picking myself up from the dusty street, I started homeward. After a couple blocks, my brother returned in his car and picked me up. I was visibly shaking; my life had passed before my eyes, and it hadn't been long enough. The hurt was not a physical pain—I was rattled because of the hardship the confrontation would cause Suzanne. This was a tempest in a teapot; neither of us had a thing to be ashamed of.

Her parents actually pulled her out of school and shipped her to Salt Lake. She was to enroll in the Alta Academy and report to Warren Jeffs. She was to have absolutely nothing to do with me from that point on. Any hope we had of being together had been crushed.

I was able to focus on my schooling and after a short bout of depression I moved forward. It's not easy trying to get a girl out of your mind, especially when you're certain she needs you. What made it worse was that we had been punished without ever committing a crime. After all this, my compassion for what Jeromy had gone through was elevated somewhat. I had always known he wasn't a bad guy, and neither was I, but the both of us were treated like spawn of Satan. Jeromy had been kicked out for dating, whereas I was on the chopping block for even communicating, but we had to take our chances. We were Williams' kids, so if we followed the rules, we were looking at a life of celibacy. The FLDS hated Williams boys, and we knew the priesthood wasn't likely to come offering. We had to compensate for an unfortunate surname, but it was a surname we wore proudly.

# VIII
# KEEP SWEET

The next weekend was priesthood meeting, which was held once a month. I had no sooner entered the front door, when I was accosted by Nephi Barlow, the same scarecrow watchdog that had hounded my dad so many times. I was in the cross hairs of the leader of the God Squad.

"Frank Jessop has reported having problems with you," he announced, shoving me back out through the door. "You are prohibited from attending any meetings or other priesthood functions until you go talk to The Man."

It was a wet spring morning. I plodded through the mud homeward, reflecting on what a mess this had become. I wasn't sure I wanted to be part of an organization that would disown a member for talking to a girl. We hadn't done anything wrong—hadn't even held hands for more than just a few dances.

When I got home and told my mom what happened, she was disappointed because I had been getting into trouble with the priesthood. She would rather me get into trouble with the law, than with the priesthood. With the exception that the law was usually more heavily armed, I couldn't really tell the difference.

"You need to call the Prophet right now," she declared, "and get an appointment set up. Don't wait, Jason. You can't afford to have anything interrupt the connection between you and your file leader. Do it *now!*"

My file leader was the "Prophet," and I was expected to maintain that "connection" at all times, as though I was a Hasbro toy in danger of being unplugged. At first I was hesitant to call because I knew I'd done nothing. I didn't want to give their silly charges an ounce of legitimacy. It seemed like such a waste of time to go talk about how I was supposed to repent of nothing. But, because of my mom was hyperventilating; I finally called out and made an appointment.

This was my first chance to meet and talk one-on-one with The Man, which was a common euphemism for "Prophet." Neither were accurate descriptors. *I* felt like Dorothy going before the Wizard of Oz. Once the appointment day had arrived, I was to sit before the "Prophet" and present my plea to get back into meetings.

Entering his palatial courtyard, I felt more like the Cowardly Lion than any of the other petitioners on the Yellow Brick Road. I did work up enough courage to ring the doorbell, and I only barely talked myself out of diving behind a nearby rosebush before Wendell Nielson answered the door.

Wendell was a short, balding man who looked something like Jason Alexander. He had all the secretarial responsibilities of scheduling appointments and refereeing the group of people that was always waiting in the lobby. He was The Man's man.

"Brother Williams," he said, extending his hand. "Uncle Rulon is running a little late but he will see you very soon".

"Thanks," I replied.

Sitting in the grand foyer, waiting anxiously, I noticed everything in this home was absolutely opulent. I had never seen such plush and ornate furnishings. The entire home had been built by the estate of the late Jack Knudson. They had been building a magnificent home for Knudson's widows, when the "Prophet's" treasurer approached them.

"You should be ashamed of yourself for having a better home than the Prophet." That's what they told me he said to them. "You expect the Prophet to stay here without a godlike home?"

The Knudson estate got the hint, and donated the home and all its celestial furnishings to the "Prophet." The UEP's thinking was that since Jack Knudson was dead, neither he nor his heirs had a right to the property. It was as though the property reverted to the public domain, where it could then be scooped up by any well-meaning church leader. They didn't really allow women to inherit property. They stole homes from the widows and the fatherless, which was how Elijah once identified wicked men.

I remember wondering what kind of job Rulon had to be able to retire and still afford all of these luxuries. It was simple, really. Rulon Jeffs had undertaken the job of managing our spiritual affairs as a method of bettering his financial ones.

I waited in the room for about forty-five minutes, growing more and more nervous as each minute passed. As the hustle and bustle of handling appointments for the Prophet finally subsided, I studied Wendell cautiously; worried he might ask me about my reason for being there.

"Brother Williams," he blurted suddenly, startling me, "so you are Robert's and Susan's son, correct?"

Surprised that he already knew that much about me, I answered timidly, "Yes sir."

"We will have you in very shortly. Sorry for the delay but he is really busy today."

Thanks," I replied, unsurprised. "I'm not in any big hurry." The "Prophet" was bound to be busy, what with the God Squad rounding up so many sinners. This place was busier than the Hurricane Traffic Court on Wednesdays.

Knowing I didn't have much time before I sat in front of the Prophet, my heart began to race. I couldn't help but wonder what he might ask me to do to get back in the church's good graces. Perhaps he was going to punish me or maybe my family for what he thought was going against the priesthood. Maybe he would tell me to leave the community like my brother Jeromy. Maybe—just maybe--just when I thought my mind was going to explode, the announcement sliced into my brain like a steak knife.

"Brother Williams," Wendell alerted me, "the Prophet will see you now."

As I stood up, my knees almost buckled. I walked toward the office, like one on Death Row. The office was hardwood and classical, with embossed ceiling panels that must have cost a fortune. On the opposite side of an ornate desk sat the "Prophet" Rulon Jeffs, staring at me through his glasses.

"Brother Williams," he called, "what can we do for you?"

Humble and a little embarrassed, I walked over and shook his hand. Then I took a chair in front of him. He leaned back into his chair, his feet resting on the desk in front of me, so that I could see the soles of his slippers. I noticed he had a word on the bottom of each one: "KEEP" on his right foot and "SWEET" on his left, in big upper case yellow letters.

Keep Sweet. That was the maxim of the Jeffs administration, and it became a popular thing to say whenever they made you feel bad. There was something symbolic about telling a man to keep sweet when you stomped the words into him.

"Well," I said, answering his question, "I have been kicked out of Priesthood meeting."

Cracking open a desk drawer, he whipped out an envelope with a condescending smile. Opening it up, he pulled out a piece of paper and studied it. The few seconds of silence seemed interminable. "I want to know what I have to do to get back in church," I said, trying to fill the void.

He fixed his old saggy eyes on me. Oh, boy, I realized. Here comes the falling piano. "Brother Frank Jessop was in earlier," he said, "and he told me they are having problems with you not leaving his daughter alone. What do you have to say about this?"

"I have not really done anything with this girl," was my reply." I think she is real cute and a nice person, but I really don't know that much about her."

"She sure knows you," he insisted, unfolding the paper. I read in one corner of the reverse side a word that almost froze my blood. *Buddy.* He began to read the letter to himself, leaving me there twisting in the wind; pondering my fate.

Uncle Rulon looked up at me. "Who is Buddy?" he asked quietly.

"Uh—well, some of my friends call me that," I answered, trying to appear stoic. He nodded and continued to read.

"But this looks like more to me than just friends," Rulon accused. "This even says she loves you. Do you feel the same way? This note claims you are the most *romantical*, wonderful sweetheart. Now, what is romantical? I've never heard that word." He was mocking our feelings, deriding the words she used, "I heart you with all my heart," he pressed on, with a thin smile. He folded the letter and looked at me condescendingly. "This is juvenile drivel--its *Hollywood* love! Not anything pure or substantial!"

"I don't know her that well, but I think she's really cool," was the only answer I could manage. I couldn't feel the shame that was expected here because my brain was banging a drumbeat inside my head. She loves me—she loves me!

"Where did the two of you meet?" was his next question. I was immediately snapped out of my reverie.

"I met her at a dance at the civic center," I replied. Whoops! I thought. That might get dances canceled. I quickly added, "I have talked several times in school, also." I wasn't sure that would be enough to get the school closed down, but hey, it was worth a shot.

"What do you hope to accomplish with these clandestine meetings?" he sneered. "Do you think you have the power to choose your own bride? Your brother thought he could choose his own bride and disobey the Priesthood. Now he wants no part of this religion—he has damned himself! Is this your plan also?"

I just looked at the floor, chastised and at an utter loss for words. He just continued on, feverishly. "What the hell does your father teach in your home that makes it okay for his sons to pick their own brides?" Becoming increasingly agitated, he took his feet off the desk and leaned toward me. Keep Sweet was no longer visible, neither on his shoes nor his visage. "I will have nothing to do with it and I am warning you to leave this alone!" his voice rose in disgust. "God has left that for *me* to decide and you must not interfere."

He slapped his fist down on his desk, glaring hard at me. "Have you fornicated with this girl?"

I wasn't sure what fornication *was* at the time, but I knew we hadn't even kissed yet, I replied timidly, "No."

"I cannot use you," he counseled, "if you think you can bypass the Prophet and get inspiration from God. You must repent and wait for the proper channels."

He folded the letter, tossing it at me. "If you can stay away from her," he admonished, "I will allow you to continue to go to priesthood meetings."

I was only a junior in high school, so I thought it would be good idea to play it low-key until I finished my education. I had no idea why I was ending up in so much trouble all the time. I was just wired to be a revolutionary, I guess. I drove down my dad's driveway and squeaked the truck to a halt. And then I unfolded the letter.

Jason,

I love you!! You are the most romantical, thoughtful, wonderful sweetheart. There's just not enough words to describe how much love is in my heart. You're always there for me. I know there are alot of women out there that would do almost anything for a man like you. I do with him by hurting him in his life more than you deserve. you deserve I think and heart I give alot of times.

That was just my luck, to find that Suzanne loved me as much as I loved her, just when the powers that be were clamping down on the relationship. I felt a moment of fury at the "Prophet" and his abject cronyism. If I was a Jeffs or a Barlow, this likely would have been handled differently, but when God plays favorites, you can't win.

It would be tough to obey the rules all the time, especially the ones I found to be unfair. But I knew that however hard this probation was on me, it was much worse for her. I was in a public school, free as the day I was born, but the girl I loved was in thrall to a religious martinet. My story was working out to be a little different from the Shakespeare play. This time, it was Juliet who was banished to Mantua, and Mantua was a terrible place.

# IX
# I HEART YOU

By hiding, hermit-like, in my classes, I somehow got through to the end of the school year. I tried to get her out of my mind, but wondered every day how she was coping with reform school—a completely undeserved detention. I wondered if she ever thought of me, or missed me. Sometimes, I worried she might meet a cuter, church-approved guy and throw me under the bus. Other times, I was sure I could feel her heart, aching for the end of her exile. Once in a while, if I really felt down I would take out the letter, and read it, savoring the lines, the words, and the emotions; even if "Uncle" Rulon thought it was juvenile nonsense.

Whenever I would reread the letter, it was spring rain on the desert, it was manna from heaven. Lord Alfred Tennyson didn't write better stuff than Susie had. I was supposed to be forgetting her, but the expressed tender adoration was etching my love in stone. I would probably frame it for all my posterity to read and cherish, even the *two* exclamation marks had tiny hearts instead of periods.

It was getting so used I might wear it out. Already the smudges were spreading. The school year was over. I had volunteered to help the teachers move things around on the last day of school. I was in the Home Ec Room, helping to pack a lot of boxes with the teacher's private stuff.

I heard a voice calling. "Jase, are you in here?" My heart leaped at the soft sound of Suzanne's voice.

"Yes, back behind all the divider screens," I yelled or whispered; I could hardly make my voice work. She had dropped by the school to see her class friends and found out I was helping clean up. Almost everyone was gone and a chance meeting with Suzy Q was the last thing I expected that day, but the best thing in a long time. She came around the corner and everything I dreamed or ever wanted was standing there, kind of smiling. We were very awkward with each other at first. It seemed like a lot of things had been said and done that made our natural friendship hard to verbalize.

"How you been, Suzy?" I finally blurted out.

"I'm good, okay, but it's so cool to see you, Jase," she told me" It's been like the state prison the last few months. I hated the Alta Academy. They were so demanding and weird."

"Yeah, I can imagine. I felt so sorry for you." I needed to know if she still felt the way my letter said she did. I had clung to that like a shipwrecked mariner clings to the broken mast. "I thought about you every day since they took you."

And then she answered the question I hadn't dared ask. "Jase, I don't know quite how to say this, but I wonder if you still have—uh, you know—feelings for me?"

Tears were starting to form in my eyes when I said, "Baby, there are no words to tell you how I missed you—the whole time you've been gone."

"Jase, would you be willing to date me—in secret, just go places, and be together—whenever it is possible?" My heart was pounding. This plan was bold, and there was no turning back. I was very open to the idea, because I was quite done with the whole FLDS power struggle. I was unable to be myself and still pretend to act according to the expectations of whomever I was around.

"Suzy," I said, "Yes. I'd love to. Hell, I'm ready to walk away from all of this, if necessary. My very best friends are all considered apostates by the whole church. They got kicked out for having a girlfriend, but they will all be there for us at a moment's notice, no matter what. Everybody else is only there for us as long as we kiss up to the Prophet. If I have a problem with anything, they just won't associate with me anymore. The same goes for you, babe, on every issue, they will just tell you to stay in line with the Prophet. If he says it, it comes from God. I just think that's bull crap."

"Nothing has changed with me, Jason," Suzy Q said. "What I wrote you is how I felt, and still feel. I don't want to keep living without you in my life." I had a feeling it was all or nothing with this beautiful girl. She was tough, and I loved her. The goons at Alta had not broken her spirit. I was relieved.

"Suzy, hell yes I'll sneak out with you, but I won't be totally happy until we can be open and in love in spite of everybody," I told her. "I play in a softball league the second warders have going. Maybe on Saturday afternoons you could come by. There are a lot of people there and you would blend in. And you know the best part? There won't be a person there to rat you out."

She grinned, "I'll try everything and anything to show up."

In an impulsive hug, she threw her arms around my neck. "See you later, sweetheart"

"Bye Suzy Q," I smiled. Sweetheart. Hmmm. Damn, that sounded good!

The first time that I really got to know Suzanne, she dropped by the softball game we were playing. After the game, she came to where I was hanging with the team, walking as close to me as she could without appearing to suspicious.

"Jase," she whispered, "do you think we could get away? Just you and I?"

"Sure," I responded. "What did you have in mind?"

"Let's just go for a drive and hang out together for awhile."

"That sounds great," I answered. Not having any mode of transportation myself, I sidled up to my cousin Jared, telling him I needed to borrow his car.

"I'm not real sure what time we'll be back," I said, "but can I please, *please* borrow your car?"

"That should be fine," he answered. We bounded into his car like Bonnie and Clyde, zooming off as though we'd just robbed a bank. I was unsure how to act because I had never been alone with a girl that I was really attracted to.

I asked, "Which way?"

"It doesn't matter as long as it is away from here," she answered aimlessly. We drove for about a half hour to the little town of Fredonia and got some fuel and snacks. We talked most of the way there about how she got away. We couldn't believe she had gotten out of the house alone. On our way back, she asked if I knew a place that was off road and wouldn't be found. I thought of just the place and drove there. She told me about her days in Salt Lake City. She said she was happy for a little while because it felt like nobody was looking over her shoulder every second. She could do whatever she wanted as long as it was with a few of the girls up there that were considered righteous.

It started to get dark outside as we finally came to a place that was clear off the beaten path. She was satisfied with the place that I had picked. I wondered what she had in mind. I'd be lying if I didn't admit that the possibility of some serious physical contact crossed my mind.

"Why do you want to be clear out here in the middle of nowhere?" I queried, nonchalantly.

"I know my dad and brothers will come looking for me," she replied. I was hoping she couldn't hear the relief in the breath I exhaled. "If they find us, you'll get a severe beating. I think we were lucky the first time that he didn't kick your ass."

Satisfied with this answer, I dove right into to our predicament. "Suzanne, what do we want to do with the rest of our lives?" I asked her. "Do you plan on living in a polygamous family?"

"Hell, no," she said quickly. "I can't even imagine sharing my man with another woman."

We were more alike every second. "Yeah," I said. "I'm not interested in having two wives because of how it was in my family. I remember how abusive Aunt Millie was. The two women get all jealous."

Our ideas and hopes poured out. We shared so many memories and had so many compatibilities; it was cool just thinking how good we might be together. Looking back, it was mostly the judgments and aspirations of a couple young kids trying to get a grip on the complexities of life.

We soon ran out of things to talk about, so we played some music and danced like the first time we had met, this time with the great outdoors and a canopy of stars as our background, rather than a row of dour chaperones.

I pointed out two special stars, part of the Southern Cross, hanging close together, spending eternity inseparable.

"Those are our stars," I said. "You and me."

We held each other until it seemed we would both fall asleep. We got back in the car and drove home. She was still worried about me getting beat up, so I dropped her off down the street from where she lived.

The next day, I returned Jared's car and found him to be a little angry that I had his car all night without even saying a word. He thought I might have had a run in with her menacing family. He claimed he had nightmares about them kicking my ass. Now that he knew I was okay, he wanted *all* the juicy details.

"So did you kiss her?" he asked anxiously.

"No," was my simple reply.

"I know you're lying to me; you don't spend seven hours alone with a chick you like and then just *not* kiss. Tell me the truth."

"I swear that nothing happened," I sheepishly replied.

The kiss didn't happen until later. I remember it like it was yesterday. The next weekend, Suzanne surprised me by showing up to my ball game. We borrowed another car, from my cousin Thomas this time. He knew what to expect; he decided we could keep it all night if we needed it.

We pulled into the incomplete shell of my Uncle Aaron's home. Feeling especially amorous, I had written a short poem for her, which I read aloud. I thought it was fairly good, as poetry goes, but the more poetry I read, the worse my attempt appears. But hey, it's the thought that counts, right?

She listened intently, tears in her eyes as I recited my schmaltz. She was moved; she told me no one had ever said anything that nice to her, ever. As far as I'm concerned, that doesn't speak much to the brainpower of the rest of the world, to look on a goddess and be unable to think of anything nice to say.

I put my arms around her waist and pulled her close, gazing into her eyes in the dim light, hoping to find permission to come a little closer. She held the back of my head, pulling me closer. When I leaned and kissed her lips it felt new, yet so familiar. Her lips were so soft and moist that I couldn't stop. Just as I was starting to wonder if maybe I was kissing her too long, she slowly and purposefully thrust her tongue gently into my mouth. That settled it. We stayed together, as one, kissing, and we didn't let go for a long time.

Finally I pulled my head back. "Are you all right?" I asked.

"No problems here," she said breathlessly.

We talked for a while after that and kissed several more times; each time seemed to be getting better and better. Finally, I could stand it no longer. "How many boys have you kissed?"

"Just you baby," she smiled. "What about you?"

"You're my first. And I'm real happy it was you."

We kissed for a long time—nothing to write the Guinness record keepers about, but a long time for two scared kids. So much time passed, in fact, that we lost track of it. Outside the house, through a dirty window, we could see a sliver of moonlight, but it was a dark night, especially in the unfinished house.

Once we could no longer see the moon through the window, we decided it was time to get the car back. When I turned the ignition on I was met with a dead battery. Dammit. I was sure we were going to get caught. Our careful plan was unraveling.

"That's okay" Suzanne said reassuringly, "my sister Liz lives just around the block, they will come and jump start us."

As we strolled up the road toward Liz's house, we noticed the taillights of a vehicle idling in the street. Not thinking anything of it, wondering whose voices we were hearing in the summer air, we approached the car. Centennial Park was usually still at night except for an occasional dog barking. Suddenly, like a Viking warrior on the scent of an enemy, her sister called out, "Who goes there?" I'm not making this up; that is actually what she said.

Horrified, Suzanne froze and stared at her parent's minivan. They were obviously checking around for her, because Liz and Kim were not on the social call list. She stopped dead in her tracks, sinking her fingers into my arm, her breath barely audible.

"Oh, crap!" she whispered in desperation, like a deer in the headlights. "Run!"

"No," I said, "just stay cool and stick with me."

Tiptoeing slowly around, we carefully vanished back into the night. No doubt Liz suspected it was us, and distracted the searchers, helping us get away. After about a half hour the lights pulled forward and disappeared into the night. We finally crept up to her sister's house and got help with the car. We were able to each get home without her family finding us.

We led charmed lives. All summer long we found a way to be together. We were so in love we made time for each other around our home life and my work. The creek was safer than the roads, and so we met there. In a way, Suzanne and I really were "Crickers" because we spent a lot of time there.

My brother Bobby, however, didn't share our luck. Sometimes when we were down in the creek, strolling hand in hand or lost in each other's eyes, the God Squad forced Bobby off the road and made threats against his life. He would insist he was not, in fact, Jason Williams; he was the little brother, but the God Squad knew he was lying. They continued with the harassment, four or five times. He was angrier at me every time they did it, and for that matter, *they* were angrier at him, for trying to keep the lie going, when they knew all along that he was me. We were living on the edge.

"Bobby," I told him once, "you are like a guardian angel."

"I don't even look like you," he complained. "It's really pissing me off. The damn guys are so stupid they mix us up."

I grinned. I still need to pay him back for that.

I heard a tapping on the window of my room one night in late summer. Did I hear something or imagine it? A soft knock was unmistakable; this was no dream. Peering out into the night I was pleasantly surprised to see her— Suzanne, beckoning me to join her.

Wearing nothing but boxers and a T-shirt, I climbed out the window. I had the good sense to bring a blanket, though, because the nights were cold at this elevation. We sat, wrapped up warm inside it, and talked for awhile. I had no idea what time it was, but I didn't want this closeness to end.

Suddenly she moved over close and we began to kiss passionately. The warmth in her kiss made the blanket obsolete. The heat of our bodies felt incredible in the cool air. My body was tingling all over as our lips hungrily searched and conquered. I was, for the first time, wanting her—even more—needing her.

"*I caught you this time!*" shrieked a strident voice, and the blinding beam of a flashlight splashed upon us. It was her brother David, who had followed her so he could burst our blissful bubble. "There is nowhere to hide!" he gloated.

Running up to us, he tore the blanket away from our grasp, surprised to see us with clothes on. He had expected to catch us in the act. He was a little stunned to find that the act was not taking place at all. Nevertheless, he grabbed me by the arm and kicked open our front door, screaming, "Robert, I need to see you out here immediately!"

I looked at the clock inside our living room and realized that it was almost two in the morning. I knew my dad would be far angrier about the early hour than what David thought was happening. He trudged groggily out of the house demanding, "What is all this noise about?"

"I just caught these two having sex right here on your sidewalk," David accused.

"We were just making out," I said, evenly, looking my dad in the eye, "sitting here with our clothes on. This idiot is lying."

"Good Lord above," he said, still wiping the sleep from his eyes. "Take her home to her parents. I'll deal with Jason. He *is* my responsibility."

"Aren't you going to punish them?" David asked in disbelief.

"What would you like me to do at two in the morning?" my dad responded. "Let's each take them home, sleep on it, and with cooler heads, work it out in the morning."

David disgustedly marched Suzanne to his truck. My dad turned to me and asked, "What goes through your head when you decide to do something like this?"

"She just knocked on my window so we could talk."

My dad nodded. "Talk? Right. Just go to bed. We'll discuss this in the morning."

The next morning, I knew I had an ass-chewing coming as I walked in his room. I started off with, "Dad I know you are disappointed and I will not let that happen again."

He gave me a long, hard look. "You better not have been doing anything wrong. I don't want to talk about last night; I want to know what your long term goal is."

"Dad," I said. "My long term *goal* is to marry that girl. I'm in love with her. I'd do anything for her."

He seemed surprised at my answer. After a few awkward moments he finally looked me right in the eye and said, "Jason, how old are you?"

"Almost eighteen" I replied, not liking where this conversation was headed.

"How old is she?" he continued, without missing a beat.

Resignedly, I answered him. "Almost sixteen."

He leaned forward. "Then what the hell is the hurry?" he said. "If it's right and you really love her, like you say, then what's wrong with letting her grow up? Jason, you're still in school, you don't have a full-time job, you don't have a pot to piss in, and you don't have a window to throw it out of." He pointed. "That window you climb out of at night is *my* window. Why don't you act like a normal person: grow up, finish school, and for hell's sake, try sleeping at 2:30 in the AM?"

Straight talk; straight from the hip—that's my dad. I really couldn't argue with the sense of it because he was telling me the truth of the situation. I knew I had nothing to offer, but I also knew Suzanne and I had a love that transcended time, distance, and hatred.

# X
# TWO SPARROWS

Building on the good advice of my dad, I spoke with Suzanne the next time we could talk. We were both on ice, because of David's fine investigative work. We both agreed to cool our heels and see how things developed. Finishing high school was one of my goals; I knew I needed a diploma. Seeing all my classmates again focused me; I was determined to make '94 the best year yet. Things were going good with my life, but Suzanne's parents had pulled her out of school and kept a constant vigil.

She told me that David had convinced her parents that we had sex. Every time her dad brought the subject up, she denied it, but he continued to press her for the truth.

"I feel like telling him yes just to see what he'd do," she told me.

"Lying about that won't make anyone feel better," I cautioned. "I don't want to lose you, Suzy. I plan on spending the rest of my life beside you."

"You are the first kiss of my life", she smiled, "and I expect you to be the last."

"Stay strong, baby," I pleaded. "We will fight our way through this, together."

Staying encouraged was the hardest part. We were never able to spend enough time with one another. We were like owls, up late at night, our heads on a swivel, looking for people that were looking for us. Time was on our side—we had plenty of it, and it was always dragging.

In spite of how slowly time was moving, it was moving—faster than we were prepared. The Lord, so they say, works a mysterious way. One day in the middle of October, Suzanne and her close friends came by the school and picked me up.

"Jason," her friend told me, as she drove the car toward a seldom-visited part of the creek, "you two need some time alone to work out your lives."

The minute we were alone, Suzanne started talking. "We need to decide if this is going to work out," she said, "because my parents have given me permission to marry you."

I could not believe it. Frank and Mary-Ann were, by definition, not very reasonable people. They were the shock troops of the "Prophet's" arranged marriage program. I didn't think it possible they would allow us to be in love. No more sneaking around? I almost began looking for the other six signs of the apocalypse.

"How did that happen?" I asked, incredulously.

"My parents got sick of us, so they asked Uncle Rulon if he would place me," she glowingly related. "He asked me what I thought about it. It seemed like our last chance, so I told him we've already had sex. I was in love with you and wouldn't give myself to a different man."

Not knowing how to process the mixed news, I sat silently on the rock for a few moments. Now the Jeffs regime would release the fabled dogs of war. This was not a way out. It was a way *in* to a deeper prison, with the key thrown away. "Why would you tell him that when you know it isn't true?" I finally asked.

"I was sick of telling them that," she confessed, "I've told them the truth a hundred times, and they only believed me the time I lied."

"So what did he do?" I quizzed her.

"Well, young lady," she said in a quivering voice. She was doing a decent impersonation. "I guess it's up to you!" She turned to me with a big grin, like a burglar who had just cracked the safe. "I'm not living with my parents anymore," she declared. "No way. So Uncle Rulon told them that if we don't get married, he'll place me with another guy. So...what do you want to do?"

I let out a long sigh. I was sure there would be some karmic repercussions for this. "The results are what we wanted," I reasoned, "even if they came about the wrong way."

I have trouble thinking at the best of times, but now the switchboard was overloaded. Thinking about Jeromy and Cheyrlynn, I knew I didn't like the odds of waiting. Things changed fast these days. This really was the solution and an incredible turn of fortune. I looked through new eyes at the girl I loved. She had courted certain shame and ridicule—for our future. This petite little brave girl had traded her reputation and position in the church for me. I was exultant and humbled; two emotions I had never tried together.

"Well then, baby," I exclaimed, "Let's get married."

"For young people we've been through a lot," Suzanne agreed. "All the crap has made us more mature than our friends, so I'm with you. Let's get married as soon as they'll let us."

"What do you mean, let us?" I asked, confused.

"Jase, we're still minors," she reminded me, "our parents'll have to sign the papers to give us permission."

I wasn't a minor at the time; I was past eighteen. But I was still worried that my parents might be the ones that hold it up. My dad already thought I was still a kid. I knew I was old enough to do everything but smoke and drink, but he insisted we were not prepared for what life was about to throw at us.

"Well," I acknowledged, "we're closer than we have ever been." I tried to imagine us married, with our own little apartment, our car, shopping together, fixing meals together, sleeping together. Whoa, horse, I realized; all those things take money, except making love, and we don't even have a bed. Maybe I should just mellow out and worry about one thing at a time.

The next Monday at school, our senior class was holding nominations to vote for school president. When my name was nominated, I raised my hand and asked them to please withdraw it. This was going to be the last day of my senior year. I wasn't sad about it because life seemed to have a greater purpose now. After school I cleaned out my locker and brought my belongings home. I had one long reminiscent look back as I was leaving. I had some good times while I was there, but I was full of excitement and anticipation about the future.

Suzanne came over that Tuesday. The whole family was at school, so we had the run of the house. We made up an itinerary for the rest of the week while we washed dishes. This was so cool—no school. Funny thing about perspective and attitude, I thought. These same dishes and same sink were hell when Aunt Dread made me do them, but this was heaven. It could last until after Thanksgiving again and I wouldn't care.

Then my mom drove up. We looked at each other like two rabbits seeing the shadow of a hawk—we hadn't told anybody in my family yet!

"Should I sneak out the back?" Suzanne volunteered.

"No way," I proclaimed, not a little proudly, "Let's tell everybody right now what our intentions are."

My mom came in, furious to see that I had company. "You both should be ashamed of yourselves," she lectured. "You've been taught better than this! What's going on here?"

"We are going to get married on Friday." I announced.

"Like hell you are!" my mom screamed. "Suzie, go home!"

Suzanne slipped out the door. I started to follow her, but my mom grabbed my arm.

"What are you trying to prove?" she demanded. "You're not going anywhere."

"Yes I am, Mom," I replied firmly. "She is my fiancée, and I'm going with her."

My mom looked as though a 737 had smashed into our living room. "What?" she stammered, her grip on my arm had gone limp as a dead fish. Spinning on my heels, I dashed toward my bedroom, to gather up a few belongings.

She recovered quickly and leapt into hot pursuit. "Jason, you look me in the eye!" she demanded, in a piercing voice. "*Have you been immoral with this girl?*"

"Mom," I yelled back at her, "what do you think?"

She was blocking the exit from my room. It was impossible to get by her. Tired of the subject, I jumped out the window, the one my dad always told me was *his* window, and ran up the hill to get into the car with Suzanne.

"Where are we going?" she asked.

"To Hurricane," I said, teeth clenched. "I need to tell my dad what is going on, before my mom freaks him out."

We found my dad at work. I told him we had some news and that we needed some of his time. He could see we were a little anxious and offered to drive around and discuss what was going on. That was what he always did whenever he needed to have a serious conversation. His car logged more emotional miles than physical ones.

"Dad," I told him, "we're going to get married this week."

He nodded, both hands on the steering wheel, and thought about it a minute. "This is a big step—a big decision," he said. "What is the reason that you are in such a big hurry now?"

"It's important that you know we are in a hurry because we *want* to," I rejoined, "not because we have to."

Just then, my dad's cell phone rang. If I had been in Las Vegas, I would have laid a hundred on the caller being my mom. And sure enough, it was her, frantic and hysterical. She sounded like a bag of cats on the other end of the line.

"Susan!" my dad yelled, holding the phone a foot away from his ear. "Susan! They're *right here*! I'll handle it!"

In between protests, he slammed the phone shut. Then he resumed our conversation, exactly where he'd left off. "I know that," he said. "It just seems that you ought to slow it down a little and catch your breath. Hell, you got a whole life ahead of you."

"We need to hurry while my dad is still in the mood," explained Suzanne. "He is going to sign the papers for us to get married."

"Yeah," I chipped in, "she's only sixteen. She needs permission to be legally married."

"I want to impress on your minds that I think you both should grow up," he said. I started to wonder who the hell's side was my dad on? "I can tell that you both feel strongly towards each other," he continued, "but you're rushing into marriage."

"Remember when Jeromy talked to Rulon Jeffs?" I interjected. "If he'd moved quicker, he wouldn't have had his heart broken by their tricks. Dad, Frank Jessop was told to let us get married."

Suzanne weighed in with her argument as well. "If enough time goes by," she said, "my Father will try to figure out a way around what Uncle Rulon told him. We just know if we delay and wait something will come along and blow it up."

"Yeah, think what Joe Barlow tried to do to you and Millie because Uncle Roy got sick." I implored. I knew that for a whole year, my dad wanted to marry her, but because Leroy Johnson was in a coma, Joe Barlow had a carte blanche to try whatever he wanted to convince her to the bag the idea.

"Jason, you are eighteen," my dad replied reassuringly. "You can make up your mind yourself. I'll support you. No such a thing as a throw-away kid."

We were right of course, and my dad had known all along. Every stitch the world used to keep us together was in danger of being snipped in two by Frank and his righteous pair of scissors. He drove us around the rest of the afternoon and helped with details of finding a Justice of the Peace, planning a honeymoon, and thinking of a place to live. It was cool because he was finally getting a chance to get to know my wife-to-be.

Wow, I realized, as I opened my eyes that October 14th. The day had finally arrived. We were scheduled to be married at eleven o'clock AM. I took a moment to reflect on the months leading up to this day—a day I hoped for but almost despaired of ever arriving at. We were really young; everybody was certain we were too immature to make it work. Even Bobby said we were screwing up, the Bobby that always claimed, "Don't worry. Things are going to work out, dude."

But things *had* somehow miraculously worked out. I had been paid $900 the two days before, which, added with my savings, enabled me to get a bridal gown and a tuxedo, and still have enough left on a down payment for a new car.

My dad had realized we could do this with or without him, so he had grudgingly given his support. Frank had signed the guardian permission slip for a marriage license, and Chester Adams, the Justice of the Peace in Toquerville had agreed to perform the marriage.

What a week: Monday, out of school; Tuesday, parent's okay; Wednesday; a marriage license, Thursday; the venue, attire, and invitations, and here was Friday. I had to get the hell out of bed, because I knew that with an ad hoc wedding, anything can go wrong. The first order of business was to head over to Liz's house and see if Suzy Q was still planning on being part of the wedding group.

They all said I was rushing into marriage. Hell yes, I was rushing; trying to remember everything, hurrying too fast shaving, speeding to Centennial Park, checking my watch at least five times an hour, and trying to find my dad. He had left town for the Friday, and I was concerned he wouldn't make it.

Suzanne was a nervous wreck when I got to Liz's house. I walked over and held her in my arms. "Hey babe," I whispered, "don't stress, everything is going to work out just fine. What's the worst that could happen? I mean seriously, only good stuff happens today."

She seemed to calm a little at my reassurance. But now *I* was getting nervous at the magnitude of the moment. It meant responsibility and respect; it also meant no more sneaking around. Our relationship had always been in secret, but somehow on the lips of every gossip in town. We could now hold each other in public without everyone thinking we had gone to hell. Actually, I realized, they probably would still think that. But I could hardly think straight I was so excited. There were no words to express my relief that she hadn't ended up with some crusty old man. Our love could breathe; this was a great day.

After the marriage, we were going to live with Liz, we decided. She and her husband were kind enough to let us stay with them until we get could find and afford our own place. Jared and Thomas each gave me 350 dollars as a wedding present, to enjoy a honeymoon. Better yet, Jared's sister Ada lent me her new Pontiac for a few days. This was like we had hired a wedding planner; but things just happened in spite of us. It was meant to be perfect, so it was.

Time was running out. She walked out from the hair stylists, her soft, long, blond locks framing a face that beamed with unrehearsed joy. Whatever I did to deserve this I was too nervous to fathom. She was curled and made up like a princess in our fairy tale. I held the bright red door open for her, reveling in the sight of her.

"Are you ready for this?" she innocently asked.

"Hell yeah," I grinned, "let's do this." In about two hours I would be able to call her my wife.

She had her wedding dress hanging on the hook on one side of the back seat while my tux hung on the opposite hook. Our clothes looked like the wedding couple; I was just the chauffeur, and Suzanne was nothing more than the head bridesmaid. We picked up our license at the courthouse, and we each ducked into the public restrooms to change. We were going to have to hurry if we wanted to pull this off.

I stood waiting in the lobby, like a prom date at the front porch. I watched the door to the restroom. The sign said "Woman," and then the door creaked open, and sure enough, it was. She stood there smiling sheepishly and asked, "So, what do you think?"

I melted inside, like nacho cheese sauce. We didn't have the time for me to tell her everything I thought, or that she was the most astonishingly gorgeous woman I had ever seen. I just stood there like an idiot, drunk without a hangover, and said, "You look beautiful."

The justice of the peace in Toquerville was Chester Adams, an old cowboy in a wheelchair. He held court in a converted two-car garage attached to his house. Normally he didn't deal much with weddings—traffic violations were his specialty, but every once in a while, he ended up with two kids like us, in a hurry to be married. His friends called him the "hangin' judge," and sent him a picture of Judge Roy Bean and his crush Lily Langtry. He liked the idea of being the Law, West of the Pecos, and so he hung the pictures right behind the place he'd park his wheelchair.

Frank Jessop, the father of the bride, sat stoically in his minivan with his wife, parked on the sidewalk when my dad drove up. My dad went over to talk to them for a few minutes, trying to coax them inside.

"I would rather be *burying* my daughter today," he told my dad, "than participating in this ceremony." His countenance supported his statement, and it was some time before he ever swallowed his pride enough to slink inside.

My brother Jeromy somehow made it, right that moment thundering up on his big, black Harley. He casually washed his long hair and face in the street runoff water, but his grin made up for the solemnity of Suzanne's dad. Because he was so cavalier about dunking headfirst into the gutter, we often called him "Duckie" after that.

"Glad you stopped by, bro." I said, genuinely pleased he was there.

Some of my brothers and sisters and a few of Suzanne's friends made it. Her maid of honor was April Mackert, a skinny girl who had just finished having her wisdom teeth pulled half an hour before. She looked like Ally McBeal with fat cheeks, standing beside "Easy Rider" and Bobby. This motley crew of well-wishers (and doomsayers) filed into the cramped office of the JP, who after the initial shock at the disparate clothing and attitudes of the wedding party, "hooked us up." Most of the audience seemed against it. It was like a shotgun wedding; with the difference being that *we* had the shotgun, and we were forcing everyone to attend.

Most of the witnesses thought we were ending our lives, but Suzanne and I knew they were just beginning. The ceremony lasted just a few minutes. If judged by the crowd's response, a casual observer couldn't tell if this was the happiest day of my life or if someone had just died. My parents were disappointed with me and had no problem making sure I knew. My cousins, Jared and Thomas, were taking college photography classes and volunteered to take pictures of our wedding day. Since the two-car garage was not the prettiest backdrop, several of us drove to Toquerville Falls and tried our best to capture our reflection in the water. That, we thought superstitiously, would double our happiness.

That evening we stopped at Mesquite and walked into the Oasis Resort. A hotel manager spotted us, still in our formal attire.

"You guys just been married?" he asked.

Suzanne beamed. "Yeah."

He nodded. "You're in luck, if you want to stay here. We just had a cancellation on the honeymoon suite. I'll give it to you, three days, for $150. I'll throw in some free champagne, and lobster for two at the Red Room Steak House. Congratulations."

We couldn't believe our luck. We hadn't even thought to get a reservation, on a Friday night. Our chance of scoring a good, affordable, room was slim at best. It was becoming a pattern—most of the people chosen by the Jeffs vision of

God were mean and nasty. You had to go into hell to find the truly nice people of the world.

We had originally planned on traveling to Las Vegas, but this, like everything on our magic day was destiny. We gladly accepted and spent a three day vacation in paradise. A wedding planner and a big budget couldn't have made us happier. We were content to just wing it. But then, what else can two sparrows do?

# XI
# FRANK AND EARNEST

We bounced around the world for about a year after our marriage, living free and shunned. For a while we had the extra room in Liz and Kim's house, and then rented an inexpensive studio apartment that had been attached to a auto repair garage. It was located in Centennial Park, so it was off limits for any one of our friends or family in the FLDS. Dubbing the place *Satannical Park*, the Jeffs regime had expressly forbidden the righteous from ever going there. It was less than a mile south of Colorado City but was treated like a hated foreign country, not to be entered by those who had hopes for a resurrection. Our moving to Centennial Park was like a Cold War Alaskan entering Siberia.

Fortunately, there was no rule against us crossing over into Alaska to visit those who lived there. The new situation worked well for us because we could visit our parents easily and often. However, my commute to work was close to sixty miles. I felt it was worth it because my wife had been missing her family so much and wanted to be able to visit them.

Her parents were not too keen on our visits though. It had been almost a year since we were married, and Suzanne still hadn't shown any signs of going around pregnant or barefoot, so some of the suppositions and gossip had finally started to die down. But her parents were still not overly willing to accept us back into the fold.

I had only visited shortly with them once in the eleven months that we had been married, but because she contacted them so frequently, they finally started to open their arms to her again. They were still not convinced that I was a decent person, let alone a good candidate for son-in-law of the month. I wasn't convinced they were good candidates for parenthood. They had not really given me a chance to get to know them. Whenever I wanted any news or information from them, I would have to rely on my wife as my go-between. She was doing her best to convince them that I was a tolerable human being.

Once we found out that Suzanne was pregnant, it helped ease the tension a bit; her parents now knew she needed them for a good reason. They wanted so much for their daughter to be back in the church, on the path to God and glory and all that. They continually urged us to try to regain access to the priesthood and renew our association with the "Prophet." We were both just damn tired of being ostracized by our families, so finally the two of us caved in and allowed Frank to set up an appointment with Rulon Jeffs.

I was sure that we would not be particularly well received. The last time that I had met this old man, he had told me in no uncertain terms that I must never see Suzanne again. Now, I was going into his opulent office once more to ask forgiveness for flagrantly disobeying his directive. It felt like a bank robber seeking clemency, even though I still had the money in the backseat of my getaway car. This was certain to be a great adventure.

Once Wendell gave us the cue to enter the office, Frank escorted the two of us in and plopped us down in the guest chairs, hovering over us like Castle Rock. And there, on the other side of the desk, sat our last hope for redemption, the "Prophet" Rulon Jeffs, still wearing his *Keep Sweet* Sunday shoes. The atmosphere was not as icy as I had feared. He seemed glad that we wanted to repent and surrender ourselves to the church's control.

"I understand your wishes," he said, once Frank told him what we wanted, "but I'm extremely concerned that if I allowed them back into church, other young couples would try to do the same thing."

I could have guessed that would be a concern. Already, since we had been married, a number of young lovers had followed our path. They had discovered, as we had, that claiming they'd had sex (or actually having sex) meant that their parents and their "Prophet" would allow them to marry whoever they wished, at the price of a little eternal damnation.

"People trying to force the Lord's hand in marriage," Rulon continued, "will not be tolerated. It is a sacred union, and must have divine guidance."

He swiveled his chair and stared at me. "Jason," he offered, "I will allow you to be re-baptized and receive full fellowship with the body of saints if, and when, you prove yourself worthy, and the same goes for you, young lady."

"Yes sir," I said, trying to feign interest in his church," if you would tell me exactly what things I can improve on I'm certainly willing to respond. I want to be found worthy."

Worthiness was a miserable existence, and it was almost impossible to hold onto. I couldn't believe that I had escaped this man's clutches, and here I was, asking him nicely if I could come back, like Daniel asking to return to the lion's den. I could think of nothing I wanted less than to be back in the line of fire, but it was what my wife yearned for, so I felt a little responsibility to strive for it.

"Well, the first thing would be to catch up on and keep up with your tithing," Rulon declared. "You will also be required to participate each weekend on the community work projects for Uncle Fred, under the direction of Nephi Barlow. And proving yourself worthy will consist of going to church regularly, preferably on the front rows."

"How often will you want him to check in and report to you, Uncle?" Frank interjected. I felt a jab of anger at his query. The list was getting long enough without help.

"At least once a month," Rulon replied, "so I can monitor your feelings and progress. This will be a trial basis until we see if you're serious about this. And Frank, I want you to give him a job with you; you'll be able to see how earnest he really is to reform."

After Frank promised to ensure I was earnest, we left the office. As he drove us home, Frank reopened the diatribe, lecturing us on all the different ways we could prove our worthiness. My parents still lived in Hildale, but for the most part their home had been open to me the entire time I was gone. I wanted Suzanne to be able to maintain a relationship with her family, and I was willing to do what was necessary to bring that opportunity about. The poor girl was so lost, like a raft floating at sea with nowhere to anchor.

Some of the requirements were easy enough to fulfill; I actually enjoyed donating my time to the Saturday work projects. I was able to find a bit of camaraderie in some of the people I worked with, and there is a lot to be said for helping those who need it. We met at the Civic Center and listened to some elders outline the tasks for the day. It was like being four years old again, working with the Roy's Boys. Only by this time the Roy's Boys had been changed to the Sons of Helaman. They declared fealty to the "Prophet" and Warren Jeffs, marching all over town waving banners, like the Hitler Youth. It was far less innocent than it had been when I was young. Something told me they didn't let anyone perform songs anymore.

The work day usually lasted all Saturday. A project manager would make the rounds, collecting signatures of the men that were participating. Because it was donated labor, I refused to sign—I didn't want to feel like I was being clocked in and out. I knew that once they were able to demand signatures from every participant, the Saturday work projects would be a requirement.

Suzanne and I continued to go to the Sunday services and kept our appointments with the "Prophet." Finally, after about seven months, we were told that we could at last be re-baptized. They performed the ceremonies of baptism and an ordination giving me the priesthood, and then they sealed us up "for time and all eternity." My impression was that we had already done that, since Chester Adams had married us, but it wasn't said to count if the "Prophet" was not the one performing the marriage.

Some days after that, during my monthly visit to the home of Rulon Jeffs, I was given two more conditions preparatory to getting back into priesthood meetings.

"First," he told me, "you will have to keep working with Frank. I believe your repentance is genuine, but I want you to work under his example so you don't slip again. The other condition is that you have to move into the community. You cannot abide on the devil's ground and still exhibit a desire to obey the Prophet's commandments.

"We don't have a place to stay," I protested. "There's nothing to rent."

He nodded in understanding. "I have been informed of a few vacant trailers in our trailer park," he advised. "Perhaps if you check with Brother Carling Stubbs, he'll find you a fixer-upper."

I had seen some of those ratty heaps of rot. We had been forced to update the sewer connections in that area, and I knew he was exhausting the euphemism "fixer-upper." It was more like "starter-from-scratcher."

And just like that, I needed different lodging. The skeleton of a house Carling decided should be mine was pathetic. It had holes all down the sides. Looking inside, I found it had no interior walls. It boasted several large holes in the floor. I was expected to prove my dedication *again* by turning a disaster area into a home for my pregnant wife. Moreover, Carling advised me that whatever improvements I made were considered donations to the United Effort Plan.

This was because of the UEP lawsuit some years before. After a twelve year court battle, the plaintiffs won the privilege of staying on their property as long as they were alive. The combined costs of this litigation was estimated around ten million dollars. After this ruling, the UEP went to great lengths to ensure people inhabiting any property knew it wasn't theirs and that improvements made to the property were considered a gift to the trust.

While I was remodeling the UEP's new house, I still needed a place to live. Suzanne's mother talked her brother, Erwin Fischer, into offering us an apartment in his house for the time being. That was an acceptable resolution in the eyes of the FLDS—at least now I lived in a sanctified town. This church didn't place too much stock in knowing or understanding the scriptures, or loving Christ. It adhered to the real estate mantra of location, location, location.

I was glad I had saved some money over the past several years, because renovating the trailer was going to be quite an undertaking. In order to transform this shell into a livable home, I had to pour support footings and a knee wall to stabilize it, buy new lumber because there were no walls inside, and order new windows, insulation, sheet rock, doors, and paint. I had to hire a plumber and electrician to rewire the trailer so it would work correctly. I had to install new flooring throughout. Finally, I foamed, lathed and stuccoed the outside to cover all the holes, framed a new roof, and waterproofed it.

My brothers and cousins donated their labor, and I traded my truck for the cabinets that I put in. But even with all that I had available to me, I spent the whole summer and fall getting this place ready to move into. It wasn't the Buckingham Palace, but it had evolved from its terrible beginning into a home I would dare bring a child into.

As this project went underway, I still labored in the excavation business with my new father-in-law. Having no experience in the excavation business, I wasn't allowed to run any of the machinery or heavy equipment, not even on a trial basis. Instead, I worked the trenches, fitting pipe and eating dirt and gaining an intense appreciation for other fields of work. The worst of it was putting down asphalt in temperatures never under three digits. This heat was made even worse for me, because being worthy meant that I was back to the long-sleeved shirt, with woolen long-johns underneath.

The underground company had a contract to redo a section of Telegraph Street in Washington, Utah, during the hottest months of the summer. We would leave Frank's home at 5:00 AM to try to beat the heat, but we never did. The summer was too good at beating us right back. By 10:30 we were exhausted and dehydrated in the hot sand.

To make matters worse, my dad once drove by as I sweated and cursed under the glare of the asphalt.

"Hell, Jason," he laughed at me from his air-conditioned truck, "I told you to finish school. Look where you are now."

I glared at him. The joke wasn't entirely accurate; I could have found jobs all over the county that treated me better than this. The only reason I was *here* was because Rulon Jeffs was testing me. One of the tenet's of the "Prophet's" righteousness was that I had to go through hell to get to heaven. Besides which, when I had dropped out of school, I had been only a credit shy of graduation, and I had college credits on top of that. When I took the GED, I was among the highest scorers, so the school elected to count my college credit toward my high school career. So I ended up with a bona fide diploma instead of a GED, which was a real achievement in Short Creek. Coming from a background like that, a high school diploma was as tough to achieve as a Nobel Prize, which is why I'm damn proud of it to this day.

It took a lot of willpower to find enough energy to do a little work on the trailer when I finally got home at the end of each day. The commute, the company, the hard labor, the profuse sweating, and the searing 100-plus degree heat were almost too much to bear. I harbored a lot of antipathy toward God's mouthpiece for subjecting me to hell. For that matter, I always wondered why God *needed* a mouthpiece—he wasn't mute. Hell, he once talked to Charlton Heston from a bush. Mouthpieces always got appointed out in the sticks somewhere. It would be less confusing if somebody else could hear God, too, just to make sure the first mouthpiece was translating correctly.

I worked with Frank for most of a year—a lot longer than it took to know without a doubt that I hated excavation. It might have been better, but every time I got around a machine to practice, they would go insane with fury. Instead, I was meant to be put in the trench and left to suffer there. If they were teaching me a lesson, I'm sure I learned it. By the time this was finished, I knew implicitly how the children of Israel suffered while they waited for Moses. Working for Pharaoh Frank was enough to teach anyone that.

# XII
## TWO FOR RULON

Growing up in the FLDS, you witness many events unusual to the outside world. Men have several wives. Families grow to over fifty children. Young children form labor crews in the work fields. But that is all small potatoes, compared to most unusual ceremony I was ever privy to. I had the privilege (if that's what it was) of watching Warren Jeffs perform a ceremony marrying two young women to his father, the "Prophet" Rulon Jeffs. It was a rare double play. Both were married to the man on the same evening.

I thought it was peculiar. My sisters-in-law, Velvet, age twenty-two, and Kathy, age eighteen, had both agreed to be married to a man in his nineties. I knew that placement marriage was a social trademark of the polygamous group at Short Creek. It had been developed and refined over years of experimentation and was accepted by most of the community. What I could not understand was how, first, an old feeble man could successfully phrase a double proposal, second, how two beautiful and seemingly intelligent girls would agree, even with a background of obedience, and third, how their parents could seem overjoyed at the prospect of having two innocent girls subjected to a rest home environment for two to three years at best, and then widowed thereafter.

Marriage to a "Prophet" is an insurance policy for salvation, no matter what happens from that moment forward. A female participant is guaranteed a place in the choirs of Heaven as a chosen daughter of Zion. But even with all of that, how could a sane girl possibly go through with it? How could a vestal virgin permit her young life to be sacrificed to the volcano god? In history class, we learned this type of sacrifice was barbaric—a complete violation of the girl's fundamental human rights. Never mind that the volcano god would spare the community for another year—it was still barbaric.

I remember the gratitude I felt at having risked the fury of the Beast by courting Suzy and daring to make her my wife. If I hadn't forced my will and ruined my reputation, my Suzy Q would be shackled to the "Prophet," just like her sisters. Suzanne could have ended up married to a man with an oxygen tank.

And I knew I had flown in the face of the established order. When I arrived, I was sure that Warren would have something to say about my presence there. I assumed he hated me, since I had violated his order, and the order of his father, when I deliberately *courted* Suzanne.

Courting is forbidden in the FLDS. Boys and girls are repeatedly taught that any contact with the opposite gender is wicked or will lead to wickedness. A boy should proceed with blinders on, much like a horse in the Kentucky Derby. His race will be less distracted if he is unaware of other participants, especially the cute filly on the outside. Girls, especially, are to maintain modesty, aloofness, and above all, a pure chastity that can be defined by the elders from time to time. Most girls grow up a bit backward and confused by the males because of the second-class position a patriarchal order casts them in. Throughout the last five thousand years, this was not an entirely new concept.

The forced segregation helps the moment of marriage become a major milestone in the lives of young people. Young men work hard and "magnify their Priesthood," which usually means strict obedience and "kissing up" to authority at school, church, work, family, etc. They must prove themselves worthy of receiving a mate. Without a wife (or wives) their ascent to glory and eternal salvation is impossible. These are strong motivators, when coupled with natural hormones. It makes people willing to "toe the line" and sacrifice. Being found worthy is essential for survival in this community.

Girls, on the other hand, must show obedience and home-keeping skills to become ready to "turn themselves in." This means they leave the orbit of their father and place their future in the hands of the "Prophet" to be placed. The biggest problem with this "perfect purity" is that the "Prophet's" selection overpowers the natural parental concerns. This makes mere spectators of the guardians these young, innocent children have learned to shield themselves with.

Regardless of age or maturity, if a placement is announced, it becomes the Word of God immediately. All parties either succumb or risk mortal banishment and eternal damnation. The idea of placement marriage was not introduced by early Mormon leaders. It is a system invented by the later "mouthpieces of God." Like the Hebrew matchmakers, it was intended to slow down the waves of courtship and proposals that hot girls always have to deal with in a polygamist order. The other obvious benefit of placement marriage is that it means older men could secure celestial wives. That would be difficult for them to accomplish if the competition of young, handsome, virile men was permitted.

That was the case for Rulon Jeffs. The man had lived for almost a century, had suffered a debilitating stroke, and had to be hooked to an oxygen tank to survive. But, like David, he still wanted the most beautiful women in the kingdom. At his age, marrying him essentially meant a girl vowing to a union of celibacy. He would certainly be unable to consummate the marriage.

My wife Suzanne and I were invited to witness this occasion only because the two beautiful young ladies were her closest sisters. They had requested our presence. There are not many chances to witness what happens when two frightened young girls marry a "Prophet" in his nineties. I was shocked when my wife told me we were invited. I hadn't heard of *anyone* but the actual people involved ever being invited to a celestial ceremony. It was the polygamist equivalent of a temple sealing for "time and all eternity."

Naturally, I was a little nervous driving over to the "Prophet's" house, but the normal joy of a wedding transformed into shame and guilt as I watched the events unfold.

Piano music tumbled from the upper parlor as we made our way into the big foyer. A young lady, one of the wives of Rulon Jeffs, was playing hymns skillfully upon the grand piano. We walked into the room and took a seat near the back. I looked around to see who else was witness to this occasion. Some of Suzanne's family members and a few of the "Prophet's" other wives were allowed inside. In the corner, Warren Jeffs was involved in a hushed dialogue with a few of the "Prophet's" bodyguards. The "Prophet" never went anywhere without a few men, whom he trusted with his life. He seemed to be protected almost as well as any President.

And there, in the center of the room, on a plush sofa, sat the brides. They were like those little scared porcelain dolls you see sitting in Victorian paintings. I couldn't but wish that I had been a fly on the wall when Rulon Jeffs offered up his ludicrous proposal. I wondered how he had done it.

I had overheard a respected man in the community recounting his experience of taking his daughter to 'turn herself in.' I knew the woman he was speaking about. I thought she was a very attractive girl. It certainly seemed that the most attractive girls would usually end up in the "Prophet's" home.

I could feel the pain in his voice. I was a little surprised that he was talking about it so openly, in his slow, sad voice. He said, "I was so proud of my daughter turning herself into the Priesthood. We had an appointment with Uncle Rulon and she told him that she was ready to be married. He sat there for just a few moments, reached out and grabbed her hand. He held it for a few seconds before saying plainly, "Consider this your proposal." My poor girl sort of did a double take. She looked startled---confused." The conversation stopped for a moment. I thought it was over. And then he said "I still wonder just how much revelation went into asking my beautiful daughter to marry him."

Perhaps this was how my sisters-in-law were proposed to. The proposal wasn't a question. It would have been punctuated with a period. What could they say to the man whose every word was the voice of God? It was taught from an early age that if you deny what the "Prophet" has given, it would turn into a curse. They just wanted to please their father and do whatever the "Prophet" had asked of them.

The music was soft and relaxing, but there seemed to be a lot of tension in the air. There was a deep sense of foreboding that hung over me, as I studied Suzanne's two sisters. They were waiting patiently, but their eyes were red; their faces were flushed. They had been weeping.

Does it take courage or madness to marry someone that is seventy years your senior? I think the reason they do it, though I don't agree with it, is that they believe that he will be lifted up in the Last Days and made young again. Most "Prophets" like to convince their followers that the "Last Days" are coming really soon. That way, no one disobeys, because retribution is coming in short order. Otherwise, people would have to wait until they die before they are punished. That could be a long wait. Sometimes people don't think that far ahead.

Every generation has an Armageddon that is imminent. They all think it is right around the corner, as though hellfire and brimstone are lapping at their feet. That is not unique to polygamist Mormons. All religions use this scenario to keep their followers in order.

Here, the "Prophet" reaped a double benefit from the forthcoming apocalypse. He could keep people in order *and* he could marry young girls, in preparation for being young again himself. In effect, these young ladies were being put on a shelf for storage.

Most girls in this sect were taught that there was no greater reward for a woman than to marry the "Prophet" or someone close to him. My in-laws had the satisfaction of seeing these two daughters marry into the highest level of security in the kingdom. My poor wife, on the other hand, was thought to have done the opposite. Marriage was no longer a union of two people in love. It was a proof of faith and conviction.

Suddenly, Warren and one of his friends briskly left the room. I was still wondering what was going on when the door opened again. "Uncle" Rulon, still recovering from his stroke, leaned heavily upon them as they proceeded into the room. It was as though they were dragging him in. A third man carried his oxygen tank behind them. It took three men just to walk the groom into the ceremony, plop him on the sofa, and get him breathing properly again.

Warren called the place to order. He took Velvet's hand and led her over to the couch where "Uncle" Rulon, in no condition to stand, sat waiting. As she sat down next to him, Rulon craned his neck and peered at her. He and Warren were both tall, gangly men. They were well over six feet tall and they kind of lurched their bodies forward to stare down at people. It was like two vultures hovering over a terrified rabbit. The oxygen mask, tubes coming up both sides, only added to the surreal nature of what I was witnessing.

As Warren performed the ceremony, tears streamed down her face. She did her best to hide it from the witnesses in the room, but steadily she began to sob. It made me sick to watch, but I could not turn my head or close my eyes.

In morbid fascination, I watched Warren, to see if he'd stop. I expected him to give her a moment to collect herself. At any rate I thought he might try to comfort her. But he just continued relentlessly on. "Do you give yourself to this man to be your lawgiver, to have and to hold, promising to cleave unto him and forsake all others for time and all eternity?"

A timid, shaken voice escaped her. "Y-yes. I do."

Warren nodded. He turned to his father and asked him to take the same vow. However, the words "forsaking all others" were noticeably missing. And the marriage wound down to an old man declaring "I do." The bride wept, as though she was attending a funeral.

At last Warren proclaimed, "You may now kiss the bride." The ancient groom was unable to turn his head. He just sat there, waiting passively, as Velvet stood up and kissed him on the cheek.

She crossed to the couch where her younger sister was waiting. As they traded places, Kathy began to sob more noticeably. The younger sister bravely took her place next to the "Prophet." She was eighteen. The law declared her capable of making her own decisions. I wondered if this was one of them.

It was the same circus, appearing twice in a row. If I had heard the ceremony on tape, I might have been impressed with its sanctity. But the coupling of these holy words with the visual misery of the brides didn't seem sanctified. It seemed too crazy to be happening, almost demented.

There was a notable difference between Velvet's wedding and Kathy's. Kathy had no pretense of hiding her unhappiness. I've heard people cry at weddings, but not like this. Somehow I felt I must have been in another time, or another place. This was the sobbing of a sacrificial virgin.

And it was over. She kissed her future husband softly on the cheek, with shiny tears on hers. He seemed so pleased, looking down at the newest addition to his already bulging family. I studied the parents of these beautiful brides. Frank and Mary-Ann kept their eyes forward, so proud of their little girls. But I wished I could see the workings of their minds. In spite of their pride, they hadn't given the girls a chance to choose their life. Their mantra, as always, was to keep sweet; it's a matter of life or death.

Watching our wizened "Prophet" accept his latest trophies, I hoped to God that I wouldn't have any daughters. I didn't want to stand there like Frank and be proud that my babies were crying on the happiest day of their lives. These were not tears of joy.

The wedding reception was a bit of juice and cake in the kitchen. Rulon's other wives welcomed the newest brides into the family. The two girls seemed much more relaxed, now that Rulon had been carried off to his bedroom, but I could still see in their eyes that they knew their youth was gone. They were fully aware that they would be widows in just a few years. They also had to know they would then be subject to the whims of the next "Prophet." In a sense, this was all a dress rehearsal.

I don't think I've ever attended a wedding that was so subdued. I'm sure I've never left one with that kind of emptiness in my heart. I had watched friends buried and felt less pain. I had known Velvet when I was in school—she was always so happy, all the time. But that was gone. A part of me had to respect their devotion to their religion, but mostly, I just felt pain for them. As we left that home, I wished them good luck, and I meant it. And I could tell I wasn't going to have much to do with them anymore. In a sense, that ceremony *was* a funeral. Those girls were dead to the rest of the outside world.

# XIII
# BOBBY

My brother Bobby has shared just about every one of my experiences. He is a year younger than I am, and we look a lot alike. While I was getting to know Suzanne, the powers-that-be were trying their hardest to stop the courtship. Because of our uncanny resemblance, he was mistaken for me on many occasions. He would be stopped by the police, challenged in church, and harassed at school. He was my wingman, whether he wanted it or not, and I was grateful for it.

He was a powerful young man, and had always been a good fighter, since we were kids. Back then we would fight each other a lot, but a greater threat came along in the form of our Aunt Mildred. She would terrorize us with enough viciousness that we were forced to band together. Now, the kid was loyal and fiercely protective.

After news of Suzanne and I went around the gossip track, every man in that community thought Bobby was secretly meeting with their daughters. However, this was only true in one case. There was a cute girl that caught his eye. He would sometimes drive by her house in an attempt to see her.

Unfortunately for him, he was not the only one who thought she was beautiful. It appeared that her stepfather, Con Holm, had similar ideas. Sometimes, when a man fell out of favor with "the Prophet" and he reassigned his wife and children to another man, the newest father would view his stepdaughters as potential future wives. It never seemed to bother a man to be married to a woman and one or two of her daughters at the same time. After all, they reasoned, there were no direct bloodlines involved. Bobby had unwittingly stumbled into one of these situations.

Bobby had been reduced to sneaking around, of course, because there weren't really any other options. Because there is no dating allowed, it is really, really hard to get to know a girl in the FLDS. A young man felt he was worthy to have a wife a lot sooner than "the Prophet" did. Being worthy usually hinged on waiting patiently until "the Prophet" thought of a good match for him. It could be days, or it could stretch into years. Since "the Prophet" is the only one that can place these marriages, sometimes his health can be a factor in the time it takes.

The length of the wait usually depended on how close the candidate was to "the Prophet." If the man had a friend or relative high enough in the priesthood to get himself known and sponsored, that usually seemed to cut through the religious red tape much more quickly.

A woman, on the other hand, could always expect a perfect match to be found fairly quickly, usually within a few days of the date she turned herself in. The women that "the Prophet" decided would fit best in his *own* family generally seemed to have the shortest wait. These women have been raised to follow exact instruction. It is a blessing to be placed in a marriage by "the Prophet". If they refuse the blessing, it is taught that they will have a curse put on them.

Young men who had wearied of waiting often took their chances sneaking around. For Bobby and me, sneaking around was almost a requirement, because we could wait forever and still never glimpse the green light at the end of the dock. The Williams family is almost universally reviled in the FLDS. So we had to take our chances flipping pebbles at our lovers' windows. It isn't very honorable, sure, but there was really no other way.

This came to a head one night in late summer. After my wife and I returned from a vacation, I found myself driving home over one of the unlighted dirt roads that exist at the north end of Hildale. As we crested one of the little hills, I noticed a truck, run off the side of the road, with a throng of people gathered about. Several four-wheel ATVs roared away from the scene, and there, to my amazement, I saw my oldest brother pursuing them as fast as he could.

Obviously he stood no chance of catching it. Stopping short, he cupped his hands to his mouth to yell at the riders, at the very top of his lungs. "Come back here and tell me what you've done with him, you big pussies!"

"Jeromy!" I called, leaping out of my truck and bolting over to his side. "What's going on here?"

He pointed in the direction the ATVs had gone. "These *assholes*," he spat, seething with anger, "came out of nowhere and jumped Bobby. There's blood all over the truck."

I burst through the crowd, looking at the truck. There was blood all down the driver's side. Near the rear of the truck, there were pools of the stuff.

Jeromy continued on. "Someone said they were using a bat. We can't find him anywhere."

I stood up, so wracked with fury I couldn't see straight. Someone needed to bleed for this. I wanted to break bones. Then, out of the dark, a man approached us, donning gloves as he did so. He had six or seven other men behind him. As he approached, the man would frequently make a fist, punching the palm of his other hand. He was trying to intimidate us.

I recognized them instantly. The leader was Greg Holm, and the several men behind him were his brothers. As Greg strode into the beam of our headlights, we could see at once he was smiling, like a pixie. "You fellers want to get some of what we just gave to that other young man?"

I gaped. Had I heard him correctly? The man just *stood* there, smiling serenely. I suspected he might be pushing for a brawl. At least, I hoped so. I wanted to kill him. I wanted to beat him to within an inch of his life. "You're a real tough bunch, you know that?" I suddenly realized I was screaming at him. "How many of you did it take to beat the shit out of a seventeen-year-old kid?" I took a step forward, hoping for a fight. "What have you done with him?"

From the back of the mob, Con Holm stepped forward. "He's just fine. We sent him home," was all he said.

Glancing around, I weighed the odds of a fair fight. A few of my cousins had gathered around beside Jeromy, which meant we had about as many bodies as they did. And these men ranged from twenty-five to mid-forties, generally. We were younger and more athletic. I started to like our chances. I took another step forward. "How bad did you hurt him?" I asked. I was face to face with Con Holm.

I think he might have liked his chances too. He looked me straight in the eye. "Not as bad as we plan to, next time I see him around my daughter," he said casually.

I was livid. That was the spark that was needed to set us all into overdrive again. We screamed and cursed at the vigilantes, balling our hands into fists. These men thought they could take justice into their own hands, and now we were bound and determined to return the favor.

Then Sam Roundy shoved his way between us. The Chief of Police rushed in to prevent the situation from deteriorating further. He turned to our group, one hand on his mace jar, and the other on his pistol. "Back up!" he cried. "Back up or I'll mace the bunch of you!"

It was us he threatened, of course. His back was to the Holm brothers. I felt it was a little unfair that he was challenging *us*, considering all the violence had so far been done by the other men. We hadn't hit a single person, although, in all fairness, we were certainly entertaining the idea.

Jeromy stepped forward. "These assholes won't tell us where our brother is!" He pointed at the truck. "They beat the ever living shit out of him, and they won't tell us if he's okay! Just look at all the blood!"

Sam Roundy glanced at the blood. He seemed a little perturbed by it, but he still faced us, mace jar at the ready. Behind him, the Holms looked at us impassively. I could just imagine Greg Holm opening his mouth and declaring "What are you going to do about it?" They knew they were going to get off without a hitch. That level of arrogance in the face of this injustice managed to infuriate us more than many of had ever been in our lives.

Shouting curses, we edged closer to the mob. A screaming Sam Roundy was the hopeless referee. And just then, another police car pulled up the road, lights blazing. As it screeched to a halt in front of us, Deputy Marshall Clark Cooke leapt out and pointed at the Holm brothers.

"I have just been at the residence of Robert Williams," he said matter-of-factly. "There is a young man there, who has been beaten badly. I want *every one* of these men in handcuffs and charged with aggravated assault of a minor."

The prospect of justice did a lot to calm us down. There were more pressing matters to worry about than revenge. We turned to Cooke, all asking questions of him at once. Was he going to be all right? What damage had been done to him? Had he lost a lot of blood? He fended off our questions and sent us home to see him. Then, hearing rumors that the mob had been drinking, he started to check them for alcohol.

When I walked into the front room of my father's house, I noticed Bobby, lying on the couch. His clothes were filthy with dirt and drying blood. His face had been smashed in. It was horribly swollen and still bleeding from several lacerations. My father and most of his family had gathered around to tend to his well-being, comforting him and telling him that the Holms would go to jail for their part in this.

Bobby's mouth was too swollen to talk much. After a few moments, though, C.H. Wyler came through the door. C.H. was one of Bobby's best friends, and he sported several cuts and bruises himself. He was able to tell us a little bit of what had happened.

Earlier this evening, Bobby had driven by Con Holm's house, with his stereo playing, loud enough that his girl could hear it. Con Holm was aware that Bobby had been trying to meet this girl, and he felt threatened by it. Determined to stop this sort of behavior, he gathered his brothers and set out after him.

Bobby had just dropped C.H. off at his house. He was on his way home when the ATVs came upon him. They edged up close to him and cut him off, forcing him off onto the side of the road. Bobby had rolled down the window to give them a hard time for their poor driving. Greg slammed his fist through the open window and into Bobby's face. And they dragged him bodily through the window and beat him against the side of the truck.

C.H. heard the commotion down the street. Knowing instinctively that it was Bobby who was in trouble, he scooped up a bat and ran to his aid. When he reached the group, he saw them gathered around Bobby, viciously kicking and punching at him. They were outnumbered twelve to two, and Bobby was pretty damaged already. C.H. leaped into the bed of the truck, raised the bat in the air, and shouted at them to leave Bobby alone.

A few of the attackers swarmed up onto the truck, tackling him in the pickup bed and wresting his bat away from him. Then they smacked him with the bat, hard, in the center of the back, and C.H. crumpled. They kicked and punched at him until he was a bleeding wreck as well before they swung their attention back over to Bobby.

C.H. told us that one of the attackers was Rodney Holm, who was considered one of Colorado City's finest police officers. Rodney would later claim that he was only there to ensure that the violence didn't get out of hand. Sometime after that, he would change his defense and insist that he wasn't there at all. But C.H. was certain that he was involved, and that he was the one who initially grabbed the bat away from him. Bobby, for his part, also claims to have seen Rodney Holm among the vigilantes.

About an hour after my arrival, Sam Roundy knocked on my father's door. He strode in, holding the bat in his hand. He didn't seem concerned about Bobby at all. He held the bat up for us to see. "Where did the bat come from?" he asked. "Who brought it to the scene?"

Without waiting for C.H. to claim ownership, he continued on. "It seems to me," he said, "that we can either let this go or charge both parties for assault."

I blinked. "Assault?" I asked.

Sam nodded. "Well, you brought a deadly weapon."

I almost laughed at the idiocy of the notion. C.H. could have brought a rifle along and shot four of them dead, and it would still be self-defense. But Sam was serious. As far as he was concerned, C.H. had committed a crime in coming to Bobby's aid.

Then Sam started in on Bobby. He knew why the beating had taken place, and he spent a few minutes scolding Bobby for having the audacity to have his stereo playing at his paramour's house. "We don't allow that kind of behavior in this town," Sam chided. "You know how close these brothers are. You need to just let this go and mind our own business." He smiled. "You hear me? *Leave the girls alone.*"

I was dumbfounded at what I was hearing. The Chief of Police had every intention of sweeping the entire affair under the rug. He was working double-time to convince my brother not to press charges. I could tell that, as far as he was concerned, nothing would be done about the beating.

Of course, we all knew why he was so adamant about protecting the Holm brothers. He was married to their sister. They were his brothers-in-law, and we were nothing more than his enemies. Later, we would even discover that the ATVs, which had been used to run my brother off the road, came from Sam Roundy's yard.

As Sam sauntered out the door and down the walk, I picked up the phone and called the Washington County Sheriff's Office. The sheriff at the time was Glenwood Humphries, and I told him all about what happened. After I was finished, there was a moment of silence as he mulled it over.

"Now, you're saying that the chief of police is *related* to the perpetrators?" he asked.

"Yes, he is," I replied. "Like an extended family member."

"And he didn't take himself off the investigation?"

"No, he didn't, Officer. He was just trying to convince my brother not to press charges."

He was shocked. "*What?*"

"Officer Humphries—"

"Please," he interrupted, "Call me Woody."

"Woody, then," I continued. "I just want to know if that line of crap he's putting on is *true*. Would my brother and his friend really be charged for assault?"

Woody growled. "One, they're both minor kids. And two, *hell no*, the kid wouldn't be hit with assault for coming to the aid of his friend. Tell you what, son, give me your address. I'm sending a deputy down to investigate. Make sure you're there. You can tell him what you've just told me."

"Thanks for your help, Woody," I said, relieved. "If it's okay, I'll probably wait a while before I tell the local cops I called for backup."

I knew that once the local police found out what I had just done, they would have conniption fit. It would probably cause a few problems in the long run. I wished that Sam Roundy had just excused himself once he realized he was related to the perpetrators, rather than leading the charge to get them acquitted.

Stepping outside, I was amazed at the number of people who had gathered in the yard. Most of the community's emergency response team was there, as well as the entire police force. Some of my cousins gathered at my uncle's home across the street. They were still seething, looking for someone to fight. Perhaps the rest of the people had gathered to ensure that the situation did not escalate.

My dad had already told my cousins to calm down, to let the police officers take care of it. But that enraged them even more. They felt just as I had; they knew the local police had no intention of seeing justice done. They were nothing more than a lynch mob, with the exception of Deputy Cooke. My cousins were ready to do violence on the lot of them. I trotted across the street to see if I could talk to them.

"Hey, fellas," I said, trying to reassure them. "I called the Sheriff's office and they are sending an officer to take care of this. I guarantee that they will *not* get out of this scot-free."

They seemed to feel a little better, knowing that someone other than the local police force was ready to investigate the situation. "Look, guys," I continued, "we're not gonna see justice unless we chill out before the problem gets too big to handle. I'm as frustrated as you are about the whole deal. But the Sheriff'll take care of it."

They were still furious at the arrogance of the cover-up, but they started to trickle off homeward, one at a time. As I walked back into the house, I caught Sam Roundy standing on the front lawn, watching the crowd fade away. I glared at the man. Just then, I wanted so much to have a quick, clean shot at his nose. I might have taken it too, if I thought that I could get away with it. But I went into the house instead.

The next day, my mom took Bobby to the hospital for a check-up. He was sporting a fat lip and two black eyes. But luckily, the kid is just damn tough. There was not a broken bone in him. My little sister still refused to let him out of her sight. She had been quite frightened when he first walked into the house, covered in blood. She was sure that it would happen again every time he left the house.

Bobby eventually made a full recovery. Although we brought a deputy down from the county seat, he was unable to collect enough evidence to bring people to court. Most of the people in the community flat-out refused to testify against someone when "the Prophet" told them not to. Even people like Truman and Dan Barlow, who have their families, homes, and livelihoods ripped away from them by "the Prophet" still for the most part refuse to go against his orders.

In the end, the deputy only got enough evidence to bring one man to court, and that was Con Holm, the stepfather of the girl Bobby had been trying to see. He received a fine and some time in jail. None of the officers who mishandled the case were charged with anything.

My father found himself in trouble with the church, because he had allowed the County Police to take over the case. He was kicked out of their priesthood meeting, and both he and Bobby were required to have a conference with "the Prophet." It was widely considered among the FLDS that the best way to handle situations like these was "in house." Because my father had allowed the sheriff's office to press charges, he was blackballed in the eyes of the community.

Bobby's case was used as a kind of example for the rebellious young people of the FLDS. The message was simple—it was a blessing to be placed in a marriage by the hand of "the Prophet." If they refused the blessing, it was a beating. The choice was a simple one.

This type of beating was not unique to my brother. It had happened before. It was just one of the tools in the arsenal of parents. These parents used this type of threat to ensure that their children adhered to the often repeated maxim, "perfect obedience produces perfect faith."

A lot went into trying to convince young people that they had to marry the person they were placed with. Many parents were genuinely happy that "the Prophet" felt their child was worthy, and they put a lot of pressure on their children to ensure that they did as "the Prophet" asked. If the child were to refuse, that would reflect poorly on the upbringing provided by the parents.

I have seen many girls marry a man they hate in order to please their parents. A father can put extreme amounts of pressure on his daughter. Sometimes a mother might take her aside and call up her own experience. "When I was your age, I didn't want to marry your father, but I knew it was right because the priesthood was behind it. You don't want to see your Maker in the last day and tell him you had no direction in your marriage. It is the highest level we can attain, having the Prophet place us. You might not know this man or be attracted to him yet, but I know that you can learn to love him."

The reason Bobby got beat up was because he wanted to choose his own blessing. Bobby had taken a lot of flak for me, because we look so much alike. He was harassed by many in the community who had heard what an unworthy soul I had become. He got his beating; it was severe and painful. The thrashing I was about to get wasn't quite so bloody. But there was still the intention to cause suffering that lingered behind it.

# XIV
# DIXIE DREAMS

On the surface I was trying to re-establish some kind of favor with Rulon Jeffs and the FLDS Church, simply because that was what my in-laws wanted. But in reality I was appalled at many things that were happening. The "Prophet's" double play was only the tip of the iceberg; many other programs were now in place that alarmed me to the core.

I was already an apostate, simply because I dared court a dissenting opinion. People in that community are like the tribal factions of Africa: they have a literal inability to understand the idea behind the term 'loyal opposition.'

Warren Jeffs had developed a narcissistic streak and was already in the process of editing history. Once while teaching in Alta Academy, he had come to the conclusion that the dead prophets were not as valuable a resource as the living "Prophet" that was his father. So during a history lesson, he orchestrated a fire alarm, and while the students were gone, he stole the church history textbooks from each desk. When the students came back looking for them, he gently advised them that he could tell them all the facts that it was necessary for them to know.

This process of revisionism was equally apparent in his ludicrous sermons. He would often discourage the reading of any kind of outside source, on the grounds that even a seed of doubt dooms you to hell. The preacher was perfectly capable, he argued, of making you aware of every historical tenet that was essential for righteous living. He would often back up his statements with quotes or excerpts from the Bible, the Book of Mormon, and the Journals of Discourses. It really worked for him because scriptures are by nature very ambiguous, which means that if you read them looking for messages of inspiration and peace, you will find them. If, however, you read them looking for a reason to shun or make war on your fellow man, you will find that too.

Unsurprisingly, the latter is what he found, and he capitalized on them over the next few years. There was no need to study history, or even read the scriptures because we were lucky enough to have a "Prophet" that would tell us all the important parts. Because the "Prophet" (and by extension, his son) received his revelations directly from God, he felt no need to edit his work. The result is a pamphlet so incoherent and riddled with typos and spelling errors, one wonders how he could justify his work to the congregation he forced to read it. It is highly unlikely that the Creator of All Things Seen and Unseen would be forced to do without spellcheck. The following is a scanned photocopy of one of these sermons, exactly as written, spelled, edited, taught, and distributed by Elder Warren Jeffs.

---

**Our! Prophet's Call-**
**"Leave Apostates Alone, Severely"**
**Steps of Apostasy**
**Lesson Given in General! Meeting At the LSJ Meeting House Colorado City, Arizona July 16, 2000**

Elder Warren Jeffs:

Today our Prophet is drawing another her line of guidance for this people, which he does not want us to cross anymore. There are combining against our Prophet and this work the apostates. They have .declared against him. They work against him. And he is now calling upon his people to let the apostates alone, and let there be a separation of this Priesthood people from associations, business, and doings with apostates. He is calling upon us to stop helping our enemies fight against us.

An apostate from this is the most dark person on earth. They are a liar fpm the beginning. They have made covenants to abide by the laws of God and have turned traitor to the Priesthood and their own existence and they are led about by their master; Lucifer. They can't help themselves but fight against the Prophet and all who support him. You cannot go to apostates to receive any evidence of this work. Their nature is to be a liar. What ever truths they use, they will insert a lie. And if you are choosing to socialize with apostates, to join with them in any way, you are choosing to get on the devil's' ground. You spend five minutes with an apostate and he or she will present some untruth as an effort against our Prophet, in their mind to justify their position.

He wants us to stop patronizing businesses of the apostates. Stop doing business with them, strengthening their hand, by your labors to fight our Prophet. And if they have businesses, do not patronize them. Come away from them. If you are in partnership with apostates, come away from them, is the call of our Prophet for your labors of earning money is strengthening their hand against this Priesthood We will not be that it people the L.ord can use as long as we harbor our enemies.

The great challenge among this people is, the apostates are our relatives. If a mother has apostates children, her emotions won't let her give them up, and she invites them into the home, thus desecrating that dedicated home. We want to see them and socialize with them; and every time we do, we weaken our own faith and our ability to stand with the Prophet. This is what our Prophet says about relatives, talking of Jesus:

Rulon Jeffs 7:418 September 19, 1993 Sandy

---

No one dared to question his poor writing skills, because to do so would be to question the writing skills of the Almighty. It was important to maintain your loyalty to the "Prophet." To that end, the FLDS started requiring allegiance oaths at the door of some priesthood meetings. The big idea behind these oaths was the "all-in" concept. You had to be 100% behind the "Prophet" in everything he did or said or was reputed to have said. It was this kind of unreserved obedience that got people to drink cyanide at Jonestown, or kill themselves to catch a comet zooming by San Diego. All-in was never my brand of poker-playing, and so they would never allow me to take the oath. Then I would be in trouble for not taking it.

The FLDS was not characterized by strong leadership—it had strong-*arm* leadership, but there is a difference between the two. The overall fiber of the church's elite was missing, and a disintegration of benevolence was underway. You were expected to remain faithful to the church, to keep sweet, no matter what, but now there was less to put your faith in.

The middle and upper echelons of the congregation were still bumping along though, unaffected by what was happening to us at the bottom. The town was a beehive of activity. Fred Jessop organized home projects, usually for one of the underpaid zoo staff or Twin City Courier press personnel working directly for him. Suburban renewal grant money always found those considered to be the neediest applicants; somehow Fred Jessop's employees made the cut every time. One of those deals was the November 24 Twenty-Four Hour House.

To ensure that all the contractor crews in town would participate and feel it was more than just a manipulated charity project, the idea was advanced that Thanksgiving Day and its commemorative honoring of the Pilgrims at Plymouth, was really another form of idolatry—it was worshipping Pilgrims, or worshipping a turkey, or worshipping a football game, or something silly like that. The point is that it was a holiday with no religious bearing.

Since all Thanksgiving festivities were banned, no one had an excuse to miss the work project. I'm sure Fred Jessop patted himself on the back for that one. They gathered hundreds of men and boys to turn a concrete foundation into a finished home in twenty-four hours. They made it, and they were proud, but it was at an enormous cost of idle manpower, what with everyone tripping over one another and waiting their turn to apply their trade. If they had stretched the time frame out a little, they could have built three or four homes with the same amount of work. But the house wasn't the important part—it was the symbol that mattered to the FLDS.

Considering the state of my ratty home, I thought I would have been a good candidate for a twenty-four hour house. Instead, I labored all summer on finishing my little trailer. It cost $45,000, mostly borrowed. It would take me two years to repay the debts, but I had done the impossible, for a nineteen year old kid in a depressed community. I had single-handedly turned a condemned rattrap into a home.

To ante up the physical and financial overload, my son Jay was born in the spring of 1996. We were a young couple, and found it hard to cope with the new baby, the church responsibilities, the distant work sites, my job, and the creation of a new home. Frank gave me a job hundreds of miles away in eastern Utah on the East Carbon County sewer and water contract. If I refused, I would be shunned by my in-laws and lose all the money I'd invested in my home, so I was forced to go.

This was the grossest work I have ever done in my life. We were replacing a sewage system that had been in use for over a century, excavating clay pipes filled with water and sewage waste. True to form, I was not allowed on the machinery. Instead, I had to work in the trenches, raw sewage flowing by and sometimes filling up where I was standing,

We had to reconnect all existing hookups, and people in eastern Utah are inconsiderate of men in trenches. Many of them just went ahead and used their bathrooms anyway, although we warned them we'd be out in a hole in front of their yard. Adding insult to injury, the wind blew unceasingly across the desert, flinging acres of dirt down my shirt and into my eyes. I earned every dime and no respect.

Our company never used a trench box for safety except on one occasion, after another kid from Colorado City was killed by a cave-in. Frank didn't want an OSHA inspector to catch us and fine him $25,000 for a safety violation. He didn't care about my safety—just about his money. Sometimes pebbles would cascade down onto my hard hat, when I was down twenty feet or more. I felt they wouldn't have cared if I had been buried alive. I hated every second of that project and knew I had to get away from this chain gang existence that I was commanded to endure to prove my worthiness.

I was damn proud of my newborn boy, and I wanted so much to be close to him. I hated eastern Utah, and I hated the daily routine of living with a crew who hated my presence. I was constantly subjected to the barbs and pathetic jokes of the rest of the crew, but I was stuck, doing penance for "stealing" a bride, I guess. Every day I listened to lectures on being obedient; and if the "Prophet" found something wrong with me, I needed to stand in front of a mirror until I realized the changes that were necessary. After all, he was never wrong.

The final straw came after Bobby was beaten. I spent the next several weeks grousing about it, wishing aloud that I could meet one of the vigilantes in a parking lot somewhere. Finally, Frank turned to face me and said, "Shut up already, Jason. He ain't got a right to go around fooling with somebody else's daughter."

His brother Clyde nodded in agreement. "He deserved every second of it," he concurred.

"Hell," Frank continued, "I just wish that one of 'em woulda called me so I could be there helpin' 'em kick the crap out of that little punk."

Watching that arrogant fool tell me what he would do to my brother made me realize even further how much I detested the peasant working conditions he subjected me to. I knew I was powerless to challenge him on the statement, because I would end up doing more penance for the priesthood. I felt something like Jacob, in love with a girl and subjected to seven years in the desert, enduring hard slavery for her Bedouin father. There was not an illegal immigrant in the country that had a worse job than I did.

That weekend, I decided I had dealt with enough. I asked Rulon Jeffs to let me seek employment closer to home; because of the hardship of our newborn and the fact my wife needed daily support. There was an opening for a shop foreman in a cabinet company that had just been founded in La Verkin. It was called Dixie Dreams, and for the first time, I dared to dream that I could have a life that was better than the one they'd given me.

He allowed me to apply, as long as I wasn't going to be associating with apostates. Because the owner was a Gentile, the "Prophet" considered him a better match for me than any relatives he might deem an apostate. Unbeknownst to him, Dixie Dreams was actually a subsidiary of the company my uncle Lane Blackmore owned. I was glad the angel on his shoulder forgot to tell him that.

The new job was a dream, and a good one at that. It paid better, and I was home every night so I could hold my infant son and work on my house. To top it off, the one thing I had been pining for was made possible again—I could play in the City Recreation Softball League for The Home Company. My immediate supervisor was no longer Frank Jessop; it was Earl Porter, an affable and thoughtful man from Sacramento. He was a much more tolerable human being than Frank had been. At last, my boot camp was over.

As I was nearing completion on the house, my brother Bobby, along with other friends and family, would come over and help me. The FLDS was keen to put a stop to this. The appointed landlord of the UEP Trailer Park, Carling Stubbs, told me that apostates were not welcome in the home.

Members of the FLDS routinely had their domiciles dedicated to the Lord. The elders would come to the house when it was ready to be moved into or soon afterward and bless the house against harm and evil spirits. After the dedication, Carling told me, *no* member of my family, including my father, would be welcome at the premises, because they were all declared apostates. Even my mother, who was a devout follower of the "Prophet," had been cast from the church because of the spat my family had been having with Aunt Dread right about then.

My dad had committed the crime, and both my parents were punished for it. My dad had dared challenge Rulon Jeffs on his decision to reassign Aunt Dread to another man. He thought there was a real impropriety to the idea of releasing his wife for a trumped up charge of idolatry. "Maybe you should check the spelling" he told Rulon. "The scriptures only allow breaking the covenant of a celestial sealing for the sin of *adultery*—you know, where the wife is convinced it's okay to go around having sex with other men? Maybe even when you tell her to, for example?"

The "Prophet" genuinely hated my father for questioning him on his religion, and so he broadcast to the world that my entire family was made up of apostates. This meant that Suzanne and I were the only Williams kids (besides my uncle Jerold) that were allowed to enter the church.

It also meant I couldn't see my family at all. The presence of an apostate in the home or even in the doorway would undo the consecrated blessing, and a new batch of elders would have to come over and rededicate to get rid of the spirit left by the visitor. For this reason, many members of the FLDS refused to even consider allowing apostates to enter their homes or vehicles. In fact, one ubiquitous churchgoer had left his own son stranded in Phoenix because he didn't want the apostate to pollute the sacred spirit of his Pontiac.

On that occasion, my dad had given the kid a ride in his car, and that was the example I wanted to follow. If you are so concerned about evil things that you end up doing some evil, you aren't achieving any kind of morality, no matter what the charlatans in the FLDS may argue to the contrary.

That was why I risked the evil spirits and invited Earl Porter to dinner one night. He was a considerate human being who had helped me immeasurably with my life and struggles. I gave him my truck in exchange for some cabinetry materials for my house, and he didn't mind that I was getting by far the better deal. He often allowed me to pay off my debts through trade labor I did at nights in the Dixie Dreams workshop. We felt it was only right that Suzy and I treat him to the best dinner we could come up with, but Carling Stubbs thought differently.

The morning after our dinner, he arrived at my door and told me that Gentiles were not allowed in the home any more than apostates. I took issue with this little man telling me who I could and could not have over to my house for dinner, but I swallowed my pride, because I didn't want to jeopardize the investment I had made into the home. Living in town those days was a mixed bag of new rules and aggressive surveillance, like Orwell's *1984* meets *Animal Farm*. Fortunately, Gentiles must be somewhat less evil-ridden than apostates, because the Elders didn't feel the need to come over and save my house all over again.

By this time, I was firmly fixed on the community radar, not only because I had invited a Gentile into my home, but also because I had dared to involve the Washington County Sheriff's Department in prosecuting Bobby's attackers. I had been living in my home for less than a year when trouble came down the lane—again.

Aunt Dread had just been reassigned to Tom Holm, who had gotten mumps when he was a child and as a result was completely sterile. Once Millie was married to him, he at last had some kids to raise. A matter of doctrine among them was making sure their children knew that Robert Williams existed only to give life to these kids, because Tom couldn't. As far as the Lord was concerned, though, they were Tom's children from day one.

That line of thought would have gone pretty well if my dad hadn't thrown a wrench in the gears. He wanted the simple privilege of visiting with his twelve kids, who all considered they had the last name of Holm now. This guy was a brother of the vigilantes who had attacked Bobby, but wasn't a part of the violence, as far as we knew, but he still had a pronounced dislike of my father for turning Bobby's assault over to Glenwood Humphries. Ultimately, he decided that continued visitation with my dad would disrupt the process of brainwashing the kids.

Incensed, my dad sued for parental visitation, and won the case, to a small extent. However, there was a stipulation imposed requiring that every child must have a seat belt before they could be driven away. The twelve children, plus my dad, outnumbered the eight available seat belts in his minivan, so he was denied the visitation.

Distressed, he found me and told me of his plight, and so the two of us hatched a plan for the next Saturday. He showed up in his minivan to get seven of his kids, and I brought my Toyota 4Runner over to fit the other five. Now we had exactly the right amount of seat belts, and there was nothing more they could do to challenge us.

Never in my life had I seen such an act of grief and tears and suffering. Even the misery exhibited in stage plays and movies were nothing compared to this. All twelve kids lined up on the porch, bawling as though they were all sentenced to hang at sunset. They used to be ready to go for pizza and ice cream in thirty seconds, but now it took us a good twenty minutes to pry them from the distressed clutches of their four mothers and strap them into our vehicles.

It was a production that was repeated each week with some variations. Usually there would be a feigned illness, or they would magically be gone off to town with "Father." Whenever we succeeded in getting them all, they would sit glumly at his house, waiting for the four hours to pass. If my dad took them anywhere, they would lament and quarrel with him the entire way about just leaving them alone.

"Well, kids," my dad would cheerily respond, "at least you know I love you. No sane person would endure all this crap for any other reason. None of you will ever be able to say that I abandoned you."

I was glad to have been of assistance, but it came with repercussions. I was perceived to be in rebellion against the "Prophet" for helping my father see his kids. Because of my crime, I lost my priesthood *again*. Whatever priesthood was, it was turning out to be one slippery sucker. It was downright impossible to keep it in the corral.

Once when I went back to help get those kids, Aunt Dread glared daggers at me, "I would hate to be in your shoes come Judgment Day," she warned. "You are disobeying the commandments of the Prophet." I was pretty sure my priesthood's elusiveness was somehow connected to that scolding.

Rulon told my dad a couple of weeks after that first incident that I had *absolutely* ZERO CHANCE at salvation. He hated my disobedience, and he had recently discovered that Dixie Dreams was connected to my apostate relatives. Once he found out I was playing softball again on Tuesday nights, the dogs were out. Softball was a real seducer, apparently; Samson couldn't have been more corrupted by Delilah than the peanuts and Cracker Jack pastime of America had corrupted me.

My dad accosted me one morning and asked why he hadn't been invited to my place for some time. I told him that I wasn't allowed to bring him over because I would be kicked out of the church. My wife really wanted to be a part of the FLDS, and I was determined to make that sacrifice for her. Besides which, I stood to lose the fifty thousand dollars I'd invested in my home.

My dad flicked those quibbles away with a wave of his hand. "Might as well invite me," he muttered. "You're already in the doghouse. Rulon told me you have a 100% certainty of burning in hell for the rest of eternity anyway."

The remark stunned me. A few months before I had been baptized, ordained an elder and sealed to come forth in the righteous resurrection clothed with glory and immortality. I had gone from a guaranteed salvation to an absolute zero in the eyes of the Almighty. Promises like that clearly weren't glued very tightly.

# XV
# NIGHTMARE

The day had been sweltering hot. They always were in Mesquite. After slaving in the Nevada desert all day, we were always ecstatic to get back to our hotel in the evening. Everyone on our crew engaged in their own sort of rituals to wind down after work. Jared would make a beeline for the shower. Another kid would always scoop up the remote and plop himself down on the bed.

I didn't really concern myself with that sort of thing when I first got off work. My quest was always for the telephone. I would call Suzanne every night and she would answer, generally happy to hear from me. It was just routine things we discussed—how the boys were doing, how she was getting along, would I be home this weekend, was there anything I needed, and other things that didn't matter much. Mostly, I just liked to hear her voice, and that was why I called her every night.

But one Thursday night the phone just went on ringing and ringing. This wasn't an entirely unknown occurrence, but usually when she was going to be away, she told me the night before. I didn't remember her saying anything about it when I had called her the previous evening, so I guessed she must have forgotten. Or perhaps something had come up and she hadn't been aware of it the night before. So I thought nothing of it.

After a shower and a quick dinner, I called home again. The phone still went unanswered. It was a little disconcerting by this point, but I was sure she had a reason for having the boys out late. Usually we would go to bed fairly early, because we had to wake up early the next morning to beat the heat of the day, but tonight I elected to stay up and try calling her again. So I sat on the foot of the bed, watching the fuzzy TV with the volume all the way down. It was a little after ten o'clock when I dialed her number again.

I was much more worried when she didn't answer the third call. I called my parents' house, but there was no answer there either. Maybe Suzanne had scooped up the boys and gone with my parents, I reasoned, shopping or going to dinner. It was a tall order, but I talked myself into believing it, for the time being.

Suzanne had a habit of stuffing notes in my suitcase whenever she packed them for me. I always loved cracking open my bag and finding these letters. She had left one only the previous Monday. Diving over the edge of the bed, I riffled through the suitcase to find it. I needed to hear from her.

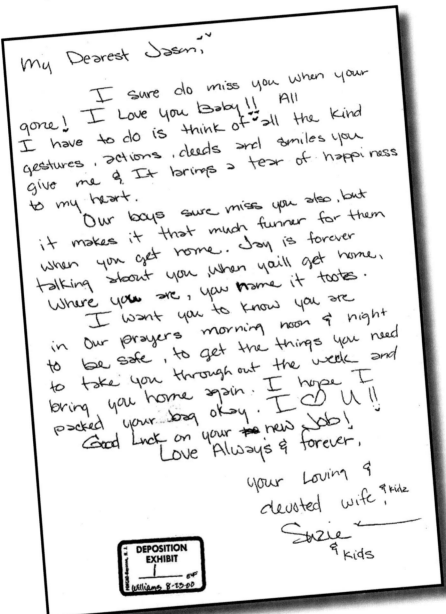

111

Reading the letter did a lot to put my mind at ease. Folding it up, I stuffed it under my pillow and drifted off into a fitful sleep, tossing and turning all night. When I awoke early the next morning, I realized I might as well have just stayed up watched TV, for all the sleep I got. Scooping up the phone, I called home once more. Every ring, I managed to convince myself that Suzanne would pick up on the next one. Needless to say, those convictions were on shaky ground.

By this time, I was truly concerned for her safety. I called my parents once more, for the second time in under twelve hours. The phone rang a few times—it had to be the two hundredth ring since I first failed to contact Suzanne, and then, thankfully, my dad answered.

"Dad!" I shouted into the phone. "It's Jason. I can't get hold of Suzy. You know where she is?"

There was a moment of silence while he processed what I said. I had awakened him pretty early in the morning. "No idea," he said after a moment. "But I did see your car out at Uncle Rulon's house the other day."

I was puzzled. Why would she do that without telling me? To my knowledge, she didn't have anything she needed to speak to the "Prophet" about that didn't need me to be there. I didn't want her to speak to that hypnotist on her own, because part of me knew that she wasn't strong enough to resist his orders. The only arguments we ever had came about because she tended to flip-flop, caving in to the pressure she received from her family and church. I hoped he hadn't made her do something she would regret. And with that, the world stopped. I realized that this might not bode well for me. Feverishly, I called Suzanne's parents' house, hoping I could find her there.

Her mother answered the phone. "Hello?"

I wasted no time. "Can I talk to Suzanne?" I demanded frantically.

"Yes, one moment." Her reply was steely, reluctant. It might have been disconcerting under different circumstances, but my mind was too busy running its own races to worry about the cold reception I got from her. My mind has always been better at asking questions than coming up with good answers. That was how I filled my time now—I stuffed it with a relentless stream of questions I couldn't answer. Why would Suzanne have spent the night at her mother's house? Why wouldn't she try to contact me?

The questions seemed to go on forever, but Suzanne finally came to the phone. "Hello?" she said. I didn't answer, but after a moment of silence she herself filled the void. "Is this Jase?" she asked.

"Yes," I said, perplexed. "What are you *doing* there? Why weren't you home last night? I—"

"Jase," she interrupted. "I went to see Uncle Rulon yesterday, and he told me to get a divorce. That is what I intend to do. My parents have offered me and the boys a place to stay until you can prove your worthiness or until he places me into another family."

Some words are worse than blows. *These* words were like knives plunged into my gut and scraping on my rib cage. They left me numb, at an utter loss for words. This was not the sort of thing I expected from the strong woman I had married. Last Tuesday, just a few days earlier, we had engaged in a long conversation about how thankful she was to be my wife. At the time, she had sworn she couldn't imagine herself with any other man. She had said in certainty that we would be together forever. This was a woman I loved very much, and she was declaring in all honesty that she was going to sever the bond that we had spent five years building. One fourth of her life had gone into this family, and she was ready to give it up over the phone.

I was quiet for a long time. I'm not sure how long it was, but finally I judged I had to say *something*. "You need to wait until I get home," I said. "Let's talk about this before you do anything permanent."

"Jase, this is what I want," Suzanne said simply. "There's nothing more that needs to be said."

I felt a massive lump in my throat. At this point I knew I was howling in the wind. "Suzanne—," I began.

"I have to go, Jase," she said. "I hope you have good luck in your life, wherever it takes you."

Then there was a click as she hung up the phone. It was the click a door makes when it shuts; a click that left me out in the cold like an Old World tramp. Most of our crew, suspecting something catastrophic was taking place, had had the good sense to find something to do outside the room. Jared, however, had remained, a silent observer leaning against the wall near the bathroom doorway.

"That has to be the worst phone call I've ever had in my life," I told him as I stuffed the phone down on the hook.

"What happened?" he asked, without changing his expression.

I recounted the phone call, although it was likely he already knew the gist of what had been discussed. Jared nodded understandingly.

"What are you going to do?" he asked.

"I have no idea," I replied. "It's too weird to think about it" I slumped down on the bed and lay my head on a pillow. I wasn't likely to contribute much at work that day. "I just wish I could have a glimpse inside her brain," I voiced aloud, "so I could see what's going on."

Jared nodded again. "Tell you what I'd do if it was my wife," he said. "I'd gather her and the boys up and I'd move as far away from that whacked-out place as I could."

It was good advice. Advice isn't the most helpful thing you can give someone who is in trouble, but it's usually more useful than sympathy is. At any rate, I always appreciated good advice, especially when it came from Jared. Jared had a kind of second sight when it came to cutting through the fluff around a problem. He could get down to brass tacks.

What he said certainly sounded like a good idea, and I was determined to try it. If I could convince her once more to leave that community with me, it wouldn't be the first time we had been forced to start over from scratch, but at least we would still be together. I decided to go home that day and see if I could persuade her to come with me.

When I arrived home, I found it had been gutted. All our ornaments, our rugs, our towels, dishes, toiletries—everything had been taken. All that remained was the sofa, our old television set, and a washer and dryer. I was just glad she had chosen to leave behind all the things we still owed money on. I walked into the bedroom and noticed that the bed also had been taken. The closet was stripped; even the hangers were gone. My clothes were left in a wrinkled pile in one corner. I slumped down next to them and leaned tiredly against our paper-thin wall. I couldn't believe that everything was gone. Slumping down in a corner, I opened the letter I had pulled out of my suitcase just the night before. It didn't seem likely that a rational human being would go from the love expressed in the letter to the rejection expressed over the phone, without someone else being involved. What was really going on here?

On the off-chance Suzanne might speak to me, I drove to her parents' house and clanged on the door. They must have known I was coming, because they both were at the door in an instant. They opened the door and stared at me.

"Can I talk to Suzanne, please?" I asked them, dully.

Frank turned and called for her, and then he turned back to face me. There was clearly no question of being invited into their home. Standing side by side, the two of them worked to fill up the frame so that I couldn't even see inside. They reminded me a lot of the married couple in a famous Grant Wood painting called *American Gothic*. The image was surprisingly fitting; all that was missing was a pitchfork. For a moment I wondered if either one of them had ever seen the picture.

I had spent a good deal of time trying to get to know the both of them. I wondered if that meant anything to them. The previous weekend they had treated me like one of their own. I would have called them my very good friends, and now they were looking at me like a vicious insect in need of a good pesticide.

After a few moments, they parted and Suzanne trudged down the steps to face me. "What do you need?" she asked.

I had expected her to break into histrionics. I had almost hoped that would be the case. But she wasn't throwing tantrums; she was just delivering recorded answers in her "keep sweet, no matter what" kind of trance. It contrasted vividly with the stomach-churning, bile tasting mass that I was trying to breathe through. This was nothing like the girl I'd married.

My eyes started burning. Choking back tears, I met her gaze. "Why are you doing this?" I asked her. "You know me. You know what I'm about. The last face-to-face conversation we had, you said we would be together forever. Remember that? How do you go from that to *this* in *two days?*"

She drooped her head, refusing to look me in the eye. "I don't feel at peace with where our life is at," was all she said.

Then the tears started flowing. I made no further move to stop them. "Peace?" I echoed. "Our life has been nothing but *peace*! What about the boys' peace? Do you really want to be a part-time parent? Do you? I know *I* don't—I brought these boys into this life so I could raise them, not so they could grow up without me!"

"I'm mainly concerned for their salvation," she explained. "My parents helped arrange a conference with Uncle Rulon. They thought it would be a good idea for me to go."

I was at a loss. I had spent five years trying to cultivate a relationship with her parents, only to find they had been waiting for a good handhold so they could whisk her away from me. One of their major motivations was probably a deep, fervent hope that she would abandon the demon she was married to, and, like her sisters, marry the "Prophet." Having three daughters married to the voice of God is a great insurance policy for the salvation of their parents.

"I went there with an open mind," Suzanne continued. "He told me that as long as I was married to you I would have no chance at salvation."

"Uncle Rulon told you this?" I snorted. "He doesn't know me. He can't even *make* that kind of statement."

"Uncle *Warren* told me that," she clarified. "The Prophet can't take appointments right now because of his health, so Uncle Warren has taken over. He is in communication with the Prophet."

I didn't know what to say to that. Rulon Jeffs had a feeble grip on reality, but his son Warren had let go entirely. This was more serious than I had first imagined. "I don't think you should decide our future so hastily," I mumbled. "Why don't we go talk about it?"

I knew what her answer was going to be, but she never did have a chance to give it. Her father opened the screen door and clumped down the steps. Foisting himself between the two of us, he smiled. "Jason, we know you want to fix this," he said. "But the Prophet has asked that you not be alone with her anymore. She has turned herself in to his judgment. You need to go through the Prophet to talk to her."

The fabled last straw that broke the camel's back had come and broken mine. "Just because he says something doesn't make it right!" I roared. "We are talking about *my* family here! *No one* has the right to interfere with my family!"

He stood there, waiting for me to finish. "Are you saying you don't believe the words of the Prophet?" he asked, a little concerned.

I was on dangerous ground and I knew it. "All I'm saying," I clarified, "is that if something is wrong, it doesn't matter *who* says it."

Then he acted as though I hadn't said anything at all. "So what are you going to do?" he asked plainly. "Are you going to obey the Prophet's wishes and let this situation take the correct course?" He put his arm around me, gently. "If I could offer any advice to you, it would be to throw yourself on your knees in front of the Prophet and beg for his forgiveness. You have to put yourself in direct line with him if you want to gain your salvation. That's what Suzanne is striving for. If you are unable to do that, I suggest you walk away."

I looked up at him. He was trying to belittle me into submission, and I knew it. "How could you ask me to walk away from my own children?" I asked him.

"As far as I'm concerned, you have no business being here until you see the Prophet," Frank proclaimed, in his even voice. "We will follow any orders that we receive from him."

Spinning around, I retreated to my car before anger could get the better of me. Last Tuesday, I had been a wonderful husband and great father; now I was a pariah. I had no idea of the nature of my crime. I thought I had demonstrated my worthiness several times in the past—why else would they have allowed her to remarry me, in a church ceremony? But now they wanted me to take steps (what steps?) to prove my worthiness *again*. In law, this type of situation would be called double jeopardy.

I didn't want to start out burning bridges I might need later; if there was a way to settle this amicably, I was determined to do that. To that end, I called to get an appointment with the "Prophet." He was in Salt Lake City at the time and would be unable to see me until December 22nd, some two weeks away. I would have to bide my time and try to find a way to communicate with Suzanne between now and then.

Communication was difficult, to say the least. Suzanne had done her best to make herself unapproachable. I would speak to her on the phone a few times over the intervening weeks. It was a rare occasion when I didn't break down into tears. She would generally listen for a few moments and then tell me, in her distant sort of voice, that she had to go. She was like a robot; her answers were always short and stoic, which made it worse. In that society, as in most others, the accepted form is that the woman will be weak and emotional, and the man must remain a disaffected rock, even when his life is collapsing all about him. It makes it hard to communicate sometimes when the pressure is on you to be something other than yourself. When I would speak to her, she sounded like she wasn't suffering at all, and I was tearing myself apart. Our roles had been reversed, and that irony sickened me even more. My misery was worse in that I felt it was mine alone.

Frank had promised me that the two of us were never to be alone. For some time, I wondered if the phone conversations were kept private. Perhaps Mary-Ann was listening in on the upstairs phone. It certainly seemed like something the "Prophet" might request. It could be that every time I bared my soul to my wife, her parents were listening and laughing at it, secure in their belief that Suzanne would never again be led into temptation by my peculiar way of living. The "Prophet" they respected most on this earth had become their son-in-law. I just couldn't stack up.

Some days had passed after I first arranged the appointment, and there came a knock at my door. Carling Stubbs was a nondescript sort of man with a pointed chin. He was handsome enough that you could imagine him as a 1950s con artist putting chumps at ease. He also had the difficult occupation of being the landlord for the trailer park in Colorado City.

"Hey, Jason," he said, smiling in his card-cheat kind of way. "I heard what happened. You're going through a tough time, and I just wanted to know if there's anything I can do for you."

"No, thanks," I told him. "I'll be all right."

He nodded. "I just wanted to know where you stood with all the events that have transpired. Now, you *do* understand that your lease on this property is conditional to your remaining faithful to the Prophet?"

He wanted to see if I was ready to move out. I was still reeling from my wife's decision to abandon her attempts at building a family, and now this man wanted to stack me, with all that was left of my furniture, on the side of the street. For a moment, I wondered how he had found out about my troubles so quickly. Then I realized what a sight it must have been to see a moving party ransack the home a few days earlier.

"I have an appointment to see the Prophet in a few days," I said, as calmly as I could. "I guess I just need some time to pray about it."

Carling smiled again. "That should be fine," he said. "Let me know if I can help you with anything."

"I'm sure I'll be okay," I lied. "Thanks for checking up on me."

And then he was gone. I wanted to lash and scream after him, to tell him to mind his own business so I could sort out my life. But I knew it was imperative to maintain some level of peace. For all I knew, he could have been specifically sent by his manipulative leader, so that Warren Jeffs could find out what I was thinking. I had to remain cautious so I wouldn't make the situation worse than it already was.

On December 21ˢᵗ, the day before my scheduled appointment, I happened to run into one of Suzanne's sisters. Her name was Rula, and she was one of the few members of Suzanne's family who would still associate with me. I had the good fortune to be able to call her a friend of mine.

She was of the opinion that everything would be okay, as long as I did everything that "Uncle" Warren asked, without question or pause. "I talked to Suzy just the other day," she told me. "She still loves you and wants things to work out between you two, but a lot of that depends on you being faithful and willing to be instructed. You have to follow the orders of the Prophet *exactly* if you want to get back together with Suzy."

It all seemed so simple to her, but I knew the walls were closing in on me. There didn't seem to be any *real* way to see my family again. I had to ask a man I barely knew if he would be so kind as to give my family back. I really didn't like my chances.

On the morning of the interview, I sought out my dad. The interview was not scheduled until sunset, and I was at a loss for something to do with my time before it came. I thought that perhaps he could help me, because he had been through a similar trial earlier in his life. If he knew what was going to happen there, though, he didn't let on. "Jason, I don't know what they'll require of you," he said, "but you just make sure you feel right about anything you decide to do. You're the only one living your life, and at the end of the day, you'll be the one answering for any decisions you make."

I nodded. "I'm just going to do whatever it takes to get my family back," I said. "I don't have to play softball, or work out of town, or any of that crap. I'd rather live dirt-poor than live without my family."

He certainly understood what I was going through. This type of situation had been the hardest part of both our lives. "I love you, Jason," he whispered. "I'll be here for you no matter what happens. I told you once before: I don't believe in throw-away kids."

He was always good at taking the teeth out of whatever came to get me. I was despairing of ever seeing my family again, but the fear had numbed by this point. A person can't spend their whole life afraid. Sooner or later they have to get out and act. I was one of the luckier ones, because I had an ally that would walk into hell if he thought it could help me. He certainly made taking action a little easier.

# XVI
## WARREN: NO PEACE

I was scheduled to walk into hell later in the evening. I did not know what to do with the time I was forced to spend waiting. I remember saying a silent prayer as I drove toward the home of my self-appointed judge. I asked God to help me understand what to do. I begged him to help me get my family back and guide me in the right path.

It was getting dark outside. After my nerves settled as much as they could, I walked to the front door and knocked a few times. One of "Uncle" Rulon's wives answered the door, which was out of the ordinary. Normally it was Wendall Nielson who handled appointments. Warren was already putting his stamp on what he felt was his.

Warren Jeffs entered the foyer, introducing himself with a wave of his hand. That man is six-foot-five. He loomed above me like a guillotine, his sharp features ready to drop. He would tower over everyone when he talked. Maybe that's why he felt he was closer to God than I was.

He motioned me over to a chair and had me sit down. Moving a chair in front of me, he sat, sizing me up a few moments. I just looked at the floor and waited for him to speak. It was a terrifying, icy silence.

And then Warren Jeffs started speaking. "I am not here to discuss what has happened because of your wickedness, but if you will listen I will tell you how you can repent."

I wasn't sure what I was expected to repent of. I just said humbly, "okay".

When he talks, he has a rhythmic way of speaking, like a hypnotist. He looks you right in the eyes, like he is trying to convince you of the truth of his words. He is not trying to control you through confrontation—he is just trying to overpower your will with every word that he says.

That's why people who obey him still feel like they made their decisions themselves. They decide one thing, and then they meet with Warren and he seduces them into believing something entirely different. Then he arranges it so they do not have the opportunity to rethink their belief. That was why Suzanne went from loving me forever to trying to take my children away from me in the space of two days. And I could not convince her to return to me because her parents would rarely let me speak with her.

His voice took on an accusing tone as he started his harangue. "You have lost your Priesthood. You have no rights to that family. Suzanne has put herself in the Prophet's hands. She has confided in me that whenever she goes to your parents' house she feels a darkness descend upon her. When she is at *her* parents' house she feels enlightened. She wants to have that feeling of light, and she can't get that with a man who has no Priesthood. I have it on great authority that you said you don't believe in the Prophet and that is just the same as saying you don't believe in God."

"Wait a minute," I replied, "All I said was just because he says it, doesn't make it true. He's human just like the rest of us."

"That is exactly what I am talking about!"exclaimed Warren, "If you are not one hundred percent with the Prophet, you are against him!" He paused and fixed me with a steely, chiseled glare. "The Prophet is sick and tired of lukewarm men and families. The time is so short that we need to follow exactly what he says. If we don't agree with his teachings and his word, maybe we should take a look in the mirror and see what we can fix with ourselves."

I didn't want to seem like I was uninterested in what he had to say. "Look," I said. "All I want is my family. Suzanne says I have to go through the Prophet to make it right. What do I need to do to get my family back?"

He looked right through me. A little irritated, his voice rose. "Haven't you been listening?" The next words came out in a sort of shriek. *"You have no rights to that family!* Do you understand? The Prophet *owns* this family now and will do with it as he sees fit. He could marry her up tomorrow and you would have to accept that. Do not try to see these boys and further confuse them. The best thing you can do for them is leave them alone. They are with the Prophet and he will make sure they get the things they need. He may, depending on your willingness to do as he asks, have the two of you get back together at a later date.

"This is all depending on how you carry yourself and demonstrate your devotion to the Prophet. You will have to be re-baptized and on probation for a few months to see if you are *truly* with us. The Prophet has instructed that Suzanne secure a divorce and stay with her parents. Frank has said that you have been going over to his home and calling on the phone. You are trying to confuse this young lady. You will have *nothing* to do with her or these children unless the Prophet *wants* you to have your family back."

I looked at him and said nothing. Any words on my part would be like adding gasoline to the fire in his eyes. This man was incensed. Licking his lips, he continued his tirade.

"Sam Barlow will take Suzanne down to Kingman tomorrow and have an attorney draw up the papers. If you are serious about repenting and regaining your Priesthood, you will travel down with them. You are instructed to sign over *full* custody to their mother and have *nothing* to do with those children."

I blinked. Why was *Sam* involved? Sam Barlow had been the Chief of Police of Colorado City. He had been a deputy sheriff for Mojave County for many years. This man should have been helping me find my children, not using his training as an enforcer for the priesthood. My mouth set into a thin line.

Warren continued laying out his sordid conditions. I felt my heart sink with every word. I felt like I was never going to see my sons again. "You are to report to me on a weekly basis and be involved in all the work projects. After we see your actions and your willingness to follow instruction we will re-baptize you. Now, we've seen your father try to confuse Mildred's children after the Prophet placed them in another family. I want you to understand how this works. The children go with the mother. It is not in their best interest for you to try to confuse them by being in their presence." He leaned forward. "I want to make this *very* clear to you. The Prophet wants you to stop *all* contact with this young family and *leave them alone!*"

He leaned back in his chair, cracking his knuckles. Now he had come to the part he must have truly enjoyed. "Now, before we continue, you must repent and confess your sins."

My only sin was that I loved my family too damn much. And that I hated him for his insistence on ruining my life, and the lives of those I held dearest. He professed to be a man of God, and he was systematically trying to destroy me. He knew I would never return to any kind of belief in his teachings. I could not possibly do what he wanted, and he knew that I couldn't do it. The only reason he set the path to retribution was because he knew that I would fail, thus cementing his claim to my sons. It was them he wanted. It was always the young they wanted—you have to start early with this kind of training.

Then the questions started. "Have you ever fornicated with another woman?"

That one was easy. "No."

He nodded. "Do you masturbate?"

"I'm not sure what that is," I lied.

He rolled his eyes, but let it pass. "Do you have pornography in the home?"

"Of course not."

"Have you ever done anything with your wife that was not pure?"

What was pure? This man's perverted questions were loaded. But I was fairly sure of the answer. We were still very young and naive. "No," I said. "Just the normal stuff."

The man didn't crack a smile. "Have you ever handled your sons inappropriately?"

I don't know whether he was referring to beating them or molestation. I was guilty of neither, and said as much.

Now his voice became sharper. He was moving in for the kill. "Do you have any idols in your home?"

This man defined everything as idols. Pictures of Jesus Christ were graven images. My softball trophy was an idol. The Chicago Bears poster that hung on my wall was an idol. Television was an idol. I evaded the question simply. "I don't worship idols, or graven images," I said. I knew my Ten Commandments.

Warren was a little disappointed at this. He was trying to connect my playing baseball with idolatry. He had once said of me that "baseball is like his second religion." I consider that baseball is a good *first* religion to have. It has rules, and they never change. It doesn't respect *anyone* above their ability to play. And it doesn't matter who you think you are—you're still out if you miss the third swing.

Warren couldn't connect me to idolatry, though. He didn't know anything about *da* Bears. He just resumed his interrogation. "Have you ever taken the Lord's name in vain?"

"No," I said, feeling a little truthful. I had never said "Oh, my God!" in vain. I am either really angry, or really scared. When I say that, I mean it.

Then came the clincher. "Do you associate with apostates?" There was a flicker in his eyes. He knew he had me pinned.

He was talking about my brother Jeromy, my father, most of my uncles, and my paternal grandparents. They were all apostates by his definition of the word, even though every one of them believed in their religion at least as sincerely as he did. I had worked for Lane Blackmore for a while. In Las Vegas I had done work with a lot of former "Crickers." These were considered the rankest of apostates. Ignoring the thrust of his question, I simply said, "Because of work and stuff, yeah, I'm near them sometimes."

Warren glared at me. "My father says that your uncles John and Thomas are his worst mortal enemies. They filed a lawsuit against the Priesthood. They have rejected—they have *attacked* the true teachings of the Lord and his Prophet. They have **zero chance** at salvation. I have it on good authority that you regularly play softball with these people."

Here we were again. A ball game? *Wow*, I thought. This man must truly lead the most boring of lives, if this is what entertains him. I had real doubts about this man. I knew I had nothing that could interest him. I had no money. I was not interested in his foolish stabs at doctrine. But he was incredibly keen to get my wife away from me.

He kept watching me. There was a fever in his eyes—this man was insane. I spoke to him in a measured voice, carefully selecting my words as I proceeded. "All I'm interested in is getting my family back."

His lip curled up in a sneer, and he said it again. "Listen closely, this time. You have *no right* to that family! Only by proving yourself worthy will you be permitted into the church."

The words hit me like an anvil. I told him I would need to pray about it overnight.

He thanked me for listening and told me I should make up my mind as soon as possible, because Sam Barlow hoped to get an early start for Kingman. I thanked him and started homeward. I knew he was not going to let me work things out with my wife. As far as Warren was concerned, Suzanne was eligible for reassignment. No amount of work crews or tithing would change that. I don't know why he hated me. I don't know why he wanted to keep her so much. Certainly he would want to bolster his ranks with my sons, but that was almost peripheral to what he was trying to do here. Why come after the little guys?

Then it hit me. Perhaps *he* wanted my wife for himself. When he was principal at Alta Academy, he may have developed a crush on her. He was known for that sort of thing. It was widely known that he had wooed Isaac Barlow's underage daughters while they were attending that school.

Warren Jeffs had a checkered past. I had heard rumors that, as principal of Alta Academy, he had sometimes engaged in several ungodly acts, which, for someone who often thought he *was* God, was not a good thing to have on the resume. A night watchman at the Jeffs home once declared that he had seen Warren staying the night in the bedrooms of various wives of his father.

Mainly, this was conjecture. But more well-known was the way he handled the United Effort Plan (UEP). This was a trust created to preserve the hard-line Mormon tenet of communal living. It was set up to protect the assets and deeds from legal proceedings. Warren and his father managed to reorganize the trust so that it was controlled entirely by the FLDS church—a family corporation. The church owned almost every piece of property in the city limits of Hildale and Colorado City. It also had a huge tract of land in Bountiful, British Columbia. The choke hold on property was always used to keep its members in check. If anyone disobeyed, they would not only lose their family; they would lose their home.

Some people have compared Warren Jeffs to the Taliban, but he could more easily be compared to certain Roman emperors after Tiberius. Nero and Caligula were both pedantic and narcissistic. They did unspeakable things for their own comfort and amusement, and they were insane enough to think that such a thing was their right.

A country only appears as strong as its leader. There may be strength in its citizens, but its leader is the face to the world. Nero and Caligula looked like morons, hell, they were insane. They coaxed their enemies to invade, destroyed citizens , and eroded the will of the empire to defend itself. They brought Rome to its knees.

Warren Jeffs seemed to be starting down the same path. He had always been a little bit like a rat. He got into his father's favor by writing silly little religious essays and bearing witness to his father about the several indiscretions of his brothers. His whole life he had played the sycophant, all as a means to concentrate more power in his hands.

Then a bolt of sudden realization slapped into my mind. He would ultimately overestimate that power. This man considered himself above the law, and he was going to break it. His father was selfish and deluded about his divine rights too, but at least he was prudent. Warren didn't have that trait. Warren thought he was invincible. He was going to bring the powers of the United States raining down on his head. I had to take serious steps to save my boys, but I had no idea what steps to take. The fight had already been brewing, and I had to find some high ground.

It was at that moment I knew that Rome was going to burn. And if I turned away from my family, they would burn with it.

# XVII
# THE MONSTERS WE DEFY

The next day, Sam Barlow and Suzanne made the trip to Kingman without me. They had come to the realization that I was a terrible human being. I must be, since I was defying the direct orders of God. They found an attorney, and Warren Jeffs opened up his pockets to pay the lady to draft a quick custody agreement.

The following weekend, Suzanne invited me over to her parents' home. She had the paperwork and wanted the two of us to finalize it. When I knocked on her door, it nearly made me sick to think that the only reason I was there was so that she would never have to see me again. I missed her so much.

"Will you sign it right away?" she asked. She looked terribly uncomfortable in my presence.

"I'm gonna read it first," I said, and sat down in one of their chairs.

I had hoped for some privacy, but it was not to be. Her parents stood nearby, watching me like a hawk. They seemed fairly confident with Suzanne at this point; I was the only variable in the equation. They listened to me even more keenly than they listened to Suzanne.

I wanted to tell them exactly what I thought of their attempts to rip her from me. I opened my mouth to speak, but thankfully, I thought better of it. Some things truly are better left unsaid. If Suzanne and I were able to work things out, I didn't want to have to deal with any wars I had started on the side.

So I generally ignored them, and settled into deciphering the agreement Suzanne's attorneys had drawn up. I don't really like reading contracts, agreements, or anything that may have been written by an attorney. Lawyers seem to shoot for ambiguity when they write, and I always have to read the provisions five or six times to make sure I understand it properly. It might as well be written in Arabic.

But this was an *important* agreement, so I made sure I understood every inch of it. There wasn't much to understand, though, except that I was being had. Suzanne was to have custody over the children. I would have one day of visitation, Saturday from eight in the morning to six in the evening. During those ten hours, I was allowed to see my children only as long as I didn't leave her parents' home with them. On special occasions, I could take them out, as long as I got Suzanne's permission, but at no point was I permitted to take them out of the community. To top it off, I was to pay five hundred dollars a month (about a third of my small paycheck) in child support. I could have laughed, but it wasn't funny.

After I got about halfway through the document, I just snorted and plopped it on the table. Suzanne took that to mean I was finished. She handed me a pen.

"I'm not signing this," I told her. "Would you?"

Suzanne looked stunned at the question. "Well—" she began.

I held up my hand. "Suzy," I said, "I just have one question. "If the shoe was on the other foot, do you think I would do this to you?"

The situation was going southward, and quickly. She tried her best to recover the fumble. "We just think," she stammered, "what with the boys' young age, they'd be better off living with their mother."

"Suzanne, you know me," I pointed out, not a little annoyed. "You know what these boys mean to me. I'm perfectly capable of taking care of them and you know it."

"We've just been advised to start *this* visitation schedule 'til something's more permanent," she said hastily. "They're very young, and they would miss their mother. So you can visit them here."

She smiled. To her it all made sense, or she was trying to convince herself it did. Something strange had certainly happened to her. She couldn't be reasoned with anymore. She had become a Stepford wife, and every time I asked her a question about our kids, she would just yammer on about their young age. On a subconscious level, I think she was trying to shield herself from difficult questions because she had no answer to them. She had made her decision; she didn't want to be confused by the facts.

"Will you sign it?" she snapped me back to attention.

I shook my head. "No."

Her parents stood up to accost me, but I swung open the door and stepped outside. Turning back, I shot her a look. "A common criminal would have been offered more than this," I said. "I haven't done a damn thing wrong." I slammed the door shut and trudged back to my truck, livid.

That day, I went off to find a lawyer. I had never really needed a lawyer before, so I didn't know much about finding one. I knew a lot of attorneys advertised in the Yellow Pages, but didn't really want to flip the pages and pick one at random.

Fortunately, I did know an attorney in Utah who was just getting started in his practice. Chris Edwards and I had played softball together for some time, and I hoped he might be able to find a good family lawyer licensed in Arizona. As soon as I could, I drove to his offices in Hurricane.

"What should I do?" I asked him.

He sat, thinking for a moment about what I'd discussed with him. "Well, you need a lawyer," he said. "That's obvious enough. I'll poke around in Kingman and try to find you a good one."

"I'm just terrified of losing my family," I confided.

"I know," he nodded. "I would be too."

"I know a couple times where the church married a woman to a guy in Canada to make sure the father couldn't see the kids anymore."

"Well, we won't let that happen," he assured me. "Worst case scenario, we'll work out a good visitation schedule."

He sounded confident. Reassured, I asked him if I could borrow his phone. Heaving a deep breath, I dialed the number to the "Prophet's" house.

"Hello, Jason," Warren said as soon as I got through to him. "What can we do for you?"

"Give my kids back," I said, full of resolve. I wondered if he knew I'd refused to sign his agreement. If he did, he was definitely cagey. "I love my family way too much to turn my back on them," I told him. "I'm not interested in signing away my rights to those kids. And I plan on retaining a lawyer."

"Jason—" he began.

"I'm not even going to discuss it."

He was silent for a long time. I wondered if he'd hung up, but finally he spoke. "I understand," he said, calmly. "What will you be doing with the property you're living in?"

"Give me two weeks to move my stuff. I'll find a place for it."

"We have some places you can store your things *now*, if you would like," he suggested, helpfully.

"Listen," I said, "If I can't have two weeks to find a proper place, I'll fight for my property too!"

"Two weeks will be fine," he said amicably.

During the next few days, I managed to find a home in Hurricane, only a half hour's drive away from Hildale. The costs looked daunting, but my brother Bobby had been longing for an opportunity to escape Short Creek as well, seeing he had been kicked out of the church as well. He thought it was a great idea to share the place and split the costs down the middle.

There weren't very many belongings I had to pack, considering Suzanne and her crew had taken most of what was there. As I finished loading the last of what I had onto the truck, I took a final look back at the trailer the FLDS had forced us to live in. It had been hard as hell to remodel this ratty-ass trailer, but it was now a fine looking home, I thought. Suzy and I had done pretty well. This place had enough memories to bring tears to my eyes.

After we'd loaded the pathetic remnants of what belongings had been left, we drove over to my parents' home to get all of Bobby's things. On the way back, I decided to take a longer route—one that went past my old trailer. As we approached it, I blinked. The lights were on inside.

"Wait a minute. Didn't we turn them all out?" I asked nobody in particular.

As I got closer, I found there was a family moving into my old home. Only four hours ago, the home was mine. It had sported an ugly sign, just like the signs in front of every other house, which had my name and address printed on it, along with an acknowledgement that it belonged to the UEP. They were adamant about keeping a tenant-at-will status with all the property. The newest family wrote over my last name and changed the sign from *Jason Williams* to *Jason Black*. They hadn't even bothered to get a new sign.

Out with the old, and in with the new, or so the saying goes. I grinned. It had cost me a lot of money to remodel and refurbish, but at that moment I was glad to be out of there. The priesthood baron could do whatever he wanted with it.

For about a week after I had refused the proposed settlement, Suzanne and I didn't speak to one another at all. We settled into a sort of détente, and the issue of custody went ignored, like an elephant in the community. I think in the back of our minds we knew that there was going to be a custody hearing, since I had refused the opportunity to settle out of court, but I tried not to entertain this idea very much, because I always hoped that Suzanne would magically come to her senses. Then the entire separation would be nothing more than a bad dream. Then we would move halfway across the United States, if we had to, to get away from the influence of Warren Jeffs. We would start over again, in Missouri maybe. I knew a few people who had gotten chased out of the area and gotten a start in that state. Or maybe we could go to the Bahamas and forget about the entire struggle—Joel Timo always said that the Bahamas was a gorgeous place to live. If she insisted on going through with this madness, maybe I would find Jimmy Buffet's island---it seemed like "there was a woman to blame."

I had to go back to work in Mesquite the following Monday, and I couldn't very well haul the boys off with me and force them to stay in a motel room for a week. I left the boys in Suzanne's care for the time being, and went to work, wishing I could see them. I stopped calling Suzanne every night, since her parents told me I would have nothing to do with her any longer. I still wanted to talk to Jay and Kyle, but I didn't have the stomach for the kind of verbal bullying it would take to get them on the phone.

When Thursday came around, I swallowed my resentments and gave her a call, because I desperately wanted to see the boys when I got home the next day.

"Hey, Suzy," I said. "I'm going to grab Kyle and Jay and take them out to get ice cream tomorrow."

"You can't!" she protested.

"Yes, I can," I told her. "They're my kids too, and I have the right to see them. We're just going to get ice cream."

The next day, when I arrived at her parents' home to get the kids, I found Kyle, rearing to go, but Jay was nowhere to be seen.

"Where's Jay?" I asked Suzanne's mother, as I pulled Kyle up into my arms.

Mary-Ann glared at me. "I don't know," she said. "Suzanne took him out somewhere. She didn't say where she was going."

Kyle and I clambered into the truck, and we sped off down the dirt road to find Jay. I was pretty confident I knew where Suzanne had taken him. It was a common practice to have the kids just magically taken somewhere whenever the hated parent showed up to get them. Suzanne knew that I had been planning on getting ice cream for the boys, and so she had whisked Jay off to get him some ice cream herself. The idea was to beat me to the punch.

There are only a couple places in the Short Creek area that serve ice cream, and so it wasn't difficult to find the two of them. They were stuffed down into a booth at the far end of a local restaurant. When Jay saw me, he grinned and leapt out of his seat.

"Daddy!" he shouted, charging toward me. I grinned and scooped him into the air, swinging him around and landing him across the broad of my back like a sack of potatoes.

"He's already had ice cream," Suzanne told me.

"Well, then he doesn't need any more," I agreed, shaking Jay and plopping him gently back down on the floor. "Come on, buddy."

"He's already had some," Suzanne said again. "You can't—"

"Suzy," I interrupted. "We've discussed this. We're both parents here. I'm just going to take them over to my dad's place. I'll have them back at eight o'clock."

Since I hadn't signed the agreement, I wasn't required to pay any form of child support yet, but I was worried that they might be a little strapped for cash. I didn't want those kids to suffer just because of *our* marital problems. Fortunately, I had just received my two weeks' pay that morning, so I was able to hand her five hundred dollars in cash, which I thought should take care of them for the next couple weeks.

On our way to my dad's house, Jay noticed some bright headlights that followed about a hundred yards behind us. Watching the car in the rearview mirror, I found it was a police car, keeping close tabs on our truck. The officer remained with us for the rest of the drive, watching us closely to make sure we didn't escape. Someone, somewhere, didn't trust me at all.

As we pulled into my dad's driveway, I could see the car coast down into a grotto just across the street. As soon as he was settled, the officer clicked off his lights so we couldn't see him. I could have lobbed a rock across the street and pelted his car; I knew exactly where it was. If he was trying to be stealthy, he was doing poorly. That was what frightened me. Maybe he *wanted* to be seen.

I shrugged it off and went inside with the boys. The three of us became engrossed with a basketball game my dad was watching on TV. After about a half an hour, the officer apparently could stand it no longer. There came a knock at our door.

"I need to see the boys," the officer said.

"No, you don't," I told him. "I'll have them back at eight."

He didn't listen. "Where are they?" he asked, stepping inside the door.

"You're trespassing," I warned. "You got a warrant?"

The officer stepped back, glaring at me furiously. "I'm required to look into the welfare of these children," he said officiously.

"Jay! Kyle!" I called "Can you come here real quick?" Then I turned back to face the officer. "Until this is settled, I have a right to see these kids, just as much as she does, and I don't have to let you into this house to prove it. Last time we let a uniformed guy, who was running errands for the Prophet, in this door, he tried to get a lynch mob off the hook."

The officer looked like he wanted to hit me. Just then, Jay and Kyle poured into the room, a little upset at being torn away from what was turning into a very exciting game. "See? They're fine," I said. "I'll have them back at eight. Go wait in your car."

He did wait in his car, for three hours or more, and then as I started up the truck, I saw him inch out of the grotto, lights ablaze. He followed our truck the entire way home. I don't think I've ever been more careful to avoid traffic violations in my entire life. I knew he had his laser fixed on me the entire while; I knew he was checking my registration, ensuring I used my blinkers correctly, checking periodically to see if we were seat-belted. If I had inched the car just one mile above the speed limit, he would have pulled me over to the side of the road, and in all probability, kept me there half the night while he searched my car. It's not an easy thing having an enemy in the police force. It's even more difficult when your enemy is Warren Jeffs, who *controlled* the police force.

When I dropped them off at their mother's house, I told her I was going to grab them again the next day and take them out for ice cream. That hadn't been an option today, since Jay had already had some, but I thought they might like going to get ice cream with their dad. I could tell her parents didn't think much of the idea, but Suzanne finally agreed.

I spent that Saturday in a kind of bliss. I couldn't wait to see them again. These boys, and their mother, were everything in the world I cared about. I knew all their favorite and second favorite flavors of ice cream, their favorite colors, favorite teams, and even how far Jay could run without stopping.

When I was finished doing my various odd jobs, I drove to Frank's house to pick the little guys up. I trotted up the steps, just about to knock on the door, when Mary-Ann opened it, eyeing me suspiciously.

"The boys are gone," she said. "They left with their mother."

"Gone?" I repeated, startled and confused. "Where've they gone?"

She sized me up and down for a moment. "I can't tell you," she said in that steely tone she'd used on me many times before, "because I don't know. They're safe with their mother. You know she'll take care of them."

"That's not the question, whether or not she'll take care of them. *I* want to take care of them! Where are they?"

She didn't answer. She just stood inside the screen door, staring blankly at me. The more I looked at her unresponsive face, the angrier I became. "She's got no right to hide my children from me!" I bellowed. "I've done nothing wrong, and I'm *tired* of being treated like this! *Where are they?*"

She knew me well. It must have been obvious to her how furious I was becoming. I couldn't very well force my way in, and she wasn't likely to be there anyway. I paced back and forth, cracking my knuckles. Finally, I turned back to her, livid and icy. "If you won't answer me, I'll just get the police involved," I warned.

She didn't waver at the prospect. She scarcely moved the entire time I talked to her. She didn't slam the door into my face; she just watched me flail against her self-righteous manipulation, knowing there was nothing I could do about it. As far as she was concerned, she had already given me all the information I was entitled to.

As soon as I reached a working phone, I called the local police dispatch. "My wife has taken my children," I cried frantically. "I was just at her parents' home and no one will tell me where they are! She must have left the community!"

"Well, do you have any court papers that prove you should have them?" the dispatch asked matter-of-factly, almost as though the whole thing had been scripted. "We can't do anything for you until we see some court papers that help settle the dispute."

"Then why is it that she can send a squad car after me and harass the hell out of me? *She* doesn't have any court papers! I know you people basically work for the church, but do you have any idea how unfair that is?"

"Well sir, I'm sorry you feel that way, but there's nothing I can do for you."

I slumped in despair against the wall of my house, rubbing my forehead. I thought I was going to be sick. "You know, officer," I said after a moment, "there *is* something you can do for me. I want you to tell her parents and whoever else is getting in the way of me seeing my children that they need to watch out. You people have treated me like shit ever since the Prophet asked Suzanne to leave me, but this is a step too far. I don't care who's in charge, but I will see them in court. I will have their face in every newspaper from here to Tulsa."

Without waiting for a reply, I slammed the phone on the hook and threw my fist into the wall. I was helpless and I knew it. I couldn't count on the cooperation by the city's police force, which meant I had to force their hands into action on anything I wanted done. I didn't know enough about the law to make them do anything, which meant the only thing I could do was wait, worrying the entire time, for Chris Edwards to call with news about an Arizona lawyer.

I spent all that day huddled up in my house, too distracted to watch TV, read, or do anything, really. Toward evening, I finally drove through the cold January rain and get whatever mail I had in the Post Office. I never expected I would crack open a handwritten letter telling me that the only chance I had at *ever* seeing my children again depended on "proving yourself faithful, your prayers, and your connection with him who holds the keys."

The letter did a lot to confirm the suspicions I had had for a long time. Frank had pointed out that Suzanne was putting herself in "direct line with the Prophet," but there is nothing quite like hearing (or reading) it from the horse's mouth. When Suzanne declared "I have put myself in the Prophet's hands," it meant that she had renounced all decision-making power in favor of strict obedience to whatever words emanated from a psychotic and deeply disturbed

"Prophet." This was a "Prophet" who put a lot of effort into making sure she would not renege on the agreement.

I was in a desperate situation. I was able to find out later that Sam Barlow had told Suzanne that the "Prophet" wanted her to "put some space between us." This was a system the church used to keep the children away from the sane parent so that the mind cleansing could begin. My boys were very young and impressionable, which worried me more than anything else. I had a strong relationship with them both, but I had no idea how long we would be apart. For all I knew, Suzy could be remarried again, to a family in the vast empty space that makes up rural Canada, or maybe in the polygamous underworld in Salt Lake City. I would never find them again. I had to act fast and get these boys back in my presence as soon as possible.

"I found you an attorney," Chris said as I entered his office that Monday. "The guy's a real bulldog. He's got a reputation as a guy who fights for his clients. His name is Stephen Lee. I called several places and his name kept coming up. So I set up an appointment for you this week. You'll have to drive down to Kingman and meet with him. You know anyone who will loan you some money for a retainer fee?"

My uncle Lane Blackmore, who had been like a second father to me, had grown up in Colorado City and was well acquainted with what I was going through. The moment I broached the subject, he had his checkbook out, writing me a check so I could retain my lawyer. Tears brimming in my eyes, I transferred my car title over into his possession until I could find the money to pay it back.

I really had no idea how I was going to take on the church. They ran the UEP, which controlled almost all of the land in the Short Creek area. The estimated value of those holdings was close to $100 million. On top of that, they had huge holdings in Salt Lake City and Canada, as well as various smaller holdings in other parts of the United States. Plus they could conceivably bilk money out of thousands of men and women who followed the teachings of the FLDS. I was defying this multi-million dollar monster with a laborer's paycheck. And my personal Atticus Finch was costing me a fortune.

# XVIII
## THE PUPPET MASTER

When I reached the law offices of Stephen Lee, I met up with a partner there, Randall Hodgkinson. I hadn't collected together much evidence to speak of, but I told him the sorts of things that had been taking place in the community over the last few years. I told him I'd been giving Suzanne regular cash outlays up to that point, so he wanted me to open a checking account and record a paper trail for every penny that I gave to her. I asked him, a little forlornly, if there was anything he could do to get my family back.

"Well, we have no control over what she's doing now," he said, "but I can guarantee this business won't help her in the long run."

"None of them will tell me where she is," I said. "For all I know she could have been remarried by now."

He looked at me like I had gone insane. It was a farfetched idea—I had never heard of anyone in the church being remarried while they were still legally married to someone else, but it could happen. These were strange times for the community, and I wasn't ready to discount the possibility.

"Tell you what," Randall said. "You contact your local police force—"

"I don't trust the local cops," I confided. "They're basically thugs for the Jeffs family."

"Well, that's the best way to contact your children for now. Ask them to do a welfare check on the children, and they're required by law to do it. If they don't, they could lose their badge. Use those words—welfare check."

I wrote the words down on a little notebook I'd thought to bring with me. "Do you know if she's taken the children out of state?" he asked. "She's not supposed to be out of this court's jurisdiction."

"I don't know," I said dully. "For all I know, they're in Canada."

Randall blinked. This was not going to be the type of case he was used to.

I left the attorney's office a lot calmer than I had been when I entered. Randall promised he was going to do everything in his power to get those boys back. He made me promise that I was going to do whatever they asked me to, and stay out of trouble. It certainly eased my mind to know there was someone fighting on my side, someone who knew what he was doing. I had been operating under the knowledge that I was alone against all the might of the Jeffs machine. It was good to know the cavalry was on its way.

Once I got home, I called the local police dispatch and asked him to do a welfare check on my children. It certainly sounded like it would be a useful tool in my arsenal. I remember when the officer had clanged on my door the night before my children disappeared, and had claimed to be interested in the welfare of the children.

A few hours later, I received a call from the Colorado City police department. "The boys are doing fine," was all they said. I didn't feel very much better, because I didn't really know if they had made the call or not. Worse than that, I knew if that was all a welfare check entailed, I would receive no opportunity at all to talk to the little guys. I missed them so much.

When I had first driven down to Kingman to speak with Randall, I had entertained the foolish hope that he would help me see them immediately. I hoped that paying his $2500 retainer fee would at least guarantee me the right to be with my children, even though I would be wracked by debt for some time. I was certainly in for a reality check. Nothing ever moves as quickly as you want it to, especially when lawyers are involved.

And it was taking a long time. I spent the better part of two weeks working days and worrying nights. The ache in my gut grew sharper every day I went without seeing them. Every time I asked for a welfare check, I got the same result. They would call back and refuse to give me any more information other than that the boys were "fine." *Fine* is a relative measure anyway—what was fine to them might not mean the same thing for me. Fine could mean anything from "nothing's broken," to "they've finally accepted the Prophet and renounced you."

Finally, three Sundays after Suzanne had left, I could stand it no longer. I needed to hear from those boys myself. I went to her parents' home and knocked, once again, on their door.

"Jason," Mary-Ann said, shocked. She stared at me through the screen door. "What can I do for you?"

"Can you call my children, please?" I asked her. "Please just let me talk to them. Please."

She looked at me as though I had sprouted a third arm. "Jason, you know I won't do that," she said. "Even if I knew where they were, I couldn't tell you."

I burst into tears of desperation. Only a few months before, she had been insisting I call her Mom. "I just hope that in your whole life, you never have to go this long without knowing where your children are," I sobbed, using the rail to keep me from slumping down on the porch like a spineless ameoba. "You know what those boys mean to me, and Jay was sick when she took them. I just want to know they're okay."

I must have been a sight for her, bawling like a baby on her porch in broad daylight. She took a few steps back. "I don't know what to say to you," she said blandly. "I know you're suffering right now, but you know Suzy will do what she thinks best for the boys."

She looked at me, a trace of sympathy in her eyes, and then she clicked the door shut. Too frustrated to argue, I stumbled blindly down the steps and into the driver's seat of my car. I wanted to speak to those boys so urgently, I was likely to die if I couldn't.

Drying my eyes, I stormed into the police station and told the dispatch I wanted him to do another welfare check on my boys. I had lost count of the number of times I'd asked.

He sighed. "What number d'you want us to call you on?" he asked in resignation.

"None," I said, settling myself into one of the visitor's chairs. "I'll just wait right here until I get confirmation that you talked to her."

The officer snorted and called Mary-Ann, asking her to have Suzanne call the station. Then he went back to his work day, and I waited in the chair as the minutes slowly ticked by. I ran out of reading material long before the day ended, so I leaned back in my chair and drummed on the armrest for an hour. I thought I would be spending the night there, but finally, the phone rang.

I walked around the counter and into the dispatch area. "Can I talk to her?" I asked.

He looked alarmed. "That's against protocol," he stammered.

Then I made a simple request. "Fine," I said, "but will you do a quick favor? She isn't supposed to be outside Arizona? Can you see where she is?"

Instantly, the dispatch shifted position so I couldn't see his board, glaring daggers at me.

"Jason," someone behind me said. "You can talk to her in here."

I was overjoyed. It was like getting a Christmas present. I had had no contact with my little guys for what was going on three weeks now. Scooping up the phone, I grinned into the receiver. "Hello?"

"Here are the boys," Suzanne said, flustered. She muffled the phone, but I could still hear what was being said on her end of the line.

"Jay!" she called, down some kind of hallway. "Phone!"

I could hear the steady thud of his footsteps as he raced down the hall. "Is it my father?" he asked. He sounded so excited to speak to me. It thrilled me to the core.

"No, it's not," Suzanne told him. "It's just your dad."

That statement infuriated me. The FLDS draws a distinction between a "father" and a "dad." A father cares for his child, and brings him up to be an upstanding human being. More than that, a father is presumed to be a celestial guardian who would be present in the afterlife. A dad has the sole purpose of giving life to the child, and doesn't contribute toward raising him. He is conveniently edited out of the hereafter.

"Hi, dad!" The voice was Jay's. I could have melted on the spot. It was so wonderful to hear from him, and he sounded overjoyed at the prospect of hearing from me. I chatted with him for a few minutes, and then Suzanne put Kyle on the phone. Kyle had missed me as much as I'd missed him. He was crying and talking all at once, trying to cram three weeks into a phone call that lasted only a few minutes. I managed to calm him down and speak to him. He loved hearing his dad's voice. I could hear him crying again as Suzanne took the phone away. I probably lost a bit of hearing by the time Kyle was finished, but I didn't care. All that mattered was that I was talking to my boys.

"Are you done?" Suzanne asked. Behind her, I could hear a baritone voice trying to calm the poor kid down.

"Whose voice is that?" I asked. "Who is that?"

"Are you finished?"

"No, I'm not finished," I told her. "I want to talk to *you*. Why have you taken the boys away from me? Where *are* you?"

"You know what you have to do to get them back," was all she said.

"And just what is that?"

She sighed. She knew she was fast approaching a heated argument. "Look, I have to go, so if you're done talking to the boys, you know they're okay, then good-bye."

I had to pass through the dispatch area on my way out. "Where'd the call come from?" I asked the dispatch, and in a flash, he was up again, trying to ensure I couldn't see the secrets his switchboard contained. I smiled, disgusted over the cover-up.

For the next two weeks I had to go to through the police to get any information at all about their well-being, but I was much more serene this time. Even though I had only gotten to talk to those boys for a few minutes, I was glad I'd made contact. I operated on that conversation for some time, like a car running on its last drips of fuel. At least now I knew for sure they were okay; no one had decided to pull an Abraham and make them into a burnt offering on the top of an apartment building.

Finally, after a full month without my children, my attorney was able to file a motion suing for sole custody of the children, on the grounds that I was the only one who would make them available to the other parent, rather than hiding their whereabouts.

That motion started the ball rolling. Randall received a call from her attorney establishing a visitation schedule for the following weekend. It firmly stipulated that I couldn't leave the community with the boys, and it only provided it for the Saturday. I was furious. They had hidden my children for a month. They had forced me to hire an attorney that would put me in the poorhouse, and the best they could offer me was the same visitation schedule I had refused to sign some time before.

Randall urged me to accept it though. "I'll make sure to stipulate it's only a temporary situation," he said. "Look, Jason, I know it isn't fair, but what's better than nothing?"

I nodded. "I'll take it," I agreed, "but you also need to point out that the *only* reason I accepted it was because I haven't seen them in a month. I don't want them to use it against me later."

The following Saturday, Valentine's Day, I was finally allowed to see them. I woke up early, excited, and drove as fast as I could to Colorado City. I was a little too eager, though--the visitation didn't start until a half an hour after I'd arrived. I drove in circles around town for a while. Every time I passed Frank's house, I wanted to wish the minutes away so I could see my sons.

It was a little before eight o'clock when I finally felt I was within my rights to stride up the steps. One of Suzanne's sisters answered the door, peering at me through the screen just as Mary-Ann had on so many occasions.

"Would you go grab the boys for me?" I asked, as pleasantly as possible.

She relented and let me into the kitchen to wait for them. I waited there until finally from the stairwell, I saw my little man appear, running at me at full speed. I grabbed my boy up and hugged him as tightly as I could without hurting him.

"Jay," I whispered in his ear, as he squeezed my neck. "I missed you guys so much! I love you, buddy."

He kissed me on the cheek and grinned. "Dad, I missed you too," he said. "I love you too."

As I set Jay on the floor, I heard a distinctive squeal. From the stairwell, Suzanne appeared, holding Kyle in her arms. As soon as Kyle noticed me, he started bawling, arms outstretched. Suzanne set him down on the floor, and the kid took his first step toward me.

I could have cried. Last time I'd seen Kyle, he couldn't walk. Now, in just five weeks, he seemed almost twice as big, and he was able to walk all the way across the kitchen floor to the point that I could grab him up into the air and hug him. I was so proud of him. To this day, I'm still upset that I wasn't there to see it when he finally learned to walk. I would give almost anything to go back in time long enough to see him take his first step.

Suzanne just stood there, at the far end of the kitchen, tears in her eyes. It was the first emotion I'd seen in her for months. I could tell she really wanted to say something, but it was just beyond her reach. It hurt to look at her. Turning my head, I strode out the door, trying to hide my tears from her.

We are all seat belted and ready to drive off, when Suzanne ran out to stop us. Leaning into the driver's side window, she started to cry. I loved her very much, and wanted her back, but I felt so betrayed. I wasn't sure I wanted to hear what she had to say.

"I know you'll probably never forgive me for what I've done to you," she said softly, "but I really want to talk. Can we go to breakfast or something?"

It was hard to speak. This was the first real glimmer of hope I'd seen in months. I was still angry that she'd smuggled the boys away, but I knew the pressure the church puts on people, especially on women, and so I felt truly sorry for her. I wanted so much to be a family again. The thought of finally being able to speak to her without her insipid parents hovering over my shoulder seemed almost too good to be true.

"Sure, I'd love to," I finally croaked, grinning at my good fortune. "I'm sure we both have a lot to talk about."

She smiled. "Hang on for a bit, and I'll tell them where we're going so they don't freak out."

I wanted to call her back. We could run away and never tell a soul where we'd gone. We'd be instantly free of the pressures of her family and the church. But we'd gotten far away before, and she'd come back. I knew this problem would just resurface again if we ran away from it. This was a decision she had to make herself.

She was visibly shaken, a few minutes later, as she walked back out to my sedan. "I've changed my mind," she said, tears forming in her eyes. "I think you just need to have some time alone with the boys."

"That's fine," I said, putting on my best happy face. "I'll see you later."

She told me later a little bit about what Frank had said when she went in and broke the news. He'd been very disappointed. "Suzanne," he'd told her, "if you do that, I will be totally embarrassed. The Prophet has done so much for you and you would be throwing it all away. You know you're not supposed to have any contact with him unless a priesthood bearer is there with you." Then he had lowered his glasses and looked at her, like an ant under a microscope. "Suzanne, that would be like watching you walk into hell. Remember how many people have helped you up to this point. You'll be turning your back on them too. If you need direction, we can just ask the Prophet."

He had then strolled over and picked up the phone. As he started to dial, Suzanne finally caved in. "Fine," she said, "I'll just stay here."

She wanted to have breakfast with me, but someone else had been pulling the strings. I had known all along that some puppet master's fingers were controlling her life. It felt great to have my sons back, but I couldn't help wishing she had been strong enough to be there with us. I wanted to force my way in and pull her out, for her own good, but I knew she'd just find a way back in again. I was already on the outside looking in. She would have to cut her strings on her own. If you love someone, they say, you have to let them go. I sure hoped she'd find her way back.

# XIX
# THE BIG 'D'

We went on about our separate lives for about a month after that, sharing an informal visitation agreement. She didn't indicate at all whether or not she was actively trying to find her way back into our family, after we'd let her go. I always hoped she would.

Then, finally, in mid-March, she ran into my family at the local grocery store. My family was busy shopping for presents for a big celebration we would hold for the "March birthdays." My son Jay was born in March, as was my dad, and my brothers Jeromy, Bobby, and Tommy. So we would celebrate them all together, in one massive blowout that would shame the best Super Bowl party.

She knew why they were there, since she had often participated in the celebration and loved every second of it. Bobby and Tommy noticed her in the parking lot, slumped over the steering wheel, crying hysterically. They did their best to comfort her, but she couldn't even look at them. She just sat and cried her eyes out.

That night, as I was dropping the boys off, she slipped furtively out the door and met me halfway to my sedan. It was the first time in weeks I had been able to talk to her alone.

"Hey, Suzy," I smiled at her.

"Jason," she said, leaning in the car window, "I know this is a rough time for both of us. I just want you to know that I still love you."

"I love you too, Suzy," I said. "I miss you---I miss what we called family."

"I know, Jase," she smiled, a little forlornly. "I really wish we could get our family back together again."

"Get in the car," I said. That was all it would take.

---

"I can't." She shook her head. "There's too much at stake. I just want you to know that if you're willing to come back in line with the Prophet, I'll wait for you."

"Thanks," I said, "I appreciate it."

She smiled again and retreated back to the house. In the window, I could see someone watching the two of us, and with a sinking heart, I realized that this scene was probably going to be reported to the "Prophet." For a moment I was genuinely worried about what he might do.

Putting my car in gear, I pulled out of the driveway, wishing that she would abandon some of the teachings of the FLDS, like I had. She, like her parents, was convinced that her way of life was the most righteous thing the Lord had ever instituted on the earth. They were so positive about the truth of their doctrine. I wondered if it had ever occurred to them that this was purely an accident of birth. If they had been born to a family with a different set of beliefs, they would have been positive of the truth of *that* doctrine instead. And they would have been convinced that the FLDS teachings were salacious lies conjured up by an opportunistic con artist. We are such programmable human beings.

During the next week, she met with my parents and repeated the same wishes about me and my family. It was not a single conversation that had me convinced we could get back together, but a whole series of them. That Thursday, my dad told me about how much she missed our life together. He had talked to her for several hours the night before. This did a lot to convince me that maybe, just maybe, she would be strong enough to reject the demands foisted upon her by the religious beliefs of her parents. I couldn't wait to see her.

I was entitled to spend that Saturday, the 27th, with the boys, but the day before, Suzanne called and asked if she could keep them that Saturday and give them to me the day after. She wasn't very clear on why she wanted them, but it seemed like a simple request.

"Sure," I said, "That'd be fine."

Since I couldn't see the boys until Sunday, I decided to go camping that weekend. I loved the outdoors, and I hadn't had an opportunity to sleep next to a tree for some time, due to my obligations to the boys. On the early morning of my visitation, though, I pulled out of our Kolob campsite, and sped off to get them. On the way, I stopped at my house and noticed there were several missed calls from a number I didn't recognize. I was sure it was important because the calls were registered so early in the morning, so I scooped up my portable and hurriedly dialed the number.

"Hello?" The voice belonged to a woman. Her phone must have been working poorly, because she sounded like she was shouting into a trash can.

"Hi," I said. "This is Jason Williams. I have a couple missed calls from this number."

The woman laughed. "I think Suzanne was trying to get a hold of you," she said.

"Why is she using this number?" I asked, confused. "Whose number *is* this?"

She laughed again, longer and louder this time, as though she thought we were playing some sort of game. I decided that I really did not like this woman. "This is Lester Johnson's home," she finally told me. "Suzanne is at her parents' place."

I spent the forty minute drive to Frank's house replaying the conversation. Who the hell was Lester Johnson, and what was Suzanne *doing* there? I wasn't sure what events these developments foreboded, but I knew it was odd, odd enough that an uneasy churning in the pit of my stomach would not settle down.

The street in front of Frank's house was littered with extra vehicles, including a big truck that looked something like an elevated Panzer. I had never seen the thing before. It seemed some sort of meeting was taking place. I hoped I wouldn't have to wait to take the boys out. I was too excited about the opportunity to see them again, and I had a lot planned for the three of us to do that day.

I trotted up the steps and banged on the door. Frank answered, swinging it open wide. As soon as he saw it was me, his mouth broke into a wide, proud sort of grin, and for the first time in months, he opened that screen door and invited me inside.

"Jason, come on in! It's great to see you!" said the spider to the fly. Frank wrung my hand, grinning at me the whole while. Smiling was not a thing he did very often, especially at me. It was a little disconcerting to be treated well by a man who regarded me as his enemy. I wondered if maybe I was about to be poisoned.

"Come on in," Frank said, leading me down the hallway into their front room. "Suzy has something to tell you."

The room was filled with several men, loitering about and toasting one another. Across the parlor, nestled under the arm of a hayseed country bumpkin--- whom I'd never met, sat Suzanne. She was practically sitting on his lap.

When she saw me, she leapt to her feet, all smiles. *"I got married yesterday!"* she squealed, celebrating.

All the color drained from my face. With those words, she'd plunged her verbal dagger straight into my heart. I knew it was over. We had gone through some difficult times because of the religious pressure she allowed the church to put on her, but until this moment I had been sure that we could work it out. The only real difference between the two of us was our belief in the FLDS. I didn't want to have my life dictated to me from a pulpit, and I took issue with anyone who thought I should. I had dared to entertain the idea that she might come around, or that we could arrive at some sort of synthesis, but now, that opportunity was gone. I had loved her, and I had let her go, and she was never coming back.

You got married?" I stammered incredulously, trying to focus enough to breathe, "How can you do that? You're still married to *me!*"

"Oh, you know how it works out here," she glibly replied.

Every person in the room was grinning at me----- like rows of leering jack o' lanterns, as though I was expected to congratulate her on the development. Leading this gloating crowd was Frank, grinning with unabashed joy. The staged situation held no semblance of anything happy or joyous; it was a surreal sick play—a dark choking drama, with demented layers that only I could see or feel . Outraged, I was ready to smash that smug grin down his throat, but I knew I was outnumbered by seven to one.

"Jason," Frank scoffed, "you know I wish nothing but the best for you. She has done what the Prophet asked. You just need to leave her alone."

"Frank," I shot back, "I don't want any *best* that you wish on me. You've done quite enough interfering with my marriage as it is."

He looked affronted, and a little frightened that I was going to rush him. As if on cue, several of Suzanne's brothers poured into the room, further tilting the odds out of my favor. The throng gathered around me, waiting to see what I would do. I tried to look past them, searching for Jay and Kyle so that I could escape the room before I ran completely out of breath, or worse, exploded and did something I would regret.

"So this is it?" I challenged Suzanne. "You've given up on our family. What about our boys? You ready to live with them part-time, because I sure as hell am not? The only fair thing to do, if this is what you really want, is to give those boys to me. I'll let you see them anytime you want, but I will *not* let them grow up in some primitive religion where a guy can randomly rip a family away from their father and shuffle them around like furniture."

The whole lot of them had taken a step back. All the pent up rage I'd kept inside me was boiling over. "What about you?" I roared, glaring at Suzanne's new husband. "Lester, or whatever your name is. What makes you think you can just come into my family and lay your damn filthy paws all over a woman that's married to me?"

He hesitated a moment before speaking. "I'm just doing as the Prophet asks," he said. "He told me to take her into my family. But don't worry—I promise you that I will treat those boys just as if they were mine."

My voice went up a few decibels. "That's just it!" I roared. "They're *not* yours! They'll never *be* yours!" I took a step toward him, and he shrank away into the couch. "Let me ask you this, Lester," I said, gaining strength from my fury. "What happens when the Prophet decides *you're* no longer worthy of a family?"

He stared at his shoes. "If the Prophet asked me to walk away from my family," he said in his even voice, "I would do just that."

"Then you're a more obedient man than I am. I would *never* abandon my family." I turned to Suzanne. "The only fair thing to do is let me have the boys. You can see them any time you want."

"We've decided to let the court handle this matter," she whispered. "We're going to let it take its course."

"I know exactly what *course* it's going to take," I exploded. "My kids are going to marry whoever they want without any shit from anybody else. They're going to make their decisions without asking some conniving Prophet if it's okay. You hear me? Those boys are gonna get an education, a real education, not the crap you people study in Sunday school."

The whole diatribe was falling on deaf ears. It was like I was on the Titanic, and I had stopped to yell at the iceberg. That was about all the good it did. "Look,"

I said, "I don't care what I have to do. If I have to go on Oprah or whatever and tell the world all about your bullshit, I will." I gave Suzanne one last, imploring look. "Please," I said. "If marrying this guy's what you really want, I won't try to stop you. But please let me take the boys."

"We'll see what the court says," she said without missing a beat.

I was utterly defeated. My entire arsenal of rage, reasoning, begging, and cajoling was used up, and none of it had worked. "Fine," I said, "we'll do that. But in the meantime, I still get my visitation. Where are the boys?"

We were deathly silent on the drive to my parents' house. They knew something was wrong with their old man, but they were too young to know what. My dad scarcely looked up from the TV, because we didn't do much to announce our presence.

When he finally heard us tiptoeing down the hallway, though, my dad grinned and spun around to face us. "Hey guys, how're you doing?" he asked.

I didn't answer right away. I just plopped into the armchair like a ghost and stared straight off into space. "What's going on?" my dad asked. "Is everything alright?"

"I guess Suzanne got married yesterday," I said without looking at him. "I have to get my kids out of this mess somehow. Has the church ever married a girl to another man while she's still legally married to the first guy?"

He considered a moment. "Can't think of any off the top of my head," he said. "Usually they land a divorce first. But you know as well as I do that it doesn't take much these days. It'll get a lot worse before it gets better. That's the problem with this place. The Prophet can do whatever he wants and he doesn't have to answer to anyone; leastways not in *this* life."

I always felt more relaxed after talking with my father. We understood each other really well, because we had gone through the same trauma. He felt the same about losing his kids to Millie as I was feeling about the risk of losing my boys to Lester Johnson. To top it off, my dad's father had lost every one of his kids for two years when the state of Arizona raided the community and committed his children to foster care. That meant I was the third generation in my family to lose my children because of the FLDS church, which is one hell of a family legacy.

We already knew there was no hope of returning to our old life, but Suzanne and I were required to meet with a court-appointed mediator to determine whether or not a hearing would be necessary. She was a matter-of-fact type of woman, good at her job. She went through her questionnaire, asking us various questions and jotting down our answers without comment.

But as she neared the end of her form, she looked a lot more hesitant to continue. Finally, she plopped the clipboard down on the table. "You know, I've got to be honest," she said. "Usually the couples in here are screaming and nasty. But I *really* think you can work this out. It's obvious the two of you still love each other. Are you sure you want to go through with the divorce?"

The silence hung in the air like a living thing, awkward and invasive. "We have to get a divorce," I said finally. "She's already married to another man."

The mediator dropped her pen, and it fell with a clatter to the floor. In disbelief, she looked at the two of us, as though hoping to find an explanation somewhere in our faces. Finally, she reached down and scooped up the pen, finishing the remaining comments on her forms. "Okay, then," she said, shaking her head, "I guess that just about does it. I'll just send this to the court and notify them of the dissolution of marriage."

She smiled at us and flounced out, still puzzling over our grounds for divorce. I didn't wait to chat, but filed out of the office as quickly as I could. The line in the sand had been drawn. I knew there would be a mighty battle waiting for me, like Hamlet fighting Laertes: *if it be not now, yet it will come. The readiness is all.*

# XX
# BATTLE LINES

The battle didn't come as quickly as I had predicted. My strategy was to take them head one, and deliver one devastating attack in exchange for the thousand they rained on me. But I didn't know just how to do that. I was fighting a multimillion dollar machine on a paycheck of $12 an hour.

There really was no way the church should have been involved, because it was a custody hearing between Suzanne and me. It really didn't involve them, but I knew they were going to force their way into the proceedings. There was too much at stake for them. They had told me to sign over full custody, but I refused, determined to fight back. If I were to win the case, it would set a precedent for other disgruntled members to jump ship and take their children with them. In a micro-cosmic way, it was like Ethan Allen's capture of Fort Ticonderoga—it would serve as a beacon of light and would demonstrate to all who came afterward that yes, you could challenge the FLDS and live to tell the tale.

The entire story was playing out something like *The Emperor's New Clothes*. The FLDS was running around naked, and no one had called them on their indiscretion because they did not want to be labeled as an apostate. I was the child who conjured up the moxie to point out that the only suit the Emperor had was the one he'd been born in.

The FLDS was determined to make an example of me so that the realization would not spread. For this reason, Warren Jeffs appointed Sam Barlow to attend every motion and preliminary hearing. Every week in church, he would give the congregation an update on what was taking place with regard to the custody battle. Then they would spend the day fasting and praying that I would lose my children.

When I had first spoken to Randall Hodgkinson about retaining Stephen Lee as my lawyer, they had required a retainer fee of $2500, which was a major loan for me. I thought that was the extent of it, but I sound found out how wrong I was. I paid Stephen Lee $200 for every hour he spent working on my case, and the FLDS saw to it that he racked up a lot of overtime. By the time the custody case was finished, I was fifty-five thousand dollars in debt.

I did everything I could to make the regular payments that were necessary. For months I ate nothing but spaghetti, panhandling and borrowing from any relative or friend I thought might help me, and it still wasn't enough. Before the battle had broken out, I had had my new Toyota 4Runner completely paid off. Now, to help cover some of the legal fees I was quickly accruing, I refinanced the vehicle and did the best I could to make the monthly installments that were necessary.

Unfortunately, once I fell behind on those payments, I had to choose between paying the bank or sending money to keep my attorney. I invariably chose my attorney, or course, on the grounds that I would rather have my boys than a good credit score any day of the week.

The inevitable result of my nonpayment was that the bank called a local tow shop to snatch my car one night, and I woke up to an empty driveway. I beseeched my uncle Lane Blackmore for more money to pay off the past due balance, but the bank refused to release the car unless I repaid the full balance that was owed on it. Lane certainly did not have that amount of money to lend, and so I was forced to write off the car—and my credit score as well. Eventually I learned that the bank was able to auction the 4Runner off for the full amount I owed, so I felt a little better knowing I hadn't swindled them out of the money they lent me.

I worked in construction, which meant that I had to travel all over the county to various worksites. Utah has fifty years of rural and suburban development under its belt, and at the time there were virtually no systems of mass transit whatsoever. This meant that you literally could not function in southern Utah without a car. My financial situation had already been precarious—I was just one injury away from utter bankruptcy and the loss of my children. Now, I was unable to get to work at all, which meant I could not collect a paycheck.

Fortunately, I had become good friends with a fellow softball player, Phil Sajack, who took me aside one evening and asked me what was wrong. I told him all about the pressure I had been dealing with for the past several months. I was stressed to the point I could not function—sometimes I stayed awake for most of the night, just worrying.

"I'm just so sick and tired of being broke all the time," I confided.

Phil nodded. "Tell you what," he said, "even if you lose, when those boys get older, they're going to have a lot of respect for you because you fought so hard."

It was good to hear. I just had to keep looking to the future, because under the circumstances that was all I could do. I did my best to keep a Pollyanna attitude about the entire desperate situation. I was walking a razor's edge between hope and despair, and the sheer effort of keeping the course was causing me an inordinate amount of stress and insomnia. No doubt that was a major factor contributing to my current baldness—my hair could not take that level of stress, so it just shriveled up and died.

Some days later, Phil dropped his car at my house and told me I could drive around in it for the next few months. It would keep me afloat, so that I could get to work and keep sending my paychecks to Stephen Lee. The case was costing an arm, leg, and soul—it was a good thing gasoline was somewhat cheaper in those days, so I could afford to make the payments I made. If it wasn't for the inexpensive partnership I formed with Top Ramen, I might have starved.

The church was trying to bankrupt me, and they were doing a hell of a job already. Still they were constantly on the lookout for some way to twist the knife. Their first opportunity came when they demanded a home evaluation be conducted.

At first, I was ebullient about the idea of a home evaluation, because I had a good-sized home that left the boys with plenty of space. It had three bedrooms and two bathrooms, and when the boys stayed over they were the only ones there, aside from Bobby and me. Suzanne, on the other hand, lived in a modest home with only a few rooms altogether. There was only one bathroom, and it had to be shared by the two ladies, Lester, and a legion of children still learning how to hold it long enough to reach the toilet.

My anticipated advantage was short-lived, however. Days before the evaluation was ordered, the church sent a army of young men and boys to construct a massive addition to the home. This was one of the church's "24 hour house" community work projects, and it almost quadrupled the size of the home. The additional costs would have reached the mid-six figures if they reached a dollar. I knew Lester made only a little more than I did, and he had many more mouths to feed. He wasn't likely to be able to afford that mansion on his salary, especially when coupled with the staggering legal fees his three attorneys would have been charging.

To some extent, I was glad of the addition, because now my boys would get a full bedroom, rather than being forced to share a stained mattress in one corner of the house. At the same time, I knew it greatly impacted my chance of winning custody, which I thought was by far the more important struggle. I wished *I* had a religion with deep pockets that would fund my legal squabbles.

The church knew I had to be feeling the economic pinch they put upon me. They filed a heavy number of motions, which meant that I received multiple subpoenas to appear in court, with my $200-an-hour lawyer in tow, to listen to and refute the newest batch of arguments the church had come up with. I would look over across the aisle and see Suzanne, sitting patiently among her three attorneys, every one of them trying to convince the judge to postpone the trial another few weeks.

It was almost comical to watch. I knew how much *one* good lawyer was costing, and here she had three. When we had filled out an income statement some months earlier, she had written that her monthly income was $893, her total salary from one part-time job. Further, among the attorneys representing her were Scott Berry, who was known to represent the UEP, and Rodney Parker, who made a living representing the FLDS church in its numerous legal quarrels.

Suzanne later validated my suspicions that the church was funding her lawsuit. She even knew that the specific strategy was to bankrupt me. Sam Barlow had said to her on more than one occasion that "we'll just see how deep his pockets are, 'cause we don't have to worry about it." The church knew that if it could bankrupt me before we went to trial, I would no longer be able to afford the bulldog Stephen Lee as my defender. I would end up essentially defenseless and vulnerable, and they would mop the floor with me.

The church also hoped to hit me with a few charges by demanding an evaluation on the part of a child psychologist. The court appointed Daniel Malatesta to interview Suzanne and me and watch us interact with the children in our homes. The home evaluation had come up as a stalemate, which meant a lot was riding on the Dr. Malatesta's verdict in determining who should be the custodial parent.

The court decided the psychologist would spend several hours with us and then use the information he gleaned to decide the outcome of the children's lives. The stakes riding on the verdict of this evaluator worried me. Every time he spent the evening with us, I was sorely tempted to offer him every present I could think of, but I had no doubt he would have seen right through it.

When I spoke with Dr. Malatesta, I tried to make it clear that I was sure they would try to phase me out of those boys' lives. The idea of "putting space between us" by disappearing for five weeks demonstrated the kinds of actions they might take if they had the legal authority to do so.

Already they were consistently referred to as Jay and Kyle Johnson, which irritated me. Their name was Williams, and for that matter, so was Suzanne's, because she was still legally married to me. Even if she had reverted to her maiden name, which was her right, it would still be Jay and Kyle *Jessop*, rather than Johnson. I didn't appreciate her forcing her husband's name onto my sons, because I knew that was just the first step in an overall insidious process.

Once she had dropped the boys off for visitation wearing the new coats I had purchased for them, and the words "Lester's Boys" were scrawled in permanent marker above each of their front pockets. It made me very worried. And pissed.

I had many reasons why I felt I should retain sole custody, but I'm certain that Suzanne had a litany of arguments herself. She would certainly be arguing that they boys must stay with their mother on account of their youth.

I hoped the boys would not be punished just because they were young—because I did view that church as a punishment. I had seen several families destroyed because the mother was placed into a different family. The problems my dad had faced with his twelve children were a daily reminder. Once Aunt Millie was placed with Tom Holm, they had always done their best to instill the children with a healthy hatred for their biological father. They refused to even call him dad. It was true that he still had visitation rights, but the kids always felt they were being handed a jail sentence when he tried to see them.

Watching my dad taught me that visitation wasn't even an option. We currently split the time down the middle, and already I was being forced to deal with some of the brainwashing my kids had undergone. If I was reduced to visitation, I would watch my kids slip away as surely as if I didn't receive any visitation at all. I had to fight now with all I had to save them from that fate.

I certainly hoped my ideas would carry the field, but there was no way to tell from looking at him. Dr. Malatesta was a very tight-lipped man. Sometimes I thought he would have made a great poker player. So I waited feverishly, worried about what his conclusions might amount to. As soon as I had the chance to read his report I wasted no time in flipping to the back page, where I could view his decision.

---

**CONCLUSIONS:**

In determining Jay and Kyle Williams best interest, several factors stand out: First, both children are positively attached to the parents; however, there is a high risk that these children will be permanently alienated from the father given the mother's chosen lifestyle. This is supported by her initial actions to black parental access of Jason with the children with the church's support. Secondly, Jason will likely continue to be outraged by the religious beliefs of the pluralistic community that his children would likely be exposed to should they be living with their mother. Conflict and divisiveness are likely to continue between the parents with these children suffering greatly should they remain in the care of their mother. Thirdly, the father demonstrates better ability to invest emotional energy from himself to the children compared to the mother. The father demonstrates considerable emotional stability and there is no evidence of any emotional disturbance other than his outrage over what has happened to his family. The mother, in contrast, exhibits a constricted emotional range which likely reflects underlying emotional and personality conflicts that have been exacerbated by her recent life choices. Therefore at this time, it is the opinion of this evaluator that the father is better equipped to make reasonable decision about the children's welfare and should have sole custody of them.

---

The findings exploded like a bomb in a fireworks factory. Before this, the church had sought to make an example of me because it was angry at my effrontery over the custody battle. But now the church was hit with the realization that I had a fair shot at winning, and so they knuckled down in an effort to drag the case out further.

The first order of business was to counter Malatesta's findings. Suzanne's attorneys filed a petition claiming that Malatesta was biased because of her religious choices. They recruited a Dr. Davies, a child psychologist out of Salt Lake City, to challenge the conclusions and undo the damage that their first recruit had done. Dr. Davies was paid six thousand dollars to call their three thousand dollar psychologist a liar. Interestingly enough, Dr. Davies never actually met me or gave me any kind of evaluation at all. His psychological profile on me was based entirely on data he gleaned from informed sources such as Suzanne, Lester, Sam Barlow, and Rodney Parker. This meant I was essentially paying a small fortune for a psychologist to compile a detailed analysis of my character by interviewing my enemies. In fact, Suzanne later told me that she was under the impression Dr. Davies was a good friend of good old Rodney Parker.

The attorneys also filed arguments on behalf of Lester trying to discount Malatesta's recommendations. They contended that it didn't matter how well I got along with the children, because I was rarely home. I left the boys with babysitters while I went off to work. Suzanne could be with the children every waking moment. Fortunately, I had two sisters, Heather and Heidi, who agreed to provide child care when I wasn't there. Since they had met with Maletasta on occasion and were believed to be well bonded with both children, the argument became a moot point.

It was only brought up again once more as we moved into the process of collecting depositions. Suzanne's attorneys collected my testimony early on, Scott Berry and Rodney Parker taking notes while her third lawyer, Mr. Linkowski, performed the cross-examination. One of the chief arguments he forwarded was that I wouldn't be able to spend enough time with those boys because I would be too busy trying to pay off all the legal fees I had accrued in the custody battle. I told him I was good for every cent, but he kept arguing, several times or more, that I shouldn't have the boys because it cost me too much to fight him.

"Listen," I told him, "You can't just bleed me dry and then use the fact that I'm dry as an argument against me."

"Well," he hedged, "the object is to determine who would be the best fit for those children. If you're bankrupt, no matter what the reason is, it bears a lot of relevance to those boys' well-being."

"Okay then," I contended, "why don't you guys just stop contesting everyone's findings and then I can save money and take care of them better."

Needless to say, they didn't take my suggestion. They pressed on for several hours, demonstrating all my inadequacies in glaring and exaggerated detail: I was gone too often, I was an alcoholic, I couldn't handle the boys' young ages, and worst of all, I was an incurable sex fiend.

"Isn't it true," Parker asked on that subject, "that you actually *begged* your wife for sex?"

Grinning, I shot a sidelong glance at the judge. "Doesn't everyone?" I asked sweetly.

I thought the judge was going to topple out of his seat. The entire courtroom was bursting with laughter. Parker just stood there, sheepishly, glaring at me the whole while. He was not a man I particularly liked, anyway. I just leaned back in my chair, extremely satisfied at the effects of my jab.

One aspect of my deposition did wind up in my favor though. Suzanne's attorneys had early on convinced the court to disallow my dad's testimony regarding what happened to him when he lost his custody battle, but some of the questions allowed me to insert some information on that subject. I was glad of the opportunity, because I felt it was very good evidence supporting my claims that the FLDS would seek to alienate me from my children. It had happened before.

After the depositions were taken, the date of the trial was set, and Stephen Lee and I had to go about the process of collecting witnesses. This was going to be a difficult process, because many of the more professional witnesses would have to be paid to appear. The FLDS could simply order its followers to appear without compensation. Plus, its pockets were nearly bottomless; the money required to bring in a legion of witnesses would be pocket change to the FLDS. To top it off, I had been steadily falling behind on my payments to Stephen Lee, and he was certainly starting to grumble.

Many of the people I asked to appear were unable to do so. Clay Mills felt he couldn't do it, because he felt it would be a conflict of interest. This was because at the time he worked as the psychologist for the local public school in Colorado City. DeLoy Bateman, who was the local science teacher, had similar misgivings, but he agreed to appear anyway. Unfortunately, Suzanne's attorneys moved quickly to disallow his testimony, so it was as though he had not come at all. Still, I appreciated the gesture.

My star witness turned out to be Dr. Malatesta, and to a lesser extent, Patricia Metcalf, the home evaluator. Both cost a fortune to retain, and I scraped together my last five thousand dollars to gain the testimony of Dr. Malatesta. This left me broke and desperate, and it made Stephen Lee angry that it didn't go to him. A few days before the trial was to commence, he called me at home.

"If I don't have five thousand dollars in my bank account by Monday morning," he told me, "I won't appear in court."

And with that, any chance at victory was ripped away from me. I knew very well he meant what he said—one of the things that made him a great lawyer was that he wasn't in awe or at all intimidated by the FLDS or anything that anybody found sacred. He would tear it all down in pursuit of the dollar. It made him a great ally in the battle against a corrupt church, but it also made him very apt to disappear once I was strapped for cash. And strapped I was; I wasn't due for a paycheck for a week, and I had already gotten an advance on it. Further, I was buried in debt in every other area of my life. I had a good chance of being evicted from my home, which would not have helped my case for sole custody.

I had no idea where to turn for the money. I had bled just about everyone I knew dry, asking them for loan after loan to cover my soaring legal fees. I couldn't borrow from a bank or any other institution because I owed too much already, and my credit was in shambles. To top it off, the car I drove didn't belong to me; the house I lived in wasn't mine, and most of the appliances I had were leased along with the house. I had nothing at all I could sell. This was the end.

I stayed in bed most of the next morning, wallowing in sickness and depression. If I couldn't get those boys out of that church, I thought, I might as well never climb out of bed again. I was so utterly broke by this time I couldn't even afford groceries. It had been months or more since I had splurged on any kind of luxury like a movie ticket. This was before there was a major exodus from the FLDS, and I was on my own. Many people who broke out of that church were able to find safe houses and charities to assist them in transitioning the lives of their families away from the influence of Warren Jeffs, but I had no such fortune. I was entirely on my own, and Warren Jeffs was throwing everything he could at me so that others wouldn't follow my example. It was like trying to stop an icebreaker with nothing but the strength of my arms. I just couldn't do it anymore.

As I was lying there in my bed, imagining the unimaginable, someone knocked at the door and forced me out into the world, whether I wanted to face it or not. My uncle John had heard the rumors of what had happened. He was broke himself, and he'd already lent me five thousand dollars, but he decided he could get me a little bit more. Dragging me out to his car, he drove the two of us to Cedar City, about an hour north on I-15. He whipped into the bank and bullied the loan officer into loaning him five thousand dollars, and the two of us wired it to Stephen Lee. At the time, he was almost squashed by debt himself, due to some massive medical bills and a host of legal fees of his own. Another five thousand dollars had him almost at the breaking point. There are not that many people lucky enough to have the kind of relatives I have, that would risk financial ruin on behalf of someone who just happens to share the same blood. His sacrifice damn near moved me to tears.

The five thousand dollars functioned as a pact of solidarity between Stephen Lee and I. I owed him much more than that, but he agreed to see the case through as long as I demonstrated that I would pay the money I owed, as soon as I had a chance. The FLDS was still intent on driving me so far into debt that he would jump ship, and I would have to file bankruptcy and lose all claim to the children. For that reason, they stretched the trial out until the proceedings were scheduled to go on for a week. Then they brought in a parade of expert witnesses that had no bearing whatsoever on the case. I was forced to subject my attorney, whom I was paying $200 an hour, to all sorts of irrelevant filibustering in an effort to break me.

# XXI
# KINGMAN

The judge had already predicted that it would be a difficult case, bringing all manner of religious issues and petty squabbles out into the open. "Usually we just have a drug test," he confided to us once, "and whoever passes gets the kids. But this one's gonna be tough."

I don't think even he could have predicted the volumes of irrelevant testimony that came out of the mouths of the FLDS witnesses. Among those witnesses was the state superintendent of the Arizona public school system. He was invited to praise the public school in Colorado City, the Unified School District 14, and give an oblique character reference to the local superintendent there, Alvin Barlow. Because District 14 boasted better test scores than Hurricane Elementary, he argued, Suzanne should have the kids. To this day, I don't know what made him think he could pass off a backwater school with no extracurricular programs as some kind of apex of the educational system.

As the cross-examination began, Stephen Lee moved quickly in for the kill. "Are you aware that the FLDS leadership has issued an edict for their followers to remove their children from public school?"

The superintendent looked a little wary. "Yes, I am," he said cautiously.

"And are you aware that several followers of the FLDS have resigned from their posts as teachers and administrators at the District 14 school?"

"Yes."

"Don't you think that might affect the test scores in the future?"

The superintendent snorted. "I couldn't say."

"Are you aware Suzanne Williams is a devout member of the FLDS church?"

"I wasn't."

"Well, now that you do know that, couldn't you argue that the quality of that school is irrelevant, since Suzanne and her partner would not allow the children to attend?"

Lee had a point. The classes could be taught be Demosthenes himself, and it wouldn't affect the boys. Ever since Warren Jeffs had instructed his followers to pull their children from public school so that they could be homeschooled in the ways of the Prophet, no FLDS children were able to attend the school. The enrollment was entirely apostates and Gentiles.

The church also swung in Miriam Fischer, who worked as a registered nurse in the hospital in nearby St. George. She volunteered her time at the Hildale Health Center, a local clinic for the FLDS. She wasted some more time on the witness stand pointing out the benefits of the medical system in Hildale versus those in Hurricane, another brilliant argument in favor of granting full custody to Suzanne and Lester.

The FLDS also brought a historian named Kenneth Driggs from Atlanta to give several hours of testimony concerning the history of the Mormon fundamentalist movement. Ken Driggs was considered an "expert" on the FLDS (mostly in Sam Barlow's mind) because he had written some silly little obscure book called *Twentieth century polygamy and fundamentalist Mormons in Southern Utah*. It had been out of print for years.

Most historians are very critical of the FLDS, but Driggs was supportive almost to the point of being obsequious. He had come down to write his little exposé some years before, and Sam Barlow had taken the man under his wing and shown him all the positive aspects of the community. Once the church was satisfied they had filled Driggs with all the informative propaganda that was necessary, Driggs went off to write his book. Seeing as he was the only historian that looked favorably upon the FLDS, he was a natural choice for an expert witness; one that had little bearing on the case.

Stephen Lee took care of Driggs very quickly. "Well, what makes you an expert?" he asked.

Driggs looked surprised, and not a little affronted. "Well, I've studied it! I've documented the history, and the culture, and—"

"I know that," Lee interrupted. "But have you ever been to Centennial Park?"

"No."

"Have you ever interviewed Jason, or for that matter, *any* apostates of the FLDS church?"

"No."

"Have you ever been in the home of anyone in the area that wasn't introduced to you by Sam Barlow?"

Driggs thought a moment. "No, I don't think so."

"So isn't it safe to say that writing about the peculiarities of the FLDS polygamists is more of a *hobby* of yours than an actual profession?"

"I've done symposiums," Driggs protested. "I've lived among them!"

"So has Jason, wouldn't you say?"

"Well, yes."

"So tell me the things that make you an expert and Jason *not* an expert."

It didn't matter what Driggs said at that point. He was already discredited. His arrogant belief in his own expertise was akin to a United States history professor conveniently ignoring every issue surrounding the black minority, or a World War II historian not even touching on the Japanese internment. The fact of the matter was that Ken Driggs couldn't care less.

Four days went by, each costing me over two thousand dollars and providing no useful or relevant information of any kind. Every one of these witnesses boasted only the most tenuous links to the case at hand; no Congress in history has ever stalled more effectively than the FLDS did here. Those who were in the church, like Miriam, would have done the service for free, but the church would have to have spent thousands to bring some of these expert witnesses in. I call these witnesses "testitutes," people who go around whoring out their testimony yet are still inexplicably considered to be unbiased "experts."

Stephen Lee argued that Suzanne's love of the boys, while genuine, had almost no bearing, because she had agreed to subject to herself to the agendas of the "Prophet." There was no responsibility in her; she just vacillated according to the whims of somebody else. She had left me, even though she loved me, because the "Prophet" asked her to. There was no reason to suggest that she would not abandon the boys, even though she loved *them*, if she was so instructed.

This line of reasoning was further demonstrated when Lee got Suzanne up on the witness stand. When I first glimpsed her in that courtroom, my eyes bugged out at the sight. She was as pregnant as I had ever seen her, easily seven or eight months along. This had certainly come at a surprise, although I had known that she had given birth to another of Lester's children before we ever moved to trial.

Lee moved quickly to capitalize on that issue. "Are you currently impregnated?" he asked her.

"Yes."

"Who is the father of the child you're carrying?"

"Lester Johnson."

"Have you had any previous children with Lester Johnson?"

Suzanne nodded. "Yes," she said, "one other little girl."

"Was this after you separated from Jason?"

"Yes."

"Did you realize you were still legally married to Jason?" Lee pressed.

"I did."

"Doesn't it seem at all odd to you that you're having not one, but two children by another man while you're still married to Jason?"

"No, it doesn't."

"Why not?"

"Because," Suzanne argued, "there is a difference between a legal marriage and a priesthood sealing."

"But weren't you at one point also priesthood sealed to Jason?"

"Yes, but that was broken."

"How so?"

"Because Jason didn't believe it—the church."

"Is there any kind of ceremony that accompanies the dissolution of a priesthood sealing?"

"It was broken because Jason didn't want to follow the teachings of the Prophet."

"Did you ever tell Jason that the priesthood sealing was inapplicable in your mind?"

Suzanne shifted her weight. "Jason didn't want to follow the Prophet, so he no longer had the priesthood sealing," she said.

"Oh, I see. So if you don't believe in Jason anymore, your legal marriage can be abandoned on the same capricious terms. How convenient; you could put divorce courts out of business on a whim."

"I believe you have to be sealed to a righteous person so you can be saved, and you don't understand the way our religion works. I can't make you understand," equivocated the poor witness, who I was sure couldn't make herself understand.

The gibe stopped Lee in his tracks for a moment. "Fine," he averred after a pause, "let's discuss some other facets of the case." He shot a look at Suzanne's attorneys. "What would you estimate your monthly income to be?" he asked.

"About a thousand," Suzanne offered.

"How much would you say Lester Johnson makes, on a monthly basis?"

"I'm not sure."

Lee nodded. "I notice on your side of the aisle there are several very good lawyers," he pointed out. "How are you able to afford this kind of representation?"

"Oh, well, you know," she prevaricated, "my friends are helping me out a lot."

"Your friends? Is there any organizational charity that helps pay the legal fees you're accruing here?"

"No," she shook her head, "they just wanted to help me out and so they pooled their money."

She did her best to make it sound as though it was an informal charity drive, but it was established that it was indeed the church that was providing the funding to keep the legal battle raging. This gave a lot of credence to our claim that Suzanne had no stable moral structure. She was just a pawn in a far greater chess game.

It also called into question exactly what the church was trying to accomplish here. I had always told Stephen Lee that I suspected the church would attempt to rob me of any visitation rights, just like they had my father. That's why visitation was a poor solution for my problem. Once Lee was allowed to cross-examine Lester, he sought to prove that point.

"Mr. Johnson," Lee said, handing him a pamphlet from his files, "would you say you are in good standing with the FLDS?"

"Yes."

"And would you characterize yourself as a believer in the doctrine of the FLDS?"

"Yes."

"Would you please read to the court the sections I've marked in the paper I've given you?"

The pamphlet was a copy of the Student Star, which was Alta Academy's official newspaper. When Warren Jeffs was principal there, he would write the paper and include sermons he felt were necessary in guiding the student body on the correct path. The particular section of the paper was an excerpt Warren had pulled from an old Brigham Young sermon during the early days of Mormonism.

> ### JD 5:57 Brigham Young July 19, 1857 SLC
>
> There are a few **apostates** here, and I have understood the whining and sympathy they manifested for our enemies. It makes me think of what I heard from a High Priest's house that he did not know a Saint's face from the Devil's. It is just so with a great many. They would not know the angel Gabriel, if he were to stand here to preach to them, from Lucifer, the Son of the Morning. If Lucifer were to hand out a dollar—"You are a gentleman; won't you call at my house?" "Here is another dollar." "Call over at my house; I have some daughter: perhaps you would like to be introduced to them. I have a fine family; call in, and get acquainted with my family."
>
> Do you know that there is no fellowship between Christ and Baal? Do you think that a union has taken place between them? Can you fellowship those who will serve the Devil? **If you do, you are like them, and we want you to go with them; for we do not want you.** We wish that all such men and women would apostatize and come out boldly and say, "We are going to hell upon our own road;" and I will say, "Go ahead, and may the Devil speed you in your journey! Here is sixpence for you." But do not be snooping round, pretending to be Saints, at the same time be receiving such men into your houses and such spirits into your hearts, as many do.

"Thank you," Lee said when he was finished. "Now, would you say that that is an accurate discussion of certain tenets of the FLDS church, as you understand them?"

Lester nodded. "Yes," he said dully.

"Are you aware that Jason Williams is considered to be an apostate of the FLDS church?"

"I am."

"Do you understand the role of the court in this matter? If a court order granted custody to Suzanne Jessop, would you cooperate with the visitation rights granted to Jason?"

"I would do whatever the court decided," Lester said.

"Are you aware that you would be required to *associate* with Jason in order to facilitate that visitation?"

"Yes."

Stephen Lee's thin little lips curled up into a smile. "The doctrine states that you yourself are an apostate if you associate with other apostates," he pointed out. "So you would agree to apostatize yourself in order to carry out the court's requirements?"

Lester turned pale. He was on dangerous ground, and he knew it. "Yes, I would," he spat.

"Even knowing full well that that apostasy would endanger your chance at salvation?"

Lester licked his lips in a barely contained fury. I tried to keep from grinning at the sight of this man squirming. He was a full believer in the Jeffs credo, and so in that sense he was both victim and perpetrator of the crimes the Jeffs regime committed. I felt sorry for Lester, although I really didn't like him that much. Sometimes I called him "Hannibal Lester" behind his back.

Finally the answer came, a barely audible whisper from a cornered rat. "I would do whatever the court said," Lester promised.

As the trial wound down on the fifth day, the line of witnesses started to peter out. Then we were left with nothing more than the closing statements. Rodney Parker made his statements first, telling the court that I was not a good fit for the children since I was gone so much of the time. It wasn't a good idea to leave them home with babysitters in their formative years. Furthermore, he argued, I didn't really care about the best interests of the boys—what this was really about, Parker decided, was that "Jason just wants to win. That's all he cares about is winning." I was a little affronted since Parker didn't know me nearly well enough to make that kind of judgment, and anyway, the only reason Parker was even involved was that the FLDS Church just wanted to win. They pumped hundreds of thousands into the case because they wanted to silence the first person who dared challenge them on the issue of custody. For my part, I had pumped over fifty thousand dollars into the case, money I did not have. I'm competitive enough that winning is worth a lot to me, but not that much.

In Lee's closing statements, his argument was simple. "Suzanne Williams," he began, "has moved into the home of a man she did not know and forced her children to refer to a stranger as 'Father.' She distanced herself emotionally from the troubles the children were facing and subjected her life and the lives of those children to the manipulation of a third party church. This is a form of emotional abuse.

"Jason can provide these children with emotional stability, a place to anchor themselves as they go out into the world. He can provide them with a home that doesn't require them to adjust to drastically foreign and conflicting circumstances. And Jason can provide Suzanne with equal opportunity visitation with the children. If Suzanne Williams receives custody, she may follow the stated doctrine of the FLDS church, and deprive him of visitation rights. It is not to be forgotten that without Jason's permission, she took the children out of the court's jurisdiction and withheld visitation from him for a period of five weeks."

He moved over to sit down next to me at the respondent's table. "Is that all?" he whispered as he approached.

"Baby," I whispered frantically back to him.

"Oh!" He spun around to face the judge, looking him directly in the eye. "And the court *cannot* turn a blind eye to the fact that she is pregnant with another man's second child while she is still legally married to Jason Williams. Thank you."

# XXII
# MY BOYS

Whenever I recount the proceedings of the custody trial, people are always astounded at how full of holes the opponent's case was. It seems as though it should have been easy for me to win a case like that, but it really wasn't. There were a convoluted series of motions surrounding the actual trial, and even once we went into trial and dealt with a host of witnesses who had witnessed nothing, there was always a pronounced fear that the FLDS would win.

There was quite a campaign in place that could have handed the boys over to Lester and Suzanne. In many cases, Arizona family courts tend to be very biased in favor of women. Custody agreements usually go to the mother, and for the father, child support is often enforced far more heavily than visitation rights. Any allegations of domestic abuse are automatically assumed to be true, and the idea of innocent until proven guilty is reversed so that the burden of proof is on the defendant, and without that proof he can no longer see his kids.

I was very glad to have Stephen Lee on my side. I am not sure I could have won without him. He certainly came with a price tag, as all good lawyers do, and I wasn't sure how I was going to be able to pay him fully. I knew I would do my utmost to resolve my debts, and then maybe from there I could work toward rebuilding my credit score. Filing bankruptcy because of the considerable debt I had amassed would certainly not have helped my situation. To this day, I am very appreciative of the way Stephen Lee fought for me. I still owe him some five thousand dollars, which I have yet to pay.

But the end result was that I finally won the right to raise my boys. For the past several months they had been introduced to everyone as Jay and Kyle Johnson, and now they were firmly and forever Jay and Kyle *Williams*. I would have spent my entire life utterly destitute in exchange for that. It was an unabashed joy to open up the paperwork and read the final verdict of the Arizona court system.

> Patricia Metcalf made observations similar to those of Dr. Malatesta. She described the respondent as an intelligent sensitive father, in charge but not in an authoritarian manner. Ms. Metcalf observed the father and children playing with enthusiasm. The children were observed to be well behaved, secure and happy with their father. The home was described as clean, warm, open, caring and joyful. Ms. Metcalf noted that she had "never seen a better interaction between a father and his children."
>
> IT IS THEREFORE ORDERED dissolving the marriage and awarding custody of the children to the father. The physical custody schedule as set by the temporary orders shall continue. It will be necessary to modify the schedule when the older child enters school this Fall.

The first task I was faced with was that of un-brainwashing the boys. Although they had only been taken away from me for five weeks, they had undergone a startling amount of religious indoctrination. Kyle at the time was just approaching two years old, so his beliefs weren't fully formed enough yet to have to be rigorously challenged.

Jay, however, was another story. He was four years old and wedded to the idea of an infallible "Prophet." He generally listened to the information I gave him countering the entire business, but when he would visit Lester's house, he would have all the dogma I had extracted pounded back into him again. One morning I was driving him to school, and he decided to express some of the antipathy that the FLDS wanted him to feel toward me.

"You're not my father," he said to me suddenly. "You're just my dad."

I immediately swung the car over to the side of the road and spun around to face him. He shrank away, leaning against the passenger door and looking up at me in surprise. It certainly wasn't his fault—my son was four years old. But I had seen the kind of tactics the FLDS used with my father's children. It started with the delineation between *dad* and *father*, but toward the end it got so insidious that one of my father's children told him that he was just there to give birth to the boys because Tom Holm, their impotent stepfather, couldn't.

I remember my dad bristling at the statement. He came storming home that afternoon. "If my sole purpose of existence is to be a sperm donor," he bellowed in a huff, "I can think of a few ladies I need to meet to fulfill the measure of my creation."

I thought I was going to fall off my chair at the statement, but I knew how much it hurt him. My dad was known to be a real riot, delivering one-liners that forever subjected stupid people to ridicule. But beneath that he was livid because the church was taking his children away from him. It hurt to watch, but now I knew that was nothing compared to how much it hurt to experience.

"Jay," I said evenly, "I want to make this abundantly clear to you. I am not *just* anything. I'm everything. I'm Dad, I'm Father, Pops, old man, you name it. I'm not *just* your friend; I'm your *best* friend, forever!"

Jay's face had gone white. "Okay, dad," he whispered mutely.

I grinned at him. "Okay, little buddy," I said. "No more of this *just* business, right?"

"Right."

We high-fived across the console of the car and sped onward down Main Street toward his school. I was really glad he was finally enrolled in a decent public school. When I grew up, pretty much everyone in my public school was as weird as I was, and it took me years to pull out of that strange FLDS mentality. In a true public school, kids get to meet people who are weird in all sorts of different ways, which really does a lot to help create a healthy outlook on life. There is a lot to be said for public schools.

Another thing I thought might help them adjust was the local Little League. I personally loved softball, playing it, watching it, and just reveling in the camaraderie that surrounds the sport. Jay and Kyle hadn't yet expressed any kind of affinity for it, but they enjoyed coming to my games in the evenings, as long as I didn't keep them up too late.

I was really surprised, but pleasantly so, when I enrolled them in the event. They took to baseball like a fish to water. In no time at all they were standing out amongst their teammates as the go-to batters and fielders. They were scoring runs like the Natural. Not a game went by that I didn't secretly hope they would pelt the ball into the scoreboard and send it exploding into a million pieces like the Fourth of July sky. It is probably just as well that that dream didn't come true, however, because I might have been obligated to pay for it.

I tried to get a role as a Little League coach, but I didn't land it until the next year later. Absent that, however, I attended every game they played, face pressed into the chain-link fence, watching them come into their own and escape the shadow of their former lives, just as I had, through athletic competition. I was so proud of my boys.

Suzanne generally had the boys for about the same amount of time as I had them, but once they got into school, her visitation was curtailed somewhat. She was limited at that point to being able to take the kids every other weekend and one night during the week.

It was a little disconcerting every time they would go off to Lester's home. Whenever they would return, they did so in Cricker clothing, with a flannel shirts and straight cut blue jeans, just like I looked when I was a child in the early 1980s, and just like my dad looked in the 1950s, and *his* dad in the early 1920s.

I couldn't help but wonder at their ability to change the boys' attire and demeanor so completely when they visited their mother. To this day I don't know what happened to the clothes they were wearing when they left, but somehow or other, they always came back looking different and strange.

There were a few articles of clothing that didn't disappear when they wore them to Suzanne's house. I once purchased them a pair of sturdy coats through a K-Mart blue light special. They were very proud of their new coats and generally wore them everywhere they went, even when they went to visit their mother that weekend.

That Sunday evening, when they were returned to me, they barreled in the door, all smiles as usual, but on their coats, just over the front pocket, two words had been written in black permanent marker. It said *"Lester's Boys."* My mouth set into a thin line as I escorted them into the house and smiled at Suzanne as pleasantly as I could. It sent shivers down my spine as I worried just what these children were being told while I wasn't present. I still wasn't their father, apparently. I was *just* their dad.

I became increasingly paranoid about just what they might do to my children. I had not forgotten that Suzanne had absconded with the children for those weeks, after the subject of divorce was first broached. That had come because of the direct order of Warren Jeffs, who arrogantly supposed he did not have to listen to anyone else, including the law. If Warren Jeffs issued another edict like that, she might go ahead and obey him all over again. I did not want something like that to happen again.

That was my biggest fear when I found Suzanne had volunteered her service at Jay and Kyle's school. I fully supported her spending time with them at school, and even forwarded all information regarding school programs, events, activities, and parent-teacher conferences. I had even suggested Suzanne volunteer at their school on Wednesday afternoons. But here I found she was coming in unpredictably, and I was not comfortable not knowing when she would be with the children, so I asked the teachers not to permit her to volunteer unless it was during periods we both agreed on.

That got the ball rolling again with the FLDS. They had been looking for a way to review and challenge the court's decision, and instructed their attorney, Rodney Parker, to file a motion alleging that I was in contempt of court. They argued that the judge had decreed the time be split between parents as evenly as possible, and I was not providing enough visitation time between the boys and their mother.

They claimed that I was throwing up obstructions to prevent her from contacting the children, just as I had done with her volunteering at the schools. I was violating the court's decree of dissolution of marriage by limiting her visitation to every other weekend and one night during the week, they argued; I was taking the kids into my custody when I couldn't be there with them, and that on more than one occasion Suzanne had dropped them off at a babysitter, when she herself was willing and desirous of taking care of them herself. Because I was violating all the requirements of the court, they asked that a warrant be sent out for my arrest, unless I started to comply with the court's demands. They also asked that the decree be reviewed and altered in light of my contempt.

When I received the summons I just about fainted to the floor of the Post Office. I was still tens of thousands of dollars in debt. There was no way I would make it through another court battle with Stephen Lee at my side. Lee would probably refuse to represent me again because I still owed him so much money.

Thankfully the request was now filed in Utah, since that's where I had lived for some time. This meant that I could count on Chris Edwards, a longtime friend of my family's, to come to my aid to the best of his ability. Even with a heavy discount on Chris's part, however, the expense would be debilitating.

We crafted our arguments very carefully. Chris wrote a brief to the court on my behalf arguing that neither a hearing nor a warrant was necessary because I had been complying with the directives of the court. Suzanne, on the other hand, was the one who had demonstrated contempt for the laws of the United States.

Quoting Dr. Malatesta, we argued that because our religious differences were so acute, it was unreasonable to expect boys that young to live concurrently in both worlds. The reason, we pointed out, that she was only allowed to have the kids on the times we set was because they were in school, and they needed to have a stable and constant home environment or their studies would be severely impacted.

The babysitter was not someone that the boys weren't familiar with. The babysitter was a paternal aunt, who had been evaluated by Dr. Malatesta. Conversely, I sometimes had to drop the boys off at Lester's house when Suzanne was away at her part-time job. This meant they were directly in the care of a sister-wife whom they did not know at all, and whom Dr. Malatesta had never even evaluated. She was not a reasonable substitute for child care because she lived twenty-five miles away and had two other children by Lester that she needed to care for.

Suzanne had claimed that I was infringing on her rights as a parent by insisting she bring the boys to my house instead of spending an extra half an hour with them and then dropping them off directly for school. This was out of deference to the wishes of Jay, who had asked me if he could come to my house before going to school, so he could change. Because of the religious pressure exerted on those boys, they ended up in attire not commonly worn in Hurricane elementary skills. Anyone who has ever been to a public elementary school can attest to how important it is to be liked, and the boys already received enough flak from their peers because their strangely dressed, polygamous mother fawned over them every Wednesday afternoon.

The FLDS was squared up for a fight once again. Sam Barlow had accepted totally the "Prophet's" interpretation of my character, and he told Parker everything he knew. By the time we had gone to trial the first time, I'm sure Sam had Parker convinced he was battling the Antichrist himself. Although Parker was not a believer in the FLDS church by any means, he would no doubt relish the chance to challenge me again.

Suzanne intervened, however, and fired Parker and the other two attorneys. She was tired of fighting, and I think she had come to realize she had erred in following the orders of the "Prophet." At any rate, in her heart, I doubt she was in favor of the boys being shepherded into that slaughterhouse of a church.

Once she withdrew from the contest, the court dismissed her petition, but as a precaution they insisted on mediation between the two of us. When Chris and I wandered into the mediation room, we were shocked to see her alone, without any kind of representation at all. Even the shoulder demon, that Sam Barlow had become, was conspicuously absent.

"Are you sure you want to do this without representation?" Chris asked her incredulously.

Eyes on the floor, she nodded wordlessly.

Chris shot me a look. "Maybe you'd better even the odds a little, Jason," he told me. "I'll just go ahead and excuse myself. Take as long as you need."

And he stepped out the room, clicking the doors shut behind him. I sat down in the folding chair across from her. "Hey, Suzy," I said, trying to appear casual.

"Hey, Jason," she replied.

Where could I start this awkward negotiation? It would be difficult, to say the least. Suzanne had a psychological problem to her. She had to believe whole-heartedly in everything she did. She couldn't waffle or vacillate like I do all the time; she was like a pendulum at the far end of its swing, and she could find no common ground. Maybe I could act like I understood her, her motivations, and her dilemmas.

"I know how it is with you, Suzy," I began. "You can't do anything halfway. Your beliefs are 100% or nothing. The deals you make, with counsel, are deals you are pressured into. Can we just start with what makes you happy?"

She squirmed ever so slightly, and twitch of her lips told me she was tempted to smile. I determined then that this would not be a quarrel.

She expressed her happiness that the children were with me, and that on many occasions she could tell the boys had a better life now. She told me that she was blinded by what was being told to her, so blinded that she was not even thinking about the boys, only the custody fight. I was hearing words coming out of her mouth I never thought I would hear.

It turns out she was promised by the priesthood and in public meeting that she would be given full custody. That promise had turned out void and empty, and had prompted her to fire her attorneys. Suzanne and I talked---really talked. For the first time in a couple of years, Jay and Kyle were the stars in our life's stage play, not the little runts who played the trees in the background.

# XXIII
# TEN MILLION

Over the years, Chris Edwards and I clocked a lot of lengthy conversations about the FLDS. Chris was a devout Mormon, and I suspect he secretly enjoyed seeing polygamists taken to task for their beliefs. Because of that, the conversations had started as debates. I would defend the lifestyle my father had chosen against the more mainstream tack espoused by Chris. Yet inevitably as time wore on the conversations wore down to our common outrage over the abuses of the church leadership.

"You know the worst part?" I said during one such discussion. "Those guys are just going to keep getting away with it. They think they can play God and destroy whatever they want, and they stomp on anybody who questions them."

Chris nodded. We generally agreed on our own powerlessness, but as the conversations wore on, we started to like the idea of taking on the church. There was an old tort still on the books in Utah detailing the circumstances under which someone could sue for "alienation of affection." Alienation of affection specifically referred to a respected authority, such as a "Prophet," using his position of trust to steer a person away from someone they loved without respect for the feelings of either spouse.

"I'll have to do some research on it," Chris said, excited by the prospect, "but I think we can do it. How much should we sue them for?"

"I don't know," I said. "Since he stole my family, maybe we should sue him for his." We both chuckled at the remark, but in reality I was dumbfounded. "How can you put a price tag on my family?" I asked, more seriously. "I don't think there is any sum that would replace that."

Chris nodded contemplatively. "That's true," he agreed. "So let me change the question. How much money do you think it would take to make them think twice about interfering with other families?"

The idea had merit. "I don't have any money," I told him.

"I think I could take on the case for a contingency," he said. "We got a shot. A judge might see things our way."

And with that, we made the decision to sue the FLDS for ten million dollars. We knew we were taking a difficult challenge, because the church had so much money and so many skilled attorneys, but we were certain we could build a strong case, so we felt it was worth the risk. Besides, the lawsuit made for a brilliant piece of strategy in the overall scheme of things. We had four goals in mind when we first mounted the case.

1) The first goal was financial. I had amassed an awful amount of debt already in the custody battle, and any funds we could get would go a long way toward resolving that, and it would make a more comfortable life for the boys. We knew we were unlikely to get the full ten million even if we won, because of taxes and legal fees, and a host of other issues. The FLDS would probably file bankruptcy or issue some statement to the effect that it was unreasonable to expect a payment over a few thousand dollars because of the financial burden it would place on the church. This would have been a lie, or course, since the FLDS had assets that amounted to well over $100 million, but this sort of thing was done all the time. Still, I wasn't looking to retire early. I just wanted to be able to get back to the stability I had enjoyed before they ruined my life in the first place.

2) The second goal was to provide some relief in the custody hearing. We were still facing the preliminary motions at this time before our custody case went to trial, and it was common knowledge that the church was actively involved in mounting Suzanne's case for sole custody. Once we filed this alienation of affection tort, the church would, naturally enough, try to demonstrate that they had had nothing to do with our divorce. This would be a tough argument to make if the church was still pouring funds into resolving Suzanne's legal expenses. In an effort to protect itself (we hoped) the church would back away from the custody trial and make the battle a little easier.

3) Our third goal was petty, but I would be lying if I said there wasn't a motive of revenge to the whole thing. I was still very bitter that the church had engineered the divorce in the first place and then married her up to another man so as to preempt all hope of reconciliation. I think that, subconsciously at least, a part of me wanted to inflict the kind of emotional distress on the Jeffs regime that they had been so cavalier about throwing at me.

4) Our final goal was what Chris had outlined. We wanted to hit the church's pocketbook with so much force that it would never again try the tactics it had used on me. I always asserted that if we were able to save even one family from their finagling, I would hold the lawsuit a success. My biggest pie-in-the-sky dreams had other disenfranchised members of the FLDS taking heart because of the success of my lawsuit and launching similar suits of their own—maybe even enough to sue the church out of existence. It would reincorporate later, obviously, but it would take at least two decades for the congregants to rebuild the church, which was enough time to allow a lot of people to escape. This scheme was unlikely to achieve that kind of success, but I was only 22 at the time—still very young, and I felt there was no harm in dreaming.

One thing Chris and I had failed to take into account was the media frenzy that followed our decision. The day after Chris filed the lawsuit in the Fifth District Court in St. George, Chris's office was flooded with requests for interviews. He called me that morning and asked me to hurry to his office so that I could do interviews for Channel Four and Channel Two.

"I'm telling you, Jason," he said over the phone, "all this publicity is only going to help your case. Even if you don't win the tort, all the news will shed some light on what those guys are doing, what with the custody battle and all that."

I needed no further convincing. I had never done an interview in front of any kind of a camera, but I got over my shyness in a hurry so that I could do as many interviews as possible. I did the interviews as scheduled, and then I spent the rest of the afternoon fielding calls from other potential interviewers. Court TV called, asking if they could monitor the process and threw several questions at Chris. CNN called asking for an interview, and Channel Five, our local newspaper (the Spectrum), the Salt Lake Tribune, and even a couple radio stations.

# Exile Sues Polygamous Clan Leaders

**BY GREG BURTON**
**THE SALT LAKE TRIBUNE**

A Utah man who claims a southern Utah polygamous clan persuaded his wife and children to leave him has sued clan leaders and the polygamous Fundamentalist Church of Jesus Christ of Latter Day Saints (FLDS) for $10 million.

Jason Miles Williams, who was forced out of his Colorado City, Ariz., home last December, contends fundamentalist leader Rulon Jeffs and Jeffs' son Warren coerced his wife, Suzanne, to flee his family because "she had no

Rulon Jeffs

chance of salvation if she were to remain married" to Williams.

The frosting on my cake came when a producer of the Oprah Winfrey Show called, asking me if I would consider appearing with several other former polygamists on the show. When my children had disappeared, my friend Trisha Porter had come up with the idea of shooting off an email to the producers in hopes it might help resolve my plight. So I used her email account to send an email to the show, detailing what had happened to my children. This ended up being the very first email I ever sent.

I had even threatened to go on the Oprah Winfrey Show when I first found that Suzanne had been remarried to Lester, so I thought this show would be of particular poetic significance, in that I was following through on a threat I had fired from the hip. I looked forward to doing the show, but eventually the producer called back and cancelled my appearance. They had made the decision to make it into an all-female symposium against the FLDS, in order to appeal to feminist activists.

So I just did the interviews certain local and national news programs had set up for me. Although I was nervous at the prospect of conducting on-camera interviews, I gradually relaxed once I realized just how easy the process is. The reporters generally asked the same questions, and they were usually very respectful in nature. A few reporters would develop some semi-antagonistic question, but because I had answered each one several times already, I generally did pretty well in answering them without making myself look too much like a fool.

"Why would you blame a religion for your divorce?" they would ask. "Was it the church, or are you just angry that your wife left you?"

"Both," I would answer. "I'm angry that my wife left me, but she left me *because* Rulon Jeffs and the FLDS leadership told her to. They actively tried to keep me from talking to her, and then they remarried her to another man while she was still legally married to me. They only reason they did that was because they wanted to stop us from reconciling."

"Well," they would change the subject, "what made you decide on ten million?"

"Because my lawyer wouldn't let me sue for ten *billion*," I would retort. "Ten million dollars is pocket change compared to the kind of emotional distress they put me through when they stole my family away from me."

It was a difficult experience having every facet of my life probed by the media. The opposing lawyers had already scooped all the dirt they could find for use in my custody battle, but that didn't really have relevance beyond our particular circle. The media was much more thorough, and their burden of evidence wasn't quite as acute. They spread the information they found throughout the populace like wildfire, and soon everyone knew more about me than I knew.

I was unsure about subjecting my children to this kind of scrutiny, but the damage had already been done, and the media was going to continue taking pictures until the public tired of the story. There wasn't much I could do about it. One of the factors behind my decision to file the suit, though, had been that I had hoped so much to better the lives of my sons. At any rate, if I was able to win the custody battle, they would at least have escaped the tyrannical rule of the Jeffs regime.

Especially important to me was the opportunity to have a paper trail that I would later be able to show my children. If I lost the custody battle I would at least want it to be demonstrable through news coverage and legal documentation that I had scrambled like mad with my efforts to build a life for them. I wanted to be able to show them that, even if I failed spectacularly, at least I had tried to show the UEP and the Jeffs leadership that their crimes were not being ignored.

And it was  an uphill battle, if not a sheer cliff, that I was facing. As with any good mountain, I had to keep climbing, even though I knew the higher I climbed the farther I would fall if things went south. I was pressing and prodding a beast that was still fairly dormant, and if I continued it was bound to raise its filthy head.

In the beginning I had been nothing more than an annoyance, a thorn in the side of the "Prophet." But the more the FLDS tested my resolve, the more they realized just how sharp and barbed the thorn was. I like to think that in their hearts the priesthood leaders knew that what they had done to me was wrong, even if they refused to admit it, but looking back on it, the idea that they were at fault had probably not even crossed their mind. They were the moral ones, who were living correct principle and sustaining a working relationship with God. They were certain of it. One of the interesting things about moral clarity is how completely it obfuscates the actual truth of the case.

Even if they were psychologically incapable of answering to themselves for what they had done, I worked tirelessly to ensure that they would answer to me, and to the other men that had suffered similar fates at their hands. Unfortunately, these other men were not so keen to rally behind me. When Chris had originally filed the case, it had been Jason Williams and John Does 1-5 vs. a series of defendants, including the FLDS, Rulon, Warren, Lester, the UEP, and even Frank. The reason the John Does 1-5 existed was in the hope that I could find a few who were willing to stand up to the man who had destroyed them and turn this into a sort of hybrid class action lawsuit, instead of the one man war of Jason vs. the Volcano.

This was easier said than done. With few exceptions, men who were in a position to file similar suits were either trying their best not to cause any ripples so that they could prove once again their worthiness and loyalty to the "Prophet," or they were trying to forget Short Creek even existed. After door after door ended up slammed in my face, I was forced to realize it would be just me against the church. It was a daunting battle, but I was still naively certain I could stop Warren from ever again doing what he had done to me. I was certain it was just cause, and so I pressed stubbornly forward, clinging to the Pirates of the Caribbean mantra that "no cause is lost if there be but one fool left to fight for it."

Not everyone agreed with my belief in the righteousness of my cause. My mom was in a difficult situation, because she loved me very much, but she was upset that I was fighting against the priesthood. She generally had been very careful to stay out of my affairs, but several nights after I had filed the tort lawsuit, I walked in her door for a visit and found her folding laundry, eyes bright red, as though she had been crying for days.

As soon as she noticed me, her eyes filled with tears again and she slumped against the laundry, weeping hysterically. "Please take it back!" she begged. "You don't sue the Prophet."

"Mom," I answered, "I love you very much, but you have to understand that I'm doing this for my children."

Not much was said beyond that, but I could tell she was very conflicted. She had already stood up to the community once, when her father demanded she leave my dad. Much of the community had already looked down on her because of her refusal to divorce him, and now she was almost universally spat upon because of the actions her son Jason was taking against the Prophet. It was widely believed that the actions of the children were reflections upon the parenting skills of the person who had somehow failed to indoctrinate them correctly.

Alienation of affection, I came to find, is a difficult law to navigate. I hope to go the remainder of my life without seeing another lawsuit. They require an outlay of time, energy, aggravation, and expense that makes me detest the idea of ever suing anyone again. Anyway, our legal system is pretty peculiar, in that even the winner of a case can end up the loser when all is said and done. The alienation of affection tort is particularly difficult because it was a rather vague law to begin with, and it has been refined and reevaluated so many times it is hard to know where you stand with it. Also, the law hadn't been discussed in a civil suit in so long it was practically stale, and even when it was discussed it hadn't really been in the light of religious instruction.

I was convinced that religious instruction was one of the best places such a law could be used, but Rodney Parker and Scott Berry filed a motion for summary judgment on the case without a trial. They said that allowing the case to go forward would be the greatest assault on religious freedom of our time. They also pointed out that the law should be effectively considered stale, and that Arizona law should take precedence because the marriage was domiciled in Arizona. We pointed out that although our driver's licenses and voters registrations were issued in Arizona, we were married in Utah, we lived in Utah for much of our marriage, and all of the conversations over which we were suing the church took place in Utah.

The church also argued that we shouldn't go to trial because the burden of proof would be impossible for us to meet. In Suzanne's deposition, she talked about serious irreconcilable differences in our marriage, although I don't really believe the differences were anything out of the ordinary. I still believe, and Suzanne would likely corroborate, that the church coached her to some degree on what sorts of statements she should make in her deposition. She also stated that she made the decision to leave of her own accord and met with Warren Jeffs about what to do afterward.

Warren Jeffs, in his deposition, also stated that he did not tell Suzanne to divorce me, but merely gave religious counsel about the options she had after she had acted upon her predetermined course. This was, of course, a bold-faced lie, because she didn't leave until after she had met with him, and he had told me during his interview that she was essentially acting on his instructions. However, there was nothing I could do to prove that he was perjuring himself.

Chris argued that we could demonstrate proof of Warren's involvement because I had a series of letters she had sent me. If the letters were any indication, she had gone from loving me dearly to divorcing me (albeit she dangled the hope of remarriage, "Prophet"-willing) within the span of only a few weeks. Besides which, Chris pointed out, whether or not he told her to leave me was only half the issue. He had arranged for her to be married to another man before we had even undergone any type of court mediation. The move was explicitly designed to prevent us from reconciling.

Despite our arguments, Judge Shumate did decide to grant the motion for summary judgment, which meant the case was dismissed. Because the court didn't report any specific findings, we basically had to work under the assumption that Shumate had accepted every one of Parker's arguments verbatim. He hadn't even really considered our arguments, or looked at the evidence I had compiled. It was as though we hadn't said anything at all.

"Don't worry," Chris reassured me when we read the finding. "There'll be an appeal. I promise you."

---

## POINT VII
**Does the lower court improperly condone the constitutionally prohibited act of polygamy by disregarding the polygamous nature of appellees' actions?**

Utah law expressly prohibits polygamy. It is part of the Utah Constitution; "...polygamous or plural marriages are forever prohibited." (Utah Const. Art. III Sec. 1) Utah is the only state that has made polygamy and marriage in general a constitutional issue. The state should not condone, by turning a blind eye, the polygamous nature of the defendant's actions. The facts in this case show that in March 1999, Suzanne Williams married another man while still married to Jason Williams. And the man Suzanne married was legally married to another woman. Suzanne bore a child and became pregnant in her polygamous relationship while still legally married to the Plaintiff. To find no fault in Mrs. Williams entering into a polygamous marriage which irreparably harmed her first marriage condones this illegal behavior.

---

We filed the appellate brief as quickly as possible, arguing once again that the case should be evaluated under Utah law, that we did indeed have evidence to back up our claims. Parker kept hammering that proceeding with the case would violate the religious freedoms the FLDS depended on to function. The idea was that confessions priests take under office of their church are sacrosanct and inadmissible. However, Chris rightly pointed out that the religious confession privilege did not apply in every case, and anyway it wasn't a confession that Suzanne went through at all. It was a religious solicitation, where the

Church specifically set out to counsel Suzanne to abandon our marriage and to commit a crime.

We had come a long way in battling the church, and I certainly didn't want to be stopped here. To turn and fight and then stop would do more harm than if I had not chosen to sue the church in the first place, because now Warren would have demonstrated to the frightened expatriates of his congregation that he was able and willing to crush any who dared oppose him. Like the Spanish Inquisition, it had become difficult for Short Creek residents to even think of thoughts bordering on heresy without also thinking about the repercussions. Only in this case, instead of the fires of the Holy Offices, the consequences were shame and humiliation, eviction, and abandonment, not to mention a hearty dose of hell for your future life. My lofty goal for the lawsuit was to destroy the belief that you cannot defeat the "Prophet" once and for all. The stakes were too great to be stopped by one district court judge who did not want to impose on religious freedom.

I heaved a sigh of relief when I learned that the Court of Appeals had ruled in our favor. Of course, this meant nothing in the overall scheme of destroying the church and winning ten million dollars in damages. All it meant was that I had won the right to have my case evaluated in a trial court and determined from there. We would still have to put on a good show in the trial, or the whole campaign would vanish in a cloud of smoke.

Soon after the appellate ruling was finalized, however, a know-it-all intervened. I was attending a family barbecue at my uncle's home, and the conversation veered over to my lawsuit against the church. My cousin Jennifer had brought a short-term acquaintance over. This guy fancied himself a specialist on common law regarding family matters, because he had studied legal issues while he was in jail.

The guy took it upon himself to file a friend of the court brief for my case. He even went so far as to drive to Warren Jeffs's home and serve him the new court summons. I don't know his motivation, whether he genuinely thought his input would be beneficial or not, but I imagine it was a move calculated, at least subconsciously, to impress Jennifer with his legal knowledge and expertise. Whatever the reason, he went on to file a brief, which infuriated Judge Shumate, because he was a paralegal and not an actual attorney. The court refused to even consider the brief—they just threw it right out.

Meanwhile, once Chris found out that the paralegal had submitted the brief, he assumed that I had simply elected to go with alternate legal representation. We never really discussed in depth what was actually going on, so Chris figured that the brief was taken care of. However, since the court had thrown out the paralegal's brief, it meant that I had filed no paperwork on the case. Just as I prepped to launch into the next round, the case was routinely dismissed for failure to prosecute, and there was nothing more I could do about it.

The case was dead, beyond any hope of revival. I now refer to this thing as my very own Ten Million Dollar Adventure. I had dented them financially (although I myself didn't see any cash), and I had also managed to shine a light into their wrongdoing. This was before Tapestry Against Polygamy and other anti-polygamy groups had come to full fruition, and I didn't have the assistance of attorney generals or district attorneys. I was on my own from the start, waging a war against a tyrant, and although I lost, it was a victory even in defeat. For the first time in history, it seemed to the outside world that the FLDS could be beaten. The problem was, inside the FLDS, they got the opposite feeling. Warren was now under the opinion that he had defeated the justice system, and his most serious opponent. He was invincible—and more vindictive than ever. He and other devout members now keenly felt that "something should be done" about that little Williams bastard who had the audacity to challenge the "Prophet" in a court of law.

# XXIV
# BLACKBALLED

From the moment I filed my tort suit, I was labeled Pubic Enemy Number One. The "Prophet" was livid that I challenged him, put him through deposition, and cost him millions of dollars in legal fees over the course of his trial. I spent the entire time knowing that he would find a way to retaliate, but I didn't know how he would do it.

I was having a good morning that day in early 2001 when I arrived at work. Most of my mornings were good ones. That's the great thing about life. Everyone has difficult battles to fight, battles that rip your heart out from your chest. But if you're lucky enough to come on top in those few episodes, all the day-to-day battles are silly and unimportant. It is easy to laugh about them.

I was still involved with the tort lawsuit, but I was on the offensive this time. As far as I knew, I wasn't really at risk. It was certainly important, but it was more of a campaign for justice than a bitter fight for my livelihood. So it was really easy to compartmentalize it and live the rest of my life without worrying *too* much about the verdict.

When I climbed out of my SUV, I noticed that one of the men I worked with was staring at me, genuinely worried. This man was named Milton Holm, and he had been kicked out of the FLDS a few years before I was. He was one of the good Holms--not one of them that had attacked Bobby some years before.

The stare was disconcerting, definitely, but I shook it off and went to work, framing up a house. After a few moments, I noticed he was standing next to me. I thought about shooting him a dirty look, but I decided that was a silly idea. When people stare at you for a long time, they are either making a judgment about you or they have something to tell you and can't figure out how to say it. A dirty look doesn't bring a favorable outcome in either situation.

It turned out Milton's reason for staring was the latter case. After a few moments he said, "Jason, I think you better watch your back. A couple friends told me the priesthood wants you destroyed."

I let out an uncomfortable laugh. It was a single, explosive *Ha!* "Oh, yeah?" I said, still nailing up the joists. "And why is that?"

"Not real sure." Milton was as serious as the grave. "But some of them who prayed for you to die have started to wonder what it was all about."

I stopped the work I was doing and turned to face him, shocked. "What?"

"If I were you, I'd watch my back," he said. "That's all I'm saying. You know how many crazy guys they got out there. Couple of them might take this on to show their commitment to the priesthood."

When words are thrown at you like bricks, sometimes it can take a while for them to sink in. "They might—why? What the hell are you talking about?"

As the conversation progressed, I started to understand something of what had happened. Warren Jeffs was furious about the lawsuit I had brought against him. So, the previous Sunday, he had gathered the entire FLDS congregation together in the community's Civic Center and held a full day of fasting and prayer. They spent the entire day, and even the following Monday morning, asking the Lord to destroy me.

Normally, I'm not the type to worry about what people say about me behind my back. There are enough people in this world that I would give myself a heart attack if I let that bother me. But when those mutterings involve even the slightest *mention* of my death, I get a little concerned. "What do you mean, they're praying for my destruction?" I asked. "Is it generic? Like they're praying for their enemies to be destroyed, and I am their enemy, and therefore—"

Milton shook his head. "No," he said emphatically. "They are praying for the destruction of Jason Williams. Specifically."

"Holy shit." I felt a fear gripping at me, black and horrible. It made my flesh tingle. This was above the game board. It changed the rules of the altercation. Really, I had done nothing to them, except for campaign to get my boys back and protect my family interests, which is within the right of any parent. This man claimed to represent the merciful God. I had met him once in my entire life, and yet here he was asking the Lord for the ultimate favor. More than that, he was leading an entire congregation in that sordid prayer. Most of them I had never even met. Some of them I knew and thought were wonderful, and until now I had assumed they thought the same of me.

I did my best to shake it off. "The guy is insane," I said. "God doesn't grant prayers like that."

Milton was unmoved. "God doesn't have to," he replied. "People take good care of that all by themselves. Jason, I'm not worried about God throwing a lightning bolt at you. I'm worried about one of the faithful coming to your house and shooting you dead on your doorstep."

I nodded. I knew the implications. "All I'm saying is it's gonna take more than a crazy guy praying to kill me."

"I know that, Jason," Milton smiled. "All I'm saying is keep your eyes open. You never know." And with that, he turned away and went back to work.

I had been deliberately dismissive of the threat during the conversation, but that does not mean I didn't know the score. When someone wants to ask God for something, that person prays in their closet. When Warren Jeffs, or anybody, for that matter, makes the prayer public, it means it is not a prayer so much as a hint.

When Rulon Jeffs ran the priesthood, he often promoted what he called the "Journals of Discourse." This was a collection of sermons given between 1846 and 1886. In those sermons, one of the principles that were often discussed was an antiquated tenet from the Old Testament. It was called Blood Atonement. This means that some people had committed sins so heinous they had to have their blood spilled to achieve forgiveness.

One famous case of this was Ervil LeBaron. He was not a member of the FLDS, but there were a lot of similarities. The FLDS is not the only Mormon splinter group He was a leader of another polygamous group called the Church of the Lamb of God. He used to preach the idea of blood atonement a lot, and he had drawn up a list of all the people that had to bleed to atone through their death. It was a long list, with his own brother, Joel LeBaron , at the top. The top ten included Elvis Presley, John F. Kennedy, LeRoy Johnson and Dr. Rulon C. Allred, the head of a rival fundamentalist group. His wives even helped carried out the assassinations. They had walked into Allred's office and shot him dead. Ervil eventually got locked away for life for ordering the assassination, so he couldn't arrange the deaths of Presley or Kennedy. Later, they ended up dead anyway, without his help.

Luckily, Warren Jeffs wasn't quite the same as Ervil LeBaron, or course. For one thing, he didn't have a group already formed that was ready to go murder people for him. But in reality, only one person had to take his hint seriously, and my life would be in severe danger. When "the Prophet" issues a death sentence, there are some people who would be ready to take it as gospel.

It wasn't really prosecutable, because it was just a prayer. Religious leaders often say all sorts of horrible things when they're in the heat of a sermon. So it couldn't really be proven it was a request for someone to kill me. Still, I wasn't about to leave that to chance.

After all, King Henry II had made a seemingly innocuous remark in 1170 AD. He said "Will no one rid me of this meddlesome priest?" But four knights got the hint. They went to Canterbury and smashed the Archbishop Thomas Becket's head in. It was in Henry's best interest for it to seem like just a frustrated yell, but it was too easy to interpret into a command. That was also how it worked for Warren Jeffs. If someone were to splatter *my* brains all over a monastery, Warren Jeffs could say it was just an innocent spark of anger. That way, he could avoid ending up in prison the way Ervil LeBaron had.

When I got home that evening, there was only one thing I was concerned about—my boys. They were with their mother at the time. As soon as I was through the door, I sprinted over to the phone and dialed Suzanne's number.

"Suzanne," I asked her, "Did you have those boys in church last Sunday?"

She sounded a little relieved to hear from me. "No," she replied.

I heaved a sigh of relief. Obviously, I did not want my sons praying for my death, or even sharing the same room with people who would ask their God for such a ridiculous favor. "What about you?" I asked. "Were *you* there?"

"Yes." She paused. "Jason, I couldn't believe what I was hearing. You may not agree with the path we've chosen, but I don't want you to die."

"I don't want me to die either," I said. "We have that in common. Were those people really asking God to smite me or something?"

"I looked around at them," she answered. "They didn't really want to. Most of them just kept their head down and prayed. Nobody dared to question the words of the Prophet."

"How could they pray for me to *die?*" I was genuinely upset by this point. That place had been my home. "I don't know them; they don't know me!"

"I don't know, Jason," Suzanne said. She seemed very unhappy with what "the Prophet" had asked of them. "He just went up there and talked about how much money you were costing the priesthood because of your lawsuit."

"You're telling me that, come Judgment Day, they're going to look at God and tell him they wanted him to strike me dead because of a *lawsuit?*"

"I'm sorry, Jason."

I was sorry too. I was Public Enemy Number One now, and I would need all the allies I could get. Some people have to go into hiding when they receive threats like these from religious leaders. This was the case with Salman Rushdie, who had to go underground for a few years to escape the assassination attempts from Muslim hardliners.

My problem was that the FLDS threat was not accepted widely enough for any police officers to really take seriously the threat against me. I didn't know the first thing about going underground. So I decided to put it out of my mind. I have a strong belief in God, and I was confident that those people wouldn't be able to touch me. That church had already driven me away from my life once, and I obviously wasn't going to allow them to do it again.

I put the notion away. After all, people get death threats all the time and they turn up empty. I just needed to carry on with my life as well as I could. However, an extra level of alertness couldn't hurt.

My cousin Jared, though, had other opinions. He was convinced that someone from that group would come after me, and so he chose to spend the next few weeks sleeping on my couch. He brought in a pair of guns with him.

"I'm going to carry a loaded gun with me at all times," he told me. "Better to have one and not have to use it than vice versa."

I nodded. "You have to take it with you when you leave," I said. He promised he would.

He spent the next few days teaching me how to use a .40. We drove out into the countryside and took pot shots at various targets. I wasn't that good at shooting, but eventually got to a point where I would do fairly well in a pinch. I certainly hoped the scare would be over soon. I don't like guns. Holding the cold metal things and pointing them and feeling the recoil—the entire process made me uncomfortable. I didn't even like to look at the ugly thing when it lay on the countertop. I hoped I would never have to use it. Jared thought differently than I did, though. He was an avid hunter, and very skilled with guns. I certainly felt safer with him standing by me.

One night, shortly after he moved in, Jared woke me up. It was about two o'clock in the morning. "There's a car outside your house," he said. "Come see if you recognize it."

I was out of bed in an instant, heart pounding ferociously. I couldn't believe it. Someone was after me. Someone was foolish enough to carry out a hit planned by a crazed preacher. I wondered, almost curiously who it would be. Perhaps there was someone out there who hated me to begin with, and now "the Prophet" had given him permission to finish what he'd wanted to start for a long time.

We creaked open the door to the boys' room and slunk over to the window. My house was on top of a steep hill, facing the other direction. The boys' room was at the back of the house, looking down toward the bottom of the slope.

We were at the window for some time, trying to see through the black of the night. There was no streetlight along the bottom of the hill, which meant the only source of light came from the half-moon above.

And then we saw it. The car sat with its headlights off at the very bottom of the slope, sort of tucked in behind a grapevine the people below us had planted. There were two shadows, indistinct but unmistakable, in the front seats of the car.

"I wasn't going to wake you," Jared whispered, "but that car has been there for about two hours. So far, nobody's moved." He drew an imaginary line from the car to the ledge of my bedroom window. "They're positioned so they can look up into your bedroom."

I spent about half an hour studying the car, hoping maybe I could tell whose it was. The shape was easy enough to pick out, once the clouds got out of the way of the moonlight, but I could not for the life of me discern what color it was. "I don't recognize it," I said.

Jared nodded. "You want to sit up and keep watch with me?"

I decided to stay and watch. Jared left me there to keep an eye on the car. He slipped out through the bedroom door and went to the front of the house. He readied his gun and found a place to watch through the front window. There was only one door to my house. Even the windows have to be approached from the front in order to get in. Jared was in a perfect position to see if anyone was coming.

We spent most of the night watching. My mind raced the entire time. I had pictured myself as a sort of bad-ass who did what was necessary to keep his family safe, but I was no John McClane. I didn't know what I would do if a man tried to get into the house. I'd practiced shooting guns, of course, but there is a fundamental difference between shooting a .40 at a beer can and shooting it at another human being. I would be taking a life in order to save my own. As far as reasons for taking lives, that's one of the better ones, but the thought of it still made me sick to my stomach.

The worst of it was that I didn't have a weapon with me at the time. I had left the .40 in my bedroom, simply because I know how jumpy I am. I was liable to start firing away at an attacker only to find out it had been Jared all along, and I had shot him to death in my entry. Or, if someone did get into the house, and I shot him, the blast would wake my sons, and they would come see what the commotion was and find blood running all over the tile. Or I would shoot first and miss, and the attacker would shoot at me. Then my kids would find their father collapsed on the stairs. None of those scenarios were experiences I wanted for my sons. I prayed to God that I would find a safe direction for my family. I wanted to keep those boys safe, but I didn't want them to grow up as terrified of the world as I was. It was a fine line to tread, and a tough one to stay on, especially for a parent like me, bouncing from one extreme to the other.

And then the headlights clicked on. The car reversed out into the road and drove off into the night. I watched the lights closely until they were vanished from my sight. Thanking God the ordeal was over, I slumped down on the bed between my sons, and then I woke up the next morning.

Over breakfast that morning I asked Jared to take the guns out of my house. I had had a dream, a good one, and I felt that the worst was over. I wasn't afraid any more. There are many ways to die, and I wasn't going to let the FLDS ruin my life all over again. Life is too short to keep looking backward. And I knew the longer the guns were lying around my home, the more likely it would become that Kyle or Jay would find one unattended. I couldn't live with myself if one of those boys ended up with a bullet in him. Jared agreed to remove the guns, but he refused to remove himself. He was going to stay on my couch, he told me, until it was over, even if the threat lasted into his nineties.

As months passed, the prayer started to seem more like a bad dream than a frightening reality. Jared moved back into his apartment, and I tried to forget the entire episode. I met quite a few people in the interim that had been part of that prayer. They had later been kicked out or left the church of their own accord. Most of them apologized for wishing such a thing upon me. Many were genuinely of the opinion that my life was in danger. There were several people in the congregation who had taken the message literally. Some had even discussed with one another the most appropriate methods to bring about the answer to that prayer.

I didn't know what to say to these apologies. If someone had actually followed through, and killed me, or killed one of my sons, I don't suppose that it would comfort me how sorry the congregation was. But at least these people found I was, like them, a fairly normal human being, rather than the demon "the Prophet" had made me out to be. No apology can really cover that amount of hatred, but they were just poor religious people who didn't dare challenge "the Prophet," and they were nice enough to apologize for the heartache. On the plus side, every apology meant that was one fewer person that might try to kill me.

Some even said that Warren Jeffs and his prayer had been major red flags in their lives, and they took action to get out of that oppressive church, and so in that sense some good came out of it, in the lives of those who had the brains to realize what they were asking. It didn't do any good in my life, though.

I thought it was over, and would never come back again, except in casual conversations. But then, an article appeared in The Spectrum, the local newspaper in our area. The article was an interview with Marvin Wyler. Wyler had believed Rulon Jeffs was "the Prophet" but he considered Warren to be an absolute and utter fraud. In the interview, Wyler said that he had followed Warren's preaching for a little while, until Jeffs asked them all "to fast and pray for the execution of Jason Williams." Then Wyler had decided that he couldn't go along with it any longer. He had abandoned the FLDS.

I thought it was interesting that my life was being discussed in the newspaper. Several members of my family called about the article as well, but it seemed so long ago that it surprised me we were discussing it again. I admit I was a little afraid this article might rekindle some of the intolerance the initial prayer meeting had forced into the world. That was on Thursday.

That Saturday, two days later, I ran an errand to our local grocery store. The boys were staying with their mother at the time, so I was alone. As I drove my SUV up into my driveway, I elected to leave it outside the garage for once. So I parked it on the driveway and ducked into the house to watch some college football.

It quickly turned into a wonderful game—one of those tight races where the referees have the good sense to stop calling penalties every few plays. I settled down, fingers crossed, when my sister-in-law hurried through the door. She was in hysterics.

"Jason!" she cried. "Your 4Runner is on fire!"

It looked like she was trying to get a reaction, so I just let out a chuckle.

"Jason!" she said, louder this time. "You 4Runner is on *fire!*"

I was watching the very climax of the game. I turned to her, a little annoyed by her ploy. "And what do you want me to do about it?" I asked her.

She looked at me like I was a damn idiot. "*Put it out!*" she shrieked. As she bolted back out the door, I caught smoke drifting through.

"Holy shit!" I realized. "My 4Runner is on fire!"

As I sprinted outside, I realized that was an understatement. The 4Runner was scarcely recognizable as anything but an inferno. Someone had used a bit of kerosene, or something like it, and lit the vehicle up like a fireball.

Cranking on the spigot, I scooped up the garden hose, and set to spraying. "Call the fire department!" I told my sister-in-law. "And get Bobby out here!"

The garden house was practically ineffective. Bobby, burst out, carrying a bucket of water, splashing it over the engine. The fire was licking at the eaves of my home. If my sister-in-law had shown up half an hour later, we would be homeless.

I started to spray down the engine, trying to keep the flames away from the house. Bobby pointed at the other end of the SUV. "Jason!" he roared. "The fuel tank!"

I had just filled it with gas while I was at the store. I watched with a feeling of dread as the fire burned away at the fuel tank. Those gallons of fuel were about to become a potent and frightening explosion. "Make sure the hose is at its max," I said as I sprayed away at the fuel tank. I expected, any moment, to be blown down the driveway and out into the street, but, thankfully, the flames started to recede.

With a garden hose and buckets of water, we fought those flames for what seemed like hours. My sister-in-law had declared she was unable to contact the fire department, and so we had fought it ourselves. Now, coughing up smoke and covered in soot, I stood watching the remains of my 4Runner. It had been only hours before that I had driven it. The thing had handled perfectly, and now, it was gone.

A lump formed in my throat. I watched the thing smolder, tears in my eyes. These charred remains were symbolic, in a way. I worked hard to get things, and then I would take them for granted. They worked so well for me, and then they would vanish, not quietly, but violently and nastily, with lots of commotion. It had happened so many times before—my marriage, my furniture, my home, and now my transportation. For a moment I wondered what else they were going to burn down.

It was like all the other things I owned that were ripped away from me. I had to replace them, and it cost money. It had cost money to get a new home, to restock it with furniture. And now I was forced to pony up some money in order to obtain a new vehicle. To top it off, I was still shackled making payments to the most expensive custody lawyer I have ever retained. This was not going to be an easy task on twelve dollars an hour.

One of the remarkable things about life is that it's never so bad it can't get any worse. Given the fanatics that were out to destroy me, it could have been very much worse. It had been a lot worse for some other people in similar situations. For example, three years later, a Dutch filmmaker named Theo van Gogh got shot down on a sidewalk in The Hague. He had made a film called *Submission*, and a local imam was infuriated because he thought it insulted Islam. The imam gave a sermon in which he asked God to visit an incurable disease upon Mr. van Gogh. It was basically the same thing Jeffs did here—pray for the man's destruction. Only in van Gogh's case, someone followed through. The disease took the form of eight bullets, a slit throat, and a message plunked down into his chest on the blade of a knife. I remember seeing this case on the news and realizing just how damn fortunate I had been.

It was at that point I understood that the difference between bad and worse is much more tangible than the difference between good and better. The FLDS could have done all manner of things to me, and to my sons as well, for that matter. I was extremely lucky that I had fought the Jeffs machine and the extent of the damage was nothing more than a fire-gutted Toyota 4Runner.

# XXV
# THE LIGHT CLICKS ON

Warren Jeffs and I were going in opposite directions. I was heading for normalcy. My life had evened out with my boys' school schedules and coaching Little League. I filled the emptiness left behind by Suzy Q with a ton of focus and energy poured into the raising of Jay and Kyle. There were certainly bumps in the road because of the visitation schedule, but everything was ironing out. I was safer now, and more accepted by the sane people of the world.

While I was rebuilding my life, Warren Jeffs was destroying his. His call for my death had been the tip of the iceberg. Now his descent into insanity and paranoia rivaled that of King Lear. Grand, expansive plans were forming in his mind.

Many outlying believers, in Salt Lake City and elsewhere, had been invited, threatened, cajoled, counseled, or excommunicated in order to move them to Colorado City in time for the city to be lifted into heaven. Jeffs had as many loyal newcomers as the old guard church had. Warren's father was old, sick, and fighting the effects of a stroke, and the son was emerging as the second mouthpiece of God. With his power base secure, he began to flex his position as leader of the group, in the name of his father, or course.

When the Y2K lift-off hadn't gone as planned, Warren Jeffs asserted it was because of the wicked among them, and launched an effort to identify who had halted the process. It was like living with Jonah on the boat when he ran away from his duties in Nineveh, every sailor on board clamoring to find out who had caused the terrible hurricane.

The Jeffs began lashing out at the members he distrusted the town, evicting them and turning their families into veritable hot potatoes to be passed from one husband to another. Erwin Fischer, who had been kind enough to let Suzanne and I stay with him, was one of the first to be chastised. His home, wives, children, and business were taken from him because he had confessed to having a temper and sometimes yelling at his family. He was forced to reside in a small room in the basement of one of his sons, doing his best to humble himself before the word of God. He was killed in an auto wreck a while later, but the poor man was already dead anyway, stripped of every dignity and loved one and possession he had ever had.

The times also saw many younger men, some of them thirteen and fourteen years old, ejected from the community and abandoned by their families. Their distraught mothers and fathers were warned to have nothing do to with them ever again. Neighboring towns saw an influx of over 400 homeless and practically orphaned teenagers whose faith had been ripped apart. They became known locally and in the courtrooms as the "Lost Boys."

Every one of the poor kids was culturally inept, like Chance the Gardner, forced to function in a world they knew little about. They were all supposed to have committed some sort of disobedient misdemeanor, talking to a girl or watching a television program, or even just playing a competitive sport. Six of them eventually filed a lawsuit alleging what most of them claimed all along—they were just weeded out to ensure there would be more girls for the faithful. Polygamy was a practical model in 8 B.C., when men were always doing stupid things, like dying young, but these men were consistently living to see eighty, which meant they were running out of beautiful girls to cohabit with. Desperate times called for desperate measures.

Warren had assured the community his father would never die, because the Lord would come down and rejuvenate him, so that he could lead the righteous in all his youthful vigor to Missouri, where they were destined to build a new temple and welcome the city of Enoch. Despite these prophecies from the infallible man-child, however, Rulon Jeffs did in fact die, in 2002, and the community was thrust into turmoil. Many expected Uncle Fred, who really was an uncle to half the town, to assume most of the leadership. Fred Jessop was the bishop, a kindly old gentleman, and a logical candidate to lead the group, but the idea that Rulon had identified his son Warren as a spiritual titan, had most of the followers resigned to a continuation of the Jeffs empire. After a brief power struggle, Fred Jessop finally capitulated, declaring publicly that Rulon had held his son Warren up as the next in authority.

The accepted idea was that time was extremely short until the destructions began, consequently propelling FLDS members into a rush to prepare. They spent hours canning food, memorizing scripture, listening to sermons, and whatever else was necessary in advance of being transported directly to heaven without having to go through the awkward process of dying. Many members were so certain of the impending lift-off, they took out massive loans—some upwards of a million dollars—and purchased whatever they wanted, whether it was new vehicles, home renovations, or even exotic vacations. There were so many loans taken out of the local branch of the Bank of Ephraim that the entire bank went completely bust because not many of these men could or would pay it back.

Under Warren's rule, many more underage marriages were performed, because they had to be married as quickly as possible. If they were single when the last days came about, they would never be able to achieve the highest level of glory. In an odd way, Warren's predictions of the end game turned out to be somewhat prophetic, if self-fulfilling, because his doings eventually galvanized the state and county into taking action against him.

In 2003, Fred Jessop and his supporters undertook a renovation project for one of the oldest buildings in the town. Starting in 1930, the building had served as a schoolhouse, but had since fallen in into disrepair. During the 1953 Raid on Short Creek, it had been used as both a holding pen and kangaroo court.

They decided to refurbish the place and create a library. The area already had a first-class zoo, a decent welfare system, several city parks, and a gigantic civic center, but no library. So the historic day of July 23, the fiftieth anniversary of the raid, became the dedication day for the building.

The town dignitaries proudly unveiled a monument commemorating the raid, which had embedded on it a bronze plague of LeRoy Johnson, the old pioneer who had led the people through the tough times and fought the courts until they were all home again. A detailed memorial plaque completed the monument. Everyone was very pleased with the work, except Warren Jeffs. Enraged by the idea of monuments to dead people, he attacked and defaced the monument, accusing the entire town of idolatry.

Soon, most of the old timers were kindly invited to leave town. A few courageous old fellows defied him, but most of them left everything and resettled in sorrow somewhere in the adjacent counties. Fred Jessop was called on a "mission for the Lord" late one night and was never seen again. Some rumors asserted he was being held in a town in western Colorado until he finally died. His family and his businesses were given to a much younger adopted son, William Timpson (or Jessop, as he referred to himself). William was then ordained a bishop in his stead, and expected to be a husband to the many wives of his vanished stepfather. Meanwhile, the magnificent zoo Fred had carefully and lovingly created was dismantled, and all the animals were sold. Today, all that remains of the work is a series of empty pens and weed-ridden pastures. The whole community has replaced the wild life as a zoo.

Along with Warren's newly acquired power of *magic marriage*, came the more potent authority to force divorce. After the removal of Fred turned out to be successful, the God Squad became much more aggressive, showing up on the porches of many of the most influential elders in the town, bearing the news that "the Prophet wants you to pack your bags. You're going on a mission for the Lord."

The elders' huge families were divided among the remaining men who still supported the tyrant that was Warren. Often, a year or so later, the elder who had been declared worthy of receiving the previous elder's gaggle of wives and kids was now found *unworthy*, and the family would be passed around again.

Every one of Fred Jessop's supporters had been systematically removed over the ensuing years, losing all claim to their possessions or families, including the more influential Barlow brothers, Louis, Joe, Truman, and even the mayor Dan. Some of the newly bachelorized men were directed to reside in an apartment building built specifically to house ten or twelve of these divorcees, all scrambling to prove themselves obedient enough to "get new assignments" or maybe, if they were truly optimistic, to get their old families back. We have referred to this sad housing development as "the Eunuch hotel."

I felt truly sorry for everyone reduced to living in it, and there seemed to be a morbid sort of kinship between us. The rest of these abandoned men settled in nearby towns, trying to find some balm for their feelings and carry on without animosity toward the "Prophet". It was amazing to me that so many of them agreed the problem was in *them* and refused to complain or resist. I hadn't been so docile.

Warren had for some time been using the consecrations and tithing money for real estate purchases in other states. Some property in Mancos, Colorado, Fargo, South Dakota, and El Dorado, Texas had been secured for the most righteous. Warren had despaired of ever getting an obedient enough congregation to meet the Lord and Enoch, so he began to handpick the loyal and the elite.

He preached that the Lord needed five hundred righteous families, and he, the "Prophet" had the weighty task of handpicking which ones got to be on the varsity team. He and his elite began a partial exodus to the newly formed Yearning for Zion Ranch in El Dorado. Many of the unfortunate who were left behind had the promise that continued support and money would prove their loyalty—then maybe they, too, could be gathered in Zion. So, like donkeys with a carrot dangled in front of them, the unworthy plodded on toward their unattainable horizon.

My father had already been ejected from the priesthood, much to my mother's chagrin. The "Prophet" had sent him a letter accusing him of idolatry and of allowing his wife to rule over him, thereby forfeiting his priesthood. Included in the letter was one of the more sexist excerpts from the JOURNAL OF DISCOURSES, with the name *Susan* scrawled in the margin. When my mom saw her name there, it damn near broke her heart.

She had already been denied the privilege of going to meeting on Sunday. Warren had sent word to Nephi that she had supported her son in the litigation against him and had forfeited her worthiness. The truth was that she had refused to attend any of the court proceedings and had even begged me to drop the suit and "stop fighting the Prophet." She got an appointment to plead her innocence, but every word fell on deaf ears.

"Why do you want your children back in meetings," he barked in his authoritarian way, "when you personally support your apostate son, Jason, in Kingman, in a fight against the Lord?"

"But I didn't go to Kingman," she protested, "I asked him to stop his lawsuit."

"Stop lying," he snorted. "We have it on good authority that you were there, cheering him on."

She wasn't going to argue with him, but her eyes were a little less clouded about his infallibility. She knew it was no use believing that Warren Jeffs did not make mistakes when it was so manifestly obvious he had. She was still very conflicted about my course of action, but she loved me firmly and believed I was not the ogre of the village.

Her ejection from church, not to mention her other children as well, deeply wounded my mother. It ruined her association with her family and friends. She had been commanded to leave my dad, but stayed with him in spite of the persecution she was suffering. I have always respected my mom for, when it came right down to it, refusing at last to kowtow to the FLDS. I can only imagine the demons she must have battled to see the truth for what it really was. It took tremendous strength to keep our family together through all the harassing, beating, and legal maneuvers. Emerson observed that "the mass of men live lives of quiet desperation," and that certainly fit her situation.

My younger brother Brian ended up facing his own music at the hands of the FLDS. Warren Jeffs assumed that he was covertly involved in collecting evidence for my tort lawsuit. When Brian went to his priesthood meeting, he was hauled up in front of the entire male congregation and frisked by Nephi

Barlow, who was actively searching for a recording device. It turned out that the paranoia was founded to some extent, because a member of the FLDS later ended up posting Warren Jeffs sermons on the Internet, after he had recorded them via a device hidden in his boot.

Of course, there was no reasonable evidence to suggest it was my brother who had been the one doing the recording, but the FLDS was certain that Brian would turn against them, since he was practically the last member of my family to still be active within the church. So they wanted to humiliate him publicly, to keep him in line. That was how it was always planned in that community—they did their disciplinary actions at the worst possible moments so as to inflict the most shame on the victim and garner the most awe from the spectators. A classic example was the police detaining him and his friends at the local police station for an hour after sunset, then following them, as they walked to home to Hildale, and arresting them all for curfew violations.

The harassment continued when Bobby found himself publicly accosted at a community social, when suddenly the music stopped in the middle of a round dance. The God Squad leapt out at him, pulling his dance partner away. Then the thugs roughly escorted him from the building, like a centurion and his platoon yanking a contestant out of the Coliseum. His infraction was being my brother.

There were certainly signs that the wheels were coming off the wagon, but they were not as evident during this time as they later became. Warren's work was being accomplished in several places, and the biggest fear each family had was to be labeled as apostates. To avoid that nightmare was even more important than being selected for the new project in Texas. To weed out dissent, the God Squad would canvass the neighborhoods, door to door, demanding a report on the loyalty of each household.

This was where Lester found himself under siege. He had already been castigated by the FLDS. I am not certain why, since no one will declare publicly, but I suspect the reason he was on thin ice with the "Prophet" was because he had allowed Stephen Lee to get the better of him in my custody trial. Lester had realized (somewhat) that he was a pawn, and he could not bring himself to come up with the correct answers.

So the headhunters came for Lester. Suzanne and Lester's other wife, a lady named Brenda, were instructed to meet with the "Prophet." They threw on their nicest clothing and trotted off to the palatial residence of the Jeffs family.

They met Warren there, in the office he had only just ripped from the bony clutches of his dead father.

"Your salvation depends on leaving Lester and putting yourselves back into the Prophet's hands," Warren proclaimed. "Lester Johnson has no priesthood. You *must* be saved by the power of priesthood—it is the force that calls you from the grave on resurrection morning."

The first wife heeded the call. "I am willing to do whatever it takes to gain exaltation," she assured him.

"Excellent," he congratulated her. "You will soon be moved out and placed with one more deserving. It is your right and obligation."

"Suzanne," he turned to face my poor ex-wife, "what do you intend to do?"

She was mortified at reliving the nightmare of leaving her husband a second time. She had been through hell at the hands of this boy "Prophet." After a few moments of deliberation, she finally summoned the courage to stay in the bed she had made, so to speak. "Enough is enough," she told him. "I already did that once."

He looked a little shocked at her answer. Until now she had always been a fairly docile person. "Suzanne," he said sternly, "it's a matter of priesthood. Or would you rather rot in your grave for eternity?"

"Well, I've already given up a lot," Suzanne shot back. "Lester is a good man and a good provider. I don't see the faults you're warning us about." It took her a lot of bravery to challenge him like that. I was so proud of her for finally cutting the strings.

"You are trifling with your chance in the celestial kingdom," he warned.

She stood up and faced him. "I have been sealed twice already," she said, "for time and all eternity. I'll just have to count on one them. My answer is no."

She stormed out of the office, fighting the urge to turn back and accept his demands. She knew her first husband was trying to rebuild his life, and her second husband was lost and re-inspecting his.

Brenda left that afternoon and was reassigned the same day, which just goes to show that after everything I had thrown at him, Warren had learned nothing. All he learned from his battle with me was that he hated my guts. As far as he was concerned, the whole world was still all about him, and he still had the arrogance to commit the very same crimes I had almost pilloried him for.

Lester was absolutely devastated by the developments. He was being sacrificed to Warren's pride, and he was utterly at a loss as to why. I had had my family ripped apart, which hurt me to the core, but Lester quite possibly had something worse to face. He had lost half of his family, and his very image of God, on which he had based his entire life, had turned on him ripping the footing from under him. He still had a wife and two beautiful little girls, but he was confident that meant nothing. They had never had a civil marriage; the only reason they had been united was because the "Prophet" had commanded it. Now it was clear that the "Prophet" was a man who was obviously imbalanced, who ravaged a helpless community to feed his frightened ego. Their marriage was built on a foundation of thin air, and he had a long conversation with her that evening about whether or not their marriage meant *anything* at all.

She told me all these things late that Sunday night. She had called half an hour earlier and asked if we could talk, which had certainly come as a surprise. To my knowledge, in the six years we had been separated, she had never once wanted to talk about anything but the boys, and not much of that. I was a little reluctant to have this "talk" with her. My guard was up, but I finally agreed. "Sure," I whispered hoarsely. "No problem."

But there *was* a problem. There almost had to be a problem, when a "talk" is scheduled just shy of midnight. She was waiting in her car when I stumbled blindly down my driveway. Peering through the gloom at her, I started. She was crying.

"What's going on, Suzy?" I asked quietly, opening the passenger door. She wept even more feverishly as I clambered in beside her. I had planned on being difficult when I got in the car, but this changed everything.

"I just want you to know how bad I feel—how sorry I am," she sobbed. "We had a good thing, and I messed it up. I've cried myself to sleep thinking how we were. I hope someday we can be friends again—that you can forgive me."

Crap. All my hopes at being hardnosed were dashed. I hadn't heard *I'm sorry* for almost six years. I was sure she didn't have feelings anymore. Whatever had happened, it was obvious that she was waking up. A few charred brain cells were flickering back to life, and she was starting to think about her own decisions. I had always felt like I was talking to an ice queen, and now it was apparent she was just as emotionally raw as I was.

"Suzy," I said, "something has happened. What?"

"Lester and I were kicked out of church today," she divulged, the words gushing out in torrents. "And Brenda left—and took all her girls, and Lester doesn't know what to do—or if he even cares, and—and I don't know what to think or feel. I—I'm just so sorry!"

I could see it in her eyes. She really was sorry. This little girl that had put me through hell needed me to forgive her. Damn. I had promised to love her forever, but I was angry at her, angry as all hell! How can you live through five or six years of shit and in an instant forgive and forget? But the woman I loved was here—right in my driveway—on her own power—the mother of my boys. This was not the adversary of the past five years; this was Suzy Q. My regimented world was spinning. Despite everything I had told myself, I wasn't really ready for anything like this.

"I'll forgive you, Suzy," I heard myself soothe her, not certain what I said was totally true. "You knew all you had to do was ask."

"It isn't all my fault" she proffered. "The church, and Uncle Warren—"

"He ain't your damn uncle," I interrupted gruffly.

"Okay," she almost smiled. "What I'm trying to say is I'm just so worried about going to hell."

"Warren's worried enough for both of you," I told her, "and Lester too."

"Lester doesn't know if we're even married anymore," Suzy said. "The prophet told us both to leave him."

I gasped. "No!" I said in mock horror. "Not that! I'll bet that is the first time that has ever happened."

We laughed. It was good to laugh with her again. "So," I prodded at last, "I bet you had a big ass problem with that line of crap. What are you going to do?" I was genuinely interested, but I'd be lying if I said I wasn't trying to pick a scab.

"I flat told Warren no, and walked out," she said.

Wow. That took some guts. She had placed her entire life in his hands. I don't think I have ever challenged my view of life the way Suzanne challenged hers that Sunday. Maybe Suzy was finally seeing the light.

We talked for about two hours, and she told me all about the crazy stuff that happened that Sunday, but I had to get up early and go to work. I asked her to talk some more when she brought the boys down, and she agreed. With a grin, I reached over and playfully mussed up her hair.

"Suzy," I said, "I'm sure we can be good friends. It's a lot to get past, but we'll make it. I heard a saying, 'if it doesn't kill you, it will make you stronger', and we're still kicking."

And then she drove off, leaving me standing alone in the darkened driveway, in the middle of the night. I had not been that surprised by Lester's problems— the instant I met him I had told him that he would one day fall from grace, and sure enough, he had. What surprised me was that Suzanne finally connected the dots, just at the point I had given up on her. I stayed out for a long time that night, watching the stars and realizing just how insignificant I was in the scope of things.

By this time, the conditions in the community were being discussed openly in newspapers, courts and government offices. Eventually, a warrant was issued for Warren Jeffs, charging him with accomplice to rape for an arranged marriage he had set up between fourteen-year-old Elissa Wall and her nineteen-year-old cousin. Lower on his list of crimes was his financial mismanagement of the UEP. I thought it was interesting that his father had once accused me of stealing a bride, who was in fact an unmarried girl, and now the "Prophet" was stealing brides and chasing their husbands away, so he could at last give the bride to some other, more deserving man.

Naturally enough, he looked at it as another persecution of the Lord's anointed, and he elevated himself to the ranks of previous martyrs. Like them, he flouted the law and went into hiding. The situation made the faithful even more faithful, believing the devil was persecuting the people of God. They hid him, succored him, and sent him more money. The village had created a monster that had been destroying them and their children. Now the monster was the prey and yet they still admired it.

Warren's feeble grip on reality was quickly slipping. If he had just gone into St. George and addressed the charges head on, he probably would have eventually been acquitted. But he chose to run and hide, like the rat he so closely resembled. He was driving his flock away from him, including Lester and Suzanne. I was painfully aware of the issues my kids faced while staying at Lester's home, but at least they no longer had to listen to the ravings of Warren Jeffs.

Suzanne was in the middle of an enormous volte-face. She had become a true soccer mom, who went out of her way on numerous occasions to haul the boys to games, cover for me, and just help me enjoy their progress. She could see the growth and the happiness in the boys, and she loved sharing their triumphs and consoling them when they failed. She enjoyed watching them grow up, and in my heart I think she grew up with them. She started to see things as they were, not as they were suggested to her. Responsibility was hers, not something that devolved upon another person. The strings were severed, one by one, until the puppet master finally had one fewer marionette to manipulate.

One night while she was dropping off the boys, she got me alone in the corner. "Jason," she began, grabbing my hand, "I think Lester is right. Everything is different now." She looked up at me and smiled hopefully. "Could you find a way to take me back—to marry me? We had a love that was true, it even has made it through all of this stuff, the church, the custody depositions, trial, and I—I still love you. I know the boys are better off with you."

I was stunned at this turn. "Well," I stammered, "I'll always care about you, and I know I still love you, but—this is crazy; you've got two girls with Lester. For you to leave him, and take those kids from him—that's the same deal I went through."

"He's always treated me well," she responded, "but I want to come back to you. We have a history together."

"Damn," I said. "Baby, this is way too much to process. You don't even communicate for five years and wham, we're on again?" I freed my hand from her grasp. "You know, you're damn lucky to have a guy who treats you okay. Most of those guys out there are chauvinistic retards. You could have been stuck with one of them."

"Well, I've been making a scrapbook photo album for the boys," she explained, "and you're in all the happy ones. I even made one for your birthday. I guess all the images have reminded me of what I left."

It dawned on me that she was just now letting a lot of her painful emotions rise to the surface. The breakup had been smothered or honeyed over with a new relationship. She had justified it all as God's will, but now, on her own responsibility, she couldn't sweep obvious things under the rug. Her feelings were her problems now.

"I'm happy that you've finally broken free from the First Ward," I told her. "But you can't give up a family again. You can't risk the little girls on a rebound."

"But Jase," she importuned, "I spend so much time with the boys, and their games, I could stay in the extra room and watch them during the day, even if you didn't want to start it up with me."

What do you do when a dead dream is waking up? A thousand times I had imagined a scenario like this; and here it was, now that I had kicked the last pile of dirt on its grave. "Suzy," I ventured, "it's not that I can't care, or couldn't learn to love you again. It's that, I don't think I could deal with two little girls reminding me of the saddest and most desperate moments of my life every day. You can't leave them behind and I can't deal with any of it right now."

"We could make it work, Jason." Suzy continued, "You've proven how big a person you are. You just need to trust us."

"I guess that's it, after all," I said. "I'm not that big. I have wounds that you being next to me would open. I know I could never trust that this couldn't happen again. Besides which, Lester needs you. He's lost everything, even his belief. You know I only went back for you—I never really bought into the crap Warren peddled, but Lester did. And it betrayed him, and you. Let's just leave it how it is for now."

I couldn't believe I had empathy for Lester, a man that had consciously provided the means to ruin my world. But, I reflected, it was not all his doing, nor was it Suzy's doing. They had both bet everything they had on the wrong horse.

With sadness I will never have words to express I took her into my arms and held her a few moments. When I had subdued the urge to crush her in an embrace of pain and passion, I stepped back to see tears filling her eyes. With a shaking hand I wiped them away, and gently kissed her on the lips. I didn't trust myself, and I certainly didn't trust the moment. I wasn't big enough for two little girls, whose only wrong was being born; but I was big enough—that minute—to turn and walk away.

The subject of remarriage never came up again, but she did apologize for asking, and for all the trouble and money she had caused me to lose. She is every bit the fine lady I thought she was fourteen years ago when we could only think of ourselves, and our happiness. Now we had others to think about.

I guess we had finally matured. Time and suffering had created a love to keep---my boys and her girls. Those twinkling stars in the Southern Cross we had found on our first breathless night, and had called ours forever—they were really ours; now they had names.

# XXVI
## YEARNING FOR WACO

While we were occupied with raising and loving our stars, trouble was brewing in another star—the Lone Star republic to be specific. I never had any direct experience with the compound in Texas, but I am ecstatically relieved my boys weren't there.

Early on, the place had been an exotic game preserve for wealthy hunters. Warren Jeffs purchased the land and named it the Yearning for Zion Ranch. Some of the people I heard marveling at the development opined that Texas real estate law was such that bankruptcy and other asset seizing litigation could not touch the land or homes. This was an odd concern in the light of the place rising up and leaving with the biblical city of Enoch while the world was being destroyed. I have difficulty imagining a judgment authorizing a bank to seize assets from the North Star.

The YFZ Ranch grew up out of nothing very quickly, at the cost of millions of dollars. Large homes sprung up out the scrub cedar, and work crews were sent from Colorado City to construct the infrastructure, building fences and homes and community centers.

Warren Jeffs and his handpicked faithful were scheduled to melt away and reestablish themselves there. Plopping a secretive Mormon-style cult in the middle of Southern Baptist country would seem imprudent to most men, but then so would underage marriages and trying to arrange a situation in which a cadre of wives, forced to share an inbred husband, might somehow get along.

In this ranch, for the first time since the 1890s, the fundamentalists decided to build a temple. They had disavowed temples completely the instant the mainstream LDS Church began excommunicating anyone living, teaching, or studying the principle of plural marriage. The fundamentalists believed that temples weren't needed until the apocalypse, which gives a lot of insight as to what the YFZ

settlers were thinking when they built one. They didn't know much about the ordinances that went on inside of Mormon-style temples, but for some reason, they felt they needed one too.

Unfortunately for the FLDS, erecting a gigantic monument on the horizon hardly qualifies as keeping a low profile. Several of the wealthiest men in the church were obligated to put up a tremendous amount of money and manpower to build a veneered stone edifice that lurked outside El Dorado like a mongrel dog over sausages.

The local business owners and law enforcement personnel tried to ignore the newcomers for the most part, but oddities made them wonder. As with anything characterized by that type of arrogant secrecy, the curiosity soon becomes a campaign to know. Was something illegal taking place? Was it an immoral cult worship operating in the midst of God-fearing citizens? Why were these people here? And why did they look so weird? Rumor is more inventive than any truth could ever be, and inevitably people will rear their heads demanding answers.

It was right about this time the warrant for Warren Jeff's arrest was made public. Like OJ's white Bronco on the Santa Monica Freeway, Warren's decision to run instead of face up to the charges, made him look awfully guilty. The Texas authorities were naturally looking for him to surface in the YFZ compound, which made the locals all the more uneasy.

It was known that the church was involved in hiding Warren from the law. His brother was arrested in Colorado on a DUI, carrying a large sum of cash money, with letters from the children, wishing the "Prophet" well. Also, there were jars of coins addressed to him, from each of the little kids in the church. This was part of the "Pennies for the Prophet" campaign, which asked the children to give up all the money in their piggy banks so that Warren Jeffs could lead a better life on the lam.

Because Warren had such an excellent network of safe houses, he was able to elude authorities for over 15 months, even after a $100,000 reward was issued. At one point he was even broadcast on the FBI's Ten Most Wanted list. Ample amounts of money, Lear jet leases, other people's credit cards, cell phones, and even vehicles lent a professional aura to his fugitive lifestyle.

The fallout from this fiasco meant that all polygamists everywhere, already sporting a black eye now got to watch it turning blacker. This was a departure from a century of passive law-abiding existence. Being statutory lawbreakers and actually being wanted criminals are worlds apart, and this was a first for the FLDS church. The press had a riot keeping on top of the pursuit and discussing the many peculiarities of the cult. Warren Jeffs was as good as any cult leader had ever been at getting his fifteen minutes (or months) of fame.

The luck finally ran out for the "Prophet" in August of 2006. He was pulled over in a late model red Escalade north of Las Vegas on I-15. The police were able to identify him sitting in the backseat and arrest him. I don't know how they made the identification, since Warren Jeffs was sporting a beard, dark sunglasses, and even Bermuda shorts. I have met Warren Jeffs and I am positive that there is no way I would recognize him with a beard, even if he was standing right next to me.

No one knows for sure how the Nevada Highway patrol was able to apprehend him. A silly joke going around was, "Why did the police pull his Escalade over? Because they could see his latest wife was not in her federally approved child safety seat." Whatever or whoever tipped them off couldn't anticipate the freak show about to ignite.

Besides the shorts and T-shirts, there were three or four wigs, a dozen different styles of sunglasses, sixteen cell phones, and four laptop computers included amongst his belongings. Some FLDS members, who are familiar with the wife who was with him at the time, claim that the driver, his brother Isaac, turned him in for the reward. They allege it was because he could never get any time off from running in order to see his own family. The real reasons, insiders say, is that he traded the location and travel direction for immunity from any charges as an accomplice. It is interesting to note that neither Isaac nor Warren's wife were ever charged for aiding and abetting his escape, or harboring a fugitive, or anything else one might have expected to come out of Utah and Nevada. This, however, is all speculation.

Now that he was in custody and scheduled for the hearings and the trial, the local authorities had to pave the way as scores of followers crammed into the courtroom, eager to see what would happen to their "Prophet." With much fanfare, the St. George police transported him the short distance to the courthouse. There were snipers in the hills, helicopter surveillance, SWAT teams surrounding the District Courthouse, and maximum security everywhere as finally we saw a television appearance of Warren Jeffs. The abundance of caution cost the county about half a million dollars, on top of the court costs and incarceration.

His trial was a drawn-out affair, with a secret witness and suppressed testimony, as Elissa Wall discussed her marriage, at fourteen, to her nineteen year old cousin, Alan Steed. She had been forced into the marriage and was denied a divorce when she wanted one, which was the exact opposite of what had happened to me. I loved every second of my wedding and fought like hell against a mandated divorce. But Warren Jeffs didn't really have a reputation for consistency anyway.

He was convicted for accomplice to a rape for officiating at the sealing ceremony of Elissa Wall and her ex-husband in a Caliente, Nevada motel room. I thought it was a little suspect that he was being tried as an accomplice to rape when there was no actual rapist on trial, but eventually, after Warren was trucked off to jail, a process was set in motion to charge Alan Steed as well. At any rate, I considered, Warren Jeffs deserved everything he got.

The next stop is a trial in Kingman, Mohave County Arizona for essentially the same crime, with an additional charge of incest. For my part, I don't know why Arizona wants to spend another half million dollars, when he is already pretty much scheduled to spend the rest of his life in a Utah prison anyway. I consider that a prison is a prison is a prison, and I'd rather see them use the money to help some of the people whose lives Warren destroyed, but perhaps that idea makes too much sense.

At any rate, I don't think he'll last through the trial anyway. Since his incarceration, Warren Jeffs has been trying to kill himself, by hanging, slamming his head repeatedly into the walls, and starvation. His stay has been characterized by extreme mental depression, and he has developed ulcers on his knees because he spends so much time kneeling in penitence for the wrongs he has done.

A lot of Warren's men, loyal supporters all of them, have been found in contempt of court. Many went into hiding themselves to avoid being compelled to deliver testimony against their "Prophet." Some are charged with molesting minors themselves. Perhaps sharing the fate of the persecuted "Prophet" will have some eternal significance for them.

Of particular interest was the Texas raid on the YFZ Ranch in April of 2008. An anonymous cell phone call reached Texas law enforcement, claiming to be from a girl named "Sarah" who was being abused by her husband. The call is now known to have come from Colorado, from a notorious prank caller named Rozita Swinton. I don't really understand how Texas law enforcement, who I presume would have complicated caller ID technology, were able to mistake a call from Colorado as coming from within the YFZ compound, but a judge did determine that the call justified the issuance of a warrant.

Now that law enforcement had elected to do something about the secret cult in El Dorado, they sprang into action surprisingly quickly. SWAT teams and National Guard units raided the place, which may indicate they had the raid set up before hand, simply because I know how long it would take to mobilize those kinds of units. They scooped up four hundred sixty-two children and packed them away in buses, generously provided by the anxious churches of the surrounding area. I don't know that SWAT training would have been quite as much of a requisite skill as changing Huggies, considering what the police were up against.

After all the children had been taken into welfare custody, the police began to search the ranch for evidence to prove that what they had already done was just and legal, under the circumstances. They were determined to find it.

This raid is a bit of a difficult issue to argue against, because for some reason questioning the tactics of government in the event is imputed to having sympathy towards Warren Jeffs or breaking the law. I firmly believe that Warren Jeffs is one of the most evil human beings America has ever produced. This puts him in among some tough contenders, but I think Warren can hold his own. But, like the ACLU, I also believe that a country born of liberty and individual rights should not err under the passion of the moment and resort to Gestapo tactics, no matter how insidious the crimes are thought to be.

My father, obviously still traumatized from his experience in the 1953 episode, was incensed at the farce. "I don't usually try to predict the future," he said, "but I guarantee you that not one of those kids will end up in a foster home. Every law that can be broken was. There is no way in hell an appeals court will tolerate this Barbara Walther bullshit."

He was right in the end, almost. Every child, but one was returned to the parent because there was simply no evidence to support their removal in the first place. Texas had ended up with ample amounts of egg on its face, just as it had some years before, when Janet Reno and the ATF engineered a firefight on David Koresch's Branch Davidians in the Waco mess. As a matter of fact, if the FLDS had been a more violent sort of cult, like the Branch Davidians, I have no doubt it would have ended in the same result—a pile of bodies splashed all over the compound. My father and I still suspect that before this issue dies down, someone will successfully sue the state of Texas for a lot of money.

At any rate, the presidential campaign took a backseat for a while, as the Child Protective Services smiled uncomfortably in the media spotlight. They were having severe difficulties with processing their newly acquired wards of the state. Not only was the number of kids daunting, the process of trying to figure out which family to take them away from was near impossible. Many of the children had been stripped away from their birth father, and so their names were obscured because of the FLDS penchant for attaching new surnames. Some of the birth certificates contained false data as a result, reflecting their musical chairs existence as a family. The idea is that the children follow the mother, so once the mother latches onto a new husband, the children supposedly takes on the new husband's last name. This can get really confusing, as it did in the case of Dean Cook. Dean's mother was remarried to my uncle Jerold, which meant he now considered himself a Williams, which meant his children, were also Williams' now. So his first several children have their birth certificate listed under Cook, and the last few have their birth certificate listed under Williams. So now, every time he wants to cross into Canada, for example, he has to figure out a way to prove that his children are, in fact, his children.

The CPS ended up spending a lot of time and money on DNA testing to get around the intense subterfuge and confusion inherent in the question "who's your daddy?" Their processing and raid ended up costing the state over $20 million all told, and they have nothing to show for it, except one little red-haired twelve-year-old named Maggie, who appears to be the latest bride of Warren Jeffs.

The Texas district attorneys have profited a little more from the debacle than the CPS did, though. Besides extradition papers for Warren Jeffs, they found bishop's records in the temple indicating several men in the compound may be guilty of statutory rape. Three of them have turned themselves in and are awaiting grand jury hearings on a collective $330,000 bail.

Some anti-FLDS activists, such as Flora Jessop, have expressed gratitude to Rozita Swinton, on the grounds that her tip, even if false, led to the states uncovering of other instances of alleged child abuse. However, I think that before the end, we will realize this raid has done nothing but make the FLDS even stronger. In 1953, when the state of Arizona raided the area and kidnapped the children without due process, it led to the kind of public resentment that eventually cost Governor Howard Pyle his second term. It also made it nearly impossible to prosecute crimes committed in polygamous enclaves because precedent is against it, and because public consciousness is now aligned against it to some extent. That is why, after 1953, almost fifty years went by before any major prosecution was made on a member of the FLDS. The state of Texas could have waited until they had some real evidence and destroyed the FLDS church once and for all, but they elected to raid the compound when they didn't have any evidence at all. This will probably enable the church to go on committing crimes and destroying lives for another fifty years, until some judge and some lawmen somewhere finally decide to do their jobs correctly.

Since his initial rant about the gross overstep of Texas law enforcement, my father hasn't had much to say about the entire squabble. Even when he turned out to be almost 100% correct on every one of his predictions, he resisted the urge to say "I told you so."

"Texas sucks!" was all he said instead. "And I'm a Dallas Cowboys fan!"

The real vindication for me did not come from the YFZ Ranch in Texas. It came from the appropriately named Purgatory Correctional Facility, the hell where Warren Jeffs was being held. The Sheriff's Department released a video of Warren Jeffs's confession to his brother Nephi. He said he had had a dream in which he could still be allowed into the telestial kingdom (the lowest of the glories of heaven), only as long as he issued a confession to the FLDS people.

"I'm not the prophet— I never was the prophet, and I have been deceived by the powers of evil. I have been the most wicked man in this dispensation in the eyes of God in taking charge of my father's family........the Lord God of heaven came to my prison cell two days ago to test and detect me, and he said I would rather defy him than obey him.  Get a copy of this video and let anyone who desires see it—even apostates and gentiles, that they may know I have been a liar and the truth is not in me---they will see I voiced these words myself.... the Lord told me to say that I yearn for everyone's forgiveness; for my aspiring and selfish way of life, and for deceiving the elect and breaking the new and everlasting covenant, and for being the most wicked man on the face of the earth....."

As the video ends, Nephi grows more and more emotional. "This is a test!" he finally shrieks as Warren finishes his speech. "You *are* the Prophet!"

This last statement is the most disturbing, but also the most illuminating. Warren's followers refuse to believe evidence even if it's right in front of their nose. Even after seeing the video, most members of the church still believe Warren Jeffs to be their "Prophet." Some have even asserted the video is a government conspiracy designed to undermine their religion. They call it faith—if they can believe in something not seen, it's not too far a stretch to *not* believe in what *is* seen.

Warren Jeffs is a chapter of my life that is over. I do feel a little bit of pride in that my early assessment of his mental condition turned out to be painfully correct, but I just want to forget the man. Forgive him his trespasses, and all that—that is my goal now. Still, I do think it a little strange that he still asserts the Lord came and talked to him. He asked forgiveness from the members of the cult, but he made no real effort to change the damage he had done. He even claims that William Jessop, Fred's adopted son (now in hiding) was the person who should have been the Prophet all the time.

I'm not going to say that his confession was insincere, because I believe it was very heartfelt. It's not that Warren doesn't have some remorse; it's that Warren doesn't *get it*. The confession is *still* all about Warren. The FLDS needs to make a conscious effort to join the rest of the human race, treat dissidents with respect, and treat women like human beings instead of Pokémon trading cards. But in his confession, Warren basically implies that he wants the church to go on doing the same thing, treating people like shit, but just to be worshipping a different face while they do it.

The saga in Texas is not over. Although the cult has declared it will cease all marriages of minor children, I am still suspicious about their agenda. Fanaticism reigns on both sides. Trust and understanding are the only antidotes for the future, so I remain guarded about the church's tendency to cling to secrecy like a drowning man to driftwood, and I am somewhat less than optimistic about the role of the courts and the CPS. Take away the thin ideological veneer, and there is not a lot of difference between a blind bureaucracy and a deaf theocracy—it's just somebody else trying to tell me what to do.

I don't know what will happen to Warren's wives, although I suspect they will be divided up once again, meaning that some of them will be onto their third husband. Since marrying every one of his father's three dozen *younger* wives, Warren had brought his count to over 70, including Velvet and Kathy, my former sisters-in-law, with whom I had commiserated in their first joyful wedding. For whatever reason, my name was excluded from the guest list when they were remarried to Warren.

Suzanne is at least grateful the courts overturned the first state welfare assault, so Velvet and Kathy are able to see their children once more. Since the raid, I have had a recurring thought—what if Warren had taken Suzanne after he got her to leave me? If I hadn't taken an aggressive course in order to keep Jay and Kyle, they could have been moved to Texas with Velvet and Kathy and become wards of the Lone Star, alone in a vast state that hated their guts. In a way, it was providential that Lester ended up with them—better him than Warren. I'm glad my story ends with many miles between my sons and the Texas child welfare system. If I hadn't fought so hard, and had so many allies, my story wouldn't have a happy ending at all. It would have been a tragedy. It certainly would have made me cry.

# XXVII
# THE MOOSE IS LOOSE

My story comes closer to a Hollywood ending than many other true stories you will read. It has the same bittersweet resolution to conflict that has neither been won nor lost, only survived. I made some terrible decisions along the way, and I made some good ones. No doubt there are some things certain armchair quarterbacks, in charting my life, would have done differently than I did. I think the important thing in my story, though, is not that a decision was good or bad; it is that a decision was *made*.

Many who are not exposed to the kind of mentality I met in that community will have difficulty understanding just how difficult it is to break free of it. Many people who were forced into a fork in the road lost everything because they failed to choose. I won because I acted.

I don't really have legal or business acumen, and because of that I did some things that I would not do today. However, given the chance to do everything over again, I am not sure there is much I would actually change. Although I have lost my faith in organized religion, I still have a profound belief in God, and while I won't go so far as to say everything happens for a predetermined *reason*, I do believe that you can never predict the inevitable results of an action or event. Some of the worst things that happened to me turned out in retrospect to function to my advantage.

For example, as hard as it was on me to have my boys spirited away, I now realize that if Suzanne had not done that, it is very likely she would have gained custody of the children, even though she was pregnant at the time of the trial. In the same vein, I was pretty nervous when Warren Jeffs conducted a community prayer beseeching God to destroy me, and yet that eventually helped many members of the FLDS, including Suzy Q, to finally see the light and break free. It may have even had an impact on the individuals that were finally able to prosecute Warren Jeffs for his awful crimes.

Besides which, I am unlikely to get a mulligan on life anyway, so endless reflection on what I would do differently if I had one is hardly a productive use of my time. I spent a considerable portion of my life doing things I didn't want to do, from my monthly meetings with the "Prophet" to working for Frank in the trench. If there are trench laborers reading this book, my heart goes out to you—you have the most awful job on God's good earth.

After spending so much of my time trapped in the hands of the false "Prophets," it is hardly a time I really want to revisit. Writing this book has been cathartic—it has helped me put my life into perspective so I can better understand it. But that chapter is behind me, and once I am finished writing these pages, I am unlikely to really spend much time reminding myself of it.

My real plan is what it has always been; to plunge into the uncharted future with the reckless fervor of an Alaskan moose, which is an animal with which I certainly identify. Once I broke free of Warren Jeffs and his web of power, my family really enjoyed the way I lumbered on. They named me "Moose" after Daryl "Moose" Johnston of the Dallas Cowboys, a team they all loved. Since they always resented my fondness for the Chicago Bears, the name "Moose" was perfectly calculated to get up my ire. Later, one of my cousins even presented me with a touching T-shirt depicting an inebriated bull moose mistaking a log for a pretty little lady moose. Whether this is meant to be indicative of anything, I may never know.

This nickname comes into use whenever I am fortunate enough to pull off an awe-inspiring play in softball. Everyone on my time yells in exultation, laughing at the opposing players and warning them that "the Moose is loose!" I truly do feel unfettered as I go into the future, released from a life sentence with the FLDS. Freedom beckons, and I plan to usher my boys in that direction rather than toward the slavery that characterizes the church I come from.

Suzanne is a big part of our lives, and she always will be. I love her very much, and I regret that she was taken away from me, but I was lucky enough to receive a lot of truth and wisdom in exchange. A lot of other people go through similar situations and don't even end up with that. Also, I have my sons, which is a reward that heals everything. Although the entire affair has left me fairly calloused towards love and marriage in general, I have been lucky enough to find that raising two boys as a bachelor is not as terrible as I was once taught to believe. We love every second of it.

My hope is to be a *parent* to those boys, like my father was to me. There is a shortage of real parenthood in the FLDS. Everyone is so concerned about teaching their children correctly so that they can stand aside and let a third party do with their children what he will. The parents there are not outwardly abusive (very often), but they are neglectful. They are so preoccupied with their own salvation that they would not risk their soul to save the souls of their children. They implicitly believe their children exist to help them get to heaven, when in reality the only reason *they* exist is to help their children find a meaningful life.

My children may find their meaning as a result of my actions. They will get through high school and learn about the world, and hopefully I can entice them to go through college and get a degree as well. In the FLDS, the children are part of a workforce throughout their childhood years. They generally learn enough to read and write, and maybe do a little bit of basic arithmetic, but beyond that their educational opportunities come to an end. Many children there have no idea who Abraham Lincoln was or who wrote *Hamlet*. Worse, they have even the desire to know ripped away from them at an early age. I thank the custody trial judge for his prudence in allowing my sons to go as far as dreams and dedication can take them.

And for myself, I get the privilege of shaping their lives, offering them training in athletics, and coaching their competitions. They are tremendous athletes, leading the way on All-Star teams.

In the meantime, I know I still have enemies in Colorado City who feel that my choices were, and continue to be, inspired by Satan himself. My own sister stopped me on the road in Hurricane one day and handed me every picture she had with me in it. It was a strong statement that she no longer wanted me in her life.

That, as badly as it hurts, no longer concerns me. I have spent my entire life being disliked by obnoxious people. For part of my life I campaigned hard to win the love of the people who hated me, but I realized that being liked was not worth being miserable. There are old bills that still come back to haunt me because I have never declared bankruptcy, but I'm working toward a stable future for my children, and a real of peace of mind for myself. I hope soon to have my mortgage paid off, and I will live a life relatively free from financial worry. Warren Jeffs couldn't be farther from my mind. That is excellent compensation for the fact that a few people might still resent me.

I have learned over my trials just how important my family is to me. If I had had a calmer childhood, I might have ended up burning bridges over petty disagreements, but now I realize that I need to cross them many times in life. Without the talents, compassion, and willingness of my network of brothers, cousins, uncles, aunts, and my own parents, I could not have enjoyed the success I have come to achieve. As a result of my struggle, I am closer to my relatives, even distant ones with tenuous kinships. I have even managed a friendship with some of the children of my uncle Jerold, who have managed to extricate themselves from the church despite the authority of their father.

I also learned a little of the darker side of human nature as well. There are a lot of people who are actively working to take your rights away from you, inalienable as they are. Some of them use force, threats, or coercion, but the more successful ones disguise their tyrannical natures under pretended helpfulness. The instant people release the responsibility of making their own decisions is the instant their life spins around and gets worse instead of better. I had been marked by the FLDS because I had refused to worship a man, no matter how prophetic he claimed to be.

My major goal in writing this has been to reach those who may be part of the FLDS, or another cult that is similarly styled. My hope is that my story has reached them and may help them to finally jump ship, instead of staying on the Titanic to rearrange deck furniture or yell at the iceberg. Obviously, no one knows for certain how they will react to evil when it challenges them, but my hope is that someone, somewhere, can find a little bit of courage by reading this, maybe even enough to break out of whatever chains are binding them. If they break free, they may at some point run into a stocky bald guy with a goatee who shares a kinship with them. If there are readers who are not in a similar situation, my hope for them is that this will be a little bit of a cautionary tale to ensure that they don't end up in a similar situation. I wouldn't wish a "Prophet" on anybody.

For my part, I have lived my life playing the hand I was dealt, and playing it aggressively, like a moose, the only way I know how. I always feel a little proud of my tendency to leap before looking. The Moose is finally, eternally, loose, and he couldn't be happier.

# AFTERWORD

From birth I was taught to put my faith in the Prophet, by doing so I would never be led wrong and would earn my salvation. I was taught that God and the Prophet are one. To me this meant that what the Prophet said was as if it came straight from God. For twenty-two years I believed this with all my heart.

I grew up in a plural family. My childhood memories are happy ones. My father and my two mothers loved me very much. There was no abuse or neglect like the media so often portrays of plural families. It is not always the case and was definitely not the case for me.

Jason and I first became friends in high school. I was a freshman, and he was a junior. The more time we spent together, the more serious we became. Eventually my parents found out that we were spending way more time than was acceptable together. In the religion that I grew up in marriage was by placement. It was not common for anyone to choose who they wanted to marry. If two people did choose to marry they were told to live outside the community for one year before they would be allowed back into the religion and would also have to be baptized again. Even though there was a great amount of pressure from his family and mine to not marry; but let the prophet place us, we married anyway. My parents were devastated. We were extremely young, I was only sixteen, and don't resent my parents for trying to protect me. They were doing what they thought was in my best interest, no different than any other loving father or mother. I, being a parent now, can see how they were trying to protect me from making a mistake.

It was an uphill battle from the start. Although Jason and I loved each other very much it always weighed heavily on me that we had not had the prophets blessing. I knew that I would never have the same standing in my parents eyes as their daughters that did have the prophets blessing.

When we were expecting our first son I wanted to have him at the clinic in Hildale. When asking the midwife if I would be allowed to give birth there she told me that she would have to ask the bishop first. When she returned she said that I would be allowed to give birth there, but I would have to be tested for H.I.V first. This was very embarrassing to me. It was hard to realize that they looked at me as a slut. I had never been with anyone but Jason; and I knew they would have never said that to a girl who had been placed by the prophet. It was yet another harsh reality check that I would never have the same standing as someone who had the prophets blessing from the start.

As time went on Jason and I did very well, we loved each other. We rarely fought, and when we did it was always about religion. The things being taught over the pulpit were becoming stricter. The teachings were that there was to be no contact or relationship with apostates. Jason's father and uncles were considered apostates and when he refused to give them up he fell from having some standing in the community to having no standing. This in turn put pressure on me. Women were told that if your husband didn't have full faith and obedience to the prophet he was against him, and there was no way you could get into the highest degree of heaven without the prophets blessing. For three years since Jason and I had married I listened to these teachings from the church. I believed they were true. I didn't know any different. I was now nineteen and had two beautiful little boys. I was told that I was following Jason to hell by staying with him and taking our children with me. The pressure was great. I could deal with the pressure I received from family and friends to leave Jason, but when I started being told by men in good standing that I was going to lose salvation for my children as well as myself if I stayed with Jason, that's when fear set in. It was fear of losing my children that drove me to leave him. The pressure to live exactly as the prophet had directed had become so great inside of me and now the fear of losing my children had been heaped onto the ever growing pile of feelings of not being good enough. Not being good enough to be lifted up when the destructions came, not being good enough to ever be equal to those who had the prophets blessing, not being good enough to raise my children, not being good enough because I wanted to stay with the man that I loved. The fear of losing my children in the hereafter was the greatest fear of all. I couldn't bear the thought of not having them in heaven. I left Jason. It was December 1998. It wasn't because I didn't love him. It wasn't because of neglect or abuse. It was fear. It had been four years now since we had been married. We had two little boys. They were two and a half and one year old. It was the single hardest thing I have ever done to this very day.

Three months later I was placed as a plural wife to a man who was in good standing. In three months I had buried every shred of feeling I had for Jason, fear can make people do things they wouldn't normally do. I felt happy. My sister wife was very kind at first, but once again the teachings of the church kept getting stricter. The prophet, Uncle Rulon , was getting sicker, and unknown to me then, his son had already taken over. I loved Uncle Rulon. He was always very kind to me. I was as devastated as the rest of the community when he died. Following his death there was a lot of confusion in the small town, some believed that Warren, his son, was his successor. Some believed that the bishop, Uncle Fred, was the next in line. After a short time, events took place that didn't square up to what had been previously taught and slowly my eyes began to open to the truth of the way things really were and that God and the Prophet weren't always one. The church I had been a part of was making drastic changes. My husband also had questions about what was really going on.

My eyes were fully opened when Lester's first wife left him. She had been directed by the new Prophet to leave, because Lester didn't believe he was his father's successor. I felt like God was letting me see from a distance what Jason had gone through when I left him. The shoe was on the other foot. It was now four years after I had been married to Lester, and the pressure from friends and family was now centered on me to leave him, as he did not believe in the new prophet.

In the four years that followed me leaving Jason, we had been in and out of court trying to figure who had rights to full custody because Jason and I were equally determined to get it. I felt like I had been dragged through the mud so many times I could barely stand. It had been so emotionally draining. It had been so hard living with our little boys going back and forth, seeing the hurt in their eyes, and always the question, " Why don't you and daddy like each other?" It had been so hard. There was no way I was going to put my little girls through that too. I made it very clear to friends and family that there was no way I was going to leave Lester. Previous experience had made me a little wiser. I was willing to go to hell if that was what it took, but there was no way I was going to go through that again. There was no way I was doing that to my children again. Lester had never been anything but good to me. I started to realize that the reasons I had for leaving Jason were really petty, actually quite immature and ridiculous.

The feelings I had for Jason that I had buried for so long were now resurfacing. I realized how much I still loved him. How could I ever tell anyone and have them understand? I even thought about leaving Lester, but Jason probably wouldn't want me back anyway. I felt all alone, and seriously confused. Leaving Lester would get me absolutely nowhere. It would only upset the stability that the boys had, and turn my little girls' world upside down. Eventually, I realized that I needed to make my marriage with Lester work. My family and friends in the religion would not have anything to do with me unless I was willing to repent and prove my faith in the new Prophet. That alone was hard to deal with. I was also trying to take care of Lester and Brenda's four little girls. The court had awarded custody to Lester (now I was their mom), my two little girls, Jason and my little boys and the fact that I still loved Jason, but I loved Lester equally. I was married to Jason for four years and had two little boys, now I had been married to Lester for four years and had two little girls. I dealt with this in silence until I got to the point of suicide, or at least the first step, I thought it. That's when I finally realized that I needed to ask Jason for forgiveness. It seemed impossible. I felt like there was no way I could ever even come close to saying how sorry I was, but I had to try. It was the only way I could live with myself and truly make my marriage with Lester work.

Today Jason and I have a really good relationship. We talk about the boys and how they are doing quite often. I know the boys are stable and happy as a result. Lester and I have a wonderful marriage, and our children are happy, healthy and love each other. We truly have a yours ,mine, and ours family.

I hold no grudges toward anyone in the community. I respect them for what they believe and expect the same from them. I am actually grateful for the experience because it opened my eyes. Had God not given me this experience I would have kept repeating this heart wrenching cycle. It was a million dollar experience I wouldn't give a damn dime for, but I'm thankful to be on this end of it. Life truly is a journey, and really, the thing that matters most is that, at the end of the day you've learned the lessons from life that the experiences were meant to teach.

Suzanne Johnson

Printed in the United States
216866BV00001B/6/P

9 781438 983967